KEYS TO THE PALACE

PALACE

EXPLORING THE RELIGIOUS VALUE OF READING TANAKH

RABBI HAYYIM ANGEL

KODESH PRESS

The Keys to the Palace

Cover image based on John Fulleylove (1845-1908), *Interior of the Golden Gate Jerusalem* (1901).

The Publisher extends its gratitude
to Rabbi Yeshayahu Ginsburg
for his assistance with this project.

Dedications

I thank my dear friends for their support of the publication of this book. Your friendship and commitment to the dissemination of Torah are eternally appreciated.

Yael Cohen,
in memory of Rabbi Daniel Beller

Levy Family Foundation,
in memory of Elsi Levy

Charles and Rochelle Moche,
in memory of Rochelle's father
Chaim Nasan ben Meir v'Charna

Sephardic Publication Foundation

Peshat interpretation
is the beginning of knowledge;
it is the key to open the gates.

— Malbim

TABLE OF CONTENTS

INTRODUCTION

Tanakh lies at the heart and soul of Judaism. The Talmud and Midrash, Jewish philosophy and mysticism, and Jewish thought and tradition all find their deepest roots in the Bible. For millennia, Jews and other faith communities have been transformed by this unparalleled collection of 24 books. Tanakh is accessible and enjoyable to small children and to the most sophisticated scholars and thinkers. It is a singular privilege to encounter its sacred words, to engage with its eternal messages, and to be galvanized to greater ethical and social action and spiritual growth as a result of our study.

The interface of the pursuit of *peshat* (the plain, primary sense of the text) of Tanakh with traditional Jewish faith is a potent combination. The critical starting question for a religious individual is always: What is God trying to tell me through these words? The *peshat* school, developed extensively over the past 1000 years and more, uses the best available scholarship to analyze the text.

In his introduction to the Song of Songs, Malbim (Rabbi Meir Leibush ben Yehiel Michel, 1809–1879) addresses the religious imperative to begin all learning with *peshat*:

> Most interpretations [of Song of Songs] … are in the realm of allusion and *derush* (homiletics); distant from the settlement of *peshat*…. Of course we affirm that divine words have 70 facets and 1,000 dimensions. Nonetheless, the *peshat* interpretation is the beginning of knowledge; it is the key to open the gates, before we can enter the sacred inner chambers of the King.

Peshat learning thus holds the keys to encountering God in His palace through the revealed words in Tanakh.

We have remarkable learning opportunities today. Scholars publish critical editions of our classical commentators so that we have access to the most accurate texts from our greatest teachers. Scholars discover and publish previously obscure rabbinic works, broadening our understanding of the range of interpretation in the classical period. They also advance the field of biblical study in areas including, but not limited to, literary analysis, archaeology, history, and linguistics.

At the same time, however, these opportunities also pose serious challenges to our enterprise. How do we balance this flood of knowledge and methodology with the fact that many scholars in the field are not Orthodox Jews and therefore bring their own assumptions and biases to their work? Are there means for sorting through information and methodology to determine what is beneficial for our religious growth and what must be discarded or modified? Ultimately, the litmus test of success for our study of Tanakh is that it deepens our religious commitments and inspires us to greater ethical behavior. How do we shape the contours of this discussion to maximize those benefits and characterize that process with intellectual honesty and integrity?

When we learn and teach Tanakh properly, we convey a sense of holiness and reverence, combined with respect for individuality and intellectual struggle with our most sacred texts and traditions. Tanakh has the singular ability to inspire and edify people of all ages and backgrounds. The potent combination of rabbinic commentary and contemporary scholarship enables our minds, hearts, and souls to complement one another in a holistic spiritual and intellectual experience. The maturation of sophisticated Tanakh study provides us with a system with which to navigate the complicated contours of scholarship and religious growth. Rabbis and educators have the immense responsibility to sort through available information, commentaries, and methodologies in order to steer the discussion for the benefit of the community.

It is inspiring that a growing circle of religious scholars are producing high-quality work in *peshat* study of Tanakh. Yeshivat Har Etzion remains at the vanguard of this enterprise, and others are adding their voices as well. In navigating the various approaches and interpretations, I find myself regularly returning to the writings of my teacher, Rabbi Shalom Carmy. Since I first took his Introduction to Bible course as an undergraduate at Yeshiva University, his teachings and writings have served as a guide for bridging the best in scholarship and religious thought and growth.

The twenty essays in this volume are divided into seven methodological studies, followed by thirteen individual studies in the biblical text and in Jewish thought. Most of the essays are reprinted from earlier publications, and I cite the original publications in each essay when relevant. As learning is an ongoing, living process, I have updated and modified many of the original essays.

Translations of biblical passages are generally taken from the New Jewish Publication Society *Tanakh*. Translations of passages from the Talmud are generally taken from Soncino.

This is my fifth book published with Kodesh Press, and Rabbi Alec Goldstein has again done a remarkable job in encouraging this project and bringing it into reality. His desire to produce quality work and his respect for his readers make him a pleasure to work with.

Special thanks to my friends whose generous support helped make this book possible: Yael Cohen, Charles and Rochelle Moche, the Levy Family Foundation, and the Sephardic Publication Foundation.

I am grateful to the many people with whom I learn each year: My students at Yeshiva University, and the synagogue communities, university campuses, and schools I visit through my work as National Scholar of the Institute for Jewish Ideas and Ideals.

As always, I thank my family for their constant love and support: Mom and Dad, Ronda and Dan, Elana and James, Jake, Andrew, Jonathan, Max, Charlie, Jeremy, and Kara. JoAnn, Matt and Erin, Nate and Kasey, Molly, Emily, Grace, Mimi and Papap.

Most importantly, I thank my wife Maxine for being the supreme life partner in all aspects of our lives and religious growth. The two greatest blessings of my life are being married to Maxine, and having our four children: Aviva Hayya, Dahlia Rachel, Mordechai Pinhas, and Eliyahu David. Raising our beautiful children together is the most miraculous of blessings. Doing it with Maxine makes it a world suffused with the greatest love and joy.

The most gratifying of all learning is when I learn Tanakh with my children: Aviva, Dahlia, and Mordechai (Eliyahu gets very enthusiastic as well, but as of this writing he is less than one year old). Learning with children, and especially one's own children, makes one appreciate the profound responsibility to clarify what actually is in the biblical text, to make it accessible to young children, and to allow them to engage in the layers and complexities of the stories and their religious messages at their own age-level. It is a singular joy learning Tanakh with my children, and we all have grown immensely from the experience. And this is only the beginning. We pray that we will continue to grow together through our learning and religious commitments throughout our lifetimes.

Hayyim Angel
Teaneck, NJ
September 20, 2017
Erev Rosh Hashanah, 5778

FROM ETZION COMES TORAH

YESHIVAT HAR ETZION
FACULTY ON THE BOOK OF GENESIS[1]

Introduction

Since the founding of Yeshivat Har Etzion in 1968, its *roshei yeshiva*, Rabbis Yehuda Amital, *zt"l*, and Aharon Lichtenstein, *zt"l*, made the rigorous study of Tanakh a vital component of the yeshiva's curriculum. Its affiliated Herzog College for teachers established Tanakh as one of its two primary departments, and its influence on religious education in Israel and beyond has been monumental.

For the past twenty years, the faculty of Yeshivat Har Etzion has been providing high-level Tanakh classes online. These classes are archived at the Israel Koschitzsky Virtual Beit Midrash of Yeshivat Har Etzion (http://etzion.org.il). Coupled with the journal *Megadim* from Herzog College and other publications, Yeshivat Har Etzion has become the address for some of the greatest religious Tanakh scholarship in the world today.

---

1. Review essay of *Torat Etzion: New Readings in Parashat HaShavua, Bereshit* (Hebrew), ed. Ezra Bick and Yonatan Feintuch (Jerusalem: Maggid Press, 2014), 529 pages. Page numbers in this essay refer to the Hebrew edition of *Bereshit*. This article appeared originally in *Tradition* 49:3 (Fall 2016), pp. 25-36.

Recently, Rabbi Ezra Bick has collected many of the essays on the weekly *parashah* into books. The five-volume English set, *Torah MiEtzion*, was published between 2011 and 2014. Most volumes of the Hebrew version, *Torat Etzion*, also have been published. A majority of the essays first appeared in the Virtual Beit Midrash, and they are supplemented by several other essays from *Megadim* and elsewhere published by faculty affiliated with Yeshivat Har Etzion.

Although each author has his or her own style, all are driven by several underlying methodological principles. In his introduction to the Genesis volume (11-18), Rabbi Bick enumerates the most important distinguishing principles of this school. *Peshat* is discoverable from a rigorous study of the text, as the Torah was not given as an esoteric code to confuse people. There is an Oral Law, but that does not diminish the pursuit of *peshat*. We attempt to learn in the manner of our classical commentators, with the goal of uncovering the intended meaning of the text. In addition to attempting to understand each word and verse locally, it is critical to consider the bigger picture, whether of a passage, an entire book, or parallels between different parts of Tanakh. God revealed the Torah to people, and therefore the Torah speaks in the language of people.[1] Since the Torah is divinely written, every word must be taken with utmost seriousness. Since it is written in human language, we may use literary tools that can expose dimensions of meaning in the text. There also is value to the study of the historical context of Tanakh, comparative linguistics, and archaeology. Since the Torah is divinely revealed, there is a religious obligation to understand its intended meaning and messages and to apply them to our lives.[2]

As with any literary study of Tanakh, one person's *peshat* might be another person's *derash*, and therefore what one reader finds compelling another may not. Moreover, even when one ascertains compelling features in the text, there are different ways to interpret those features. That said, the writers of these essays generally read the text carefully, present their methodology and conclusions transparently, and make strong cases for their analyses. Someone reading these essays stands to gain immensely from the learning, methodology, and religious messages taught by their authors.

Three of the greatest lights of this school whose essays appear in this volume—Rabbis Yoel Bin-Nun, Yaakov Medan, and Elhanan Samet—have merited reviews of their work.[3] An unexpected and delightful bonus is a transcribed speech by Rabbi Aharon Lichtenstein on Joseph's crying (517-529). This review essay will focus on the essays on Genesis written by some of the other authors.

Literary Parallels

One of the most popular techniques in these essays is to compare and contrast parallel passages or figures. The writers first demonstrate the close similarities between the passages, and then often exploit subtle differences to suggest additional layers of meaning.

The Sins of Adam-Eve and Cain

Rabbi Yonatan Grossman (28-33) enumerates a number of parallels between Adam and Eve's sin in Eden and Cain's sin of murder, including:

1. God opens a dialogue both with Adam and Cain with rhetorical questions (3:9; 4:9).
2. Both sinners initially attempt to escape responsibility (3:10; 4:9).
3. God asks *mah zot asit*, "what is this that you have done," to Eve (3:13), and *meh asita*, "what have you done," to Cain (4:10).
4. Eve's consequence (3:16) is a sexual urge for her husband (*teshukatekh*), and he will dominate her (*yimshol*). God tells Cain (4:7) that sin tempts him (*teshukato*) but he can dominate sin (*timshol*).
5. God curses the land after Adam's sin, *arur ha-adamah* (3:17-18), and Cain is accursed from the land, *arur attah min ha-adamah* (4:11), and the land will not be productive for him (4:12).
6. Both are banished eastward after their sins (3:24; 4:16).
7. They both procreate following their banishment (4:1; 4:17).

How should these parallel narratives be interpreted? Grossman suggests two possibilities. First, Adam and Eve's sin violated a divine command. In contrast, Cain did not need to be commanded against murder, since the Torah expects a basic level of morality from all humanity. By juxtaposing these narratives, the Torah teaches from its outset that a relationship with God requires faithfulness in both realms, and that all ethical sins are religious sins.

Alternatively, Ramban explains in his introduction to Genesis that the Torah teaches that sin leads to exile. These early Genesis narratives form the basis for later passages in the Torah that stress the necessity for Israel to be righteous to remain in its land. Holy land cannot tolerate sin, and the sins of Adam, Eve, and Cain drove humanity further and further away from the Garden of Eden.

One may suggest a complementary layer of meaning by noting an intensification between the two narratives. Adam hides from God in the garden, whereas Cain permanently hides from God. Adam will sweat when farming, whereas Cain no longer can be a farmer. Adam was exiled from the garden but remained in the vicinity of Eden, whereas Cain was forced into a permanent state of exile away from Eden. Adam caused the earth to be cursed, whereas Cain himself was cursed.

Perhaps these contrasts suggest that murder is worse than eating the forbidden fruit, and the land cannot tolerate such grave immorality. Eating of the forbidden fruit is a sin that creates a barrier with God, but one can still remain near God's presence and repent. The Torah supports this reading by speaking of the Land of Israel's absolute intolerance of child sacrifice and sexual sins: "Thus the land became defiled; and I called it to account for its iniquity, and the land spewed out its inhabitants" (Lev. 18:25).

Dreams in the Joseph Narratives

Rabbi Yonatan Grossman (397-404) analyzes the dreams of the butler and baker in chapter 40, and Rabbi Tamir Granot (417-424) explores Pharaoh's dreams in chapter 41. Both exploit subtle details within the respective pairs of dreams to suggest how Joseph correctly interpreted the dreams.

Rabbi Grossman enumerates the parallels between the presentation of the dreams of the butler and baker. However, there also are several critical distinctions:

1. The butler has vines before him, whereas the baker has baskets of bread on his head.
2. The butler sees blooming grape vines, suggesting growth. The baker, on the other hand, has fully baked bread.
3. The butler is active, squeezing the grapes for Pharaoh. In contrast, the baker is passive.
4. The butler gives wine to Pharaoh, whereas the baker has nothing left to give Pharaoh after the birds ate the bread.[4]

Overall, these differences suggest that the butler will have a favorable outcome, whereas the baker will have a negative outcome.

In addition to the above analysis, Rabbi Grossman submits that Joseph understood the butler's having the grapes "before him" to mean that he should interpret that dream literally: just as you made wine for Pharaoh in the dream, so too you will make wine for Pharaoh again. The baker, on the other hand, has the actions "above his head," suggesting that the dream should be interpreted symbolically: the bread symbolizes the baker, and the baskets symbolize the gallows. Joseph was able to ascertain entirely different meanings of the dreams as a result of the subtle differences between them.

Rabbi Tamir Granot picks up where Rabbi Grossman left off by analyzing Joseph's interpretation of Pharaoh's dreams. He asks the classical questions of how Joseph knew how to interpret Pharaoh's dreams correctly, and how Pharaoh could have known that Joseph was correct. Rabbi Granot proposes that we may ascertain these answers from a careful reading of Pharaoh's dreams. The Torah first presents its objective narrative account of Pharaoh's dreams (41:1-7), and then repeats

Pharaoh's relating of his dreams to Joseph in full (41:17-24). The Torah could have said simply that "Pharaoh told his dreams to Joseph." By presenting a complete repetition, the Torah hints that the solution lies in Pharaoh's retelling.

Pharaoh's relating his dreams to Joseph is for the most part identical to the Torah's objective account. Several minor variations are easily explained as emanating from Pharaoh's perspective. However, Pharaoh adds one critical detail to his retelling of the dream of the cows: "when they had consumed them, one could not tell that they had consumed them, for they looked just as bad as before" (41:21). The Torah's objective account of Pharaoh's dreams does not contain that detail.

Of course, Joseph heard only Pharaoh's presentation of the dreams, and not the objective Torah account. How could Joseph interpret Pharaoh's true dreams if he heard only Pharaoh's version? Rabbi Granot believes that the answer lies in Joseph's premise, that both of Pharaoh's dreams were really one (41:25). Joseph astutely observed that Pharaoh did not say anything about the bad sheaves of grain remaining as bad as they had been prior to swallowing the good sheaves. Since the dreams are otherwise parallel, Joseph concluded that Pharaoh must have added this detail regarding the cows because of Pharaoh's own worries.

Joseph interpreted Pharaoh's dreams to mean that there would be seven years of plenty followed by seven years of famine. Joseph then addressed Pharaoh's subjective worries by proposing a solution of how to rescue Egypt from this upcoming famine. Pharaoh was deeply impressed that Joseph was able to discern the objective details from Pharaoh's subjective addition, and concluded that Joseph was the man for the job.[5]

Rabbi Granot then offers a complementary theological interpretation. From Pharaoh's fatalistic pagan perspective, there would be seven years of plenty followed by seven years of famine. However, Joseph reflects the Torah's monotheistic view, that people have free will and must take responsibility to help shape their destiny. Therefore, he proposed a solution of how to benefit Egypt rather than fatalistically accepting the fourteen-year forecast. Pharaoh acknowledged the superiority of Joseph's view, and his "spirit of God" (41:38).

Both Rabbi Grossman and Rabbi Granot assume that Joseph ascertained the meaning of the dreams through his careful attention to the subtle differences between the details in the pairs of dreams. One still must ask, however: even if Joseph had the most sensitive ear, how could he have been so absolutely confident in his own interpretations and predictions? Is the Torah celebrating Joseph's ingenious listening abilities, or is it also conveying a sense of the divine hand behind Joseph's success? Joseph repeatedly credits God for the dreams and his ability to interpret (40:8; 41:16, 25, 28, 32), but the Torah never states explicitly that God inspired Joseph. However, the Torah gives a clear sense of divine providence throughout the narrative. Commentators throughout the ages have debated the balance between Joseph's wisdom and divine assistance, and even the fine literary analyses of Rabbis Grossman and Granot should not obscure this vital complexity underlying the Joseph narratives.[6]

Broader Parallels between Narratives
In addition to the compare-contrast method with individual passages discussed above, several writers analyze broader sections that compare and contrast the protagonists.

Abraham and Isaac

As is well known, Isaac follows in the footsteps of Abraham. Dr. Brachi Elitzur (229-231) enumerates many of the parallels and concludes that Isaac's role is to continue the path forged by Abraham. Rabbi Amnon Bazak (247-257) also takes these parallels as a starting point, but then suggests that the differences between the two figures demonstrate that Isaac also improves on his father's trailblazing path.

Both Sarah and Rebekah were barren, but Abraham never prayed for Sarah to have a son in the text,[7] whereas Isaac prayed for Rebekah and God answered him (25:21).

Abraham and Isaac both told foreign kings that their wives were their sisters (chapters 12, 20, 26). However, there is a progression over the three narratives. Pharaoh took Sarah, Abimelech did not go near Sarah, and Abimelech never even took Rebekah to his home. Rabbi Bazak submits that this progression mirrors how Abraham and Isaac handled each situation. In his encounter with the Egyptians, Abraham revealed his motivations for stating that Sarah was his sister: "If the Egyptians see you, and think, 'She is his wife,' they will kill me and let you live. Please say that you are my sister, that it may go well with me because of you, and that I may remain alive thanks to you" (12:12-13). Surprisingly, Abraham was not concerned exclusively about protecting his life. He also hoped to gain possessions from Pharaoh (*lema'an yitav li ba-avurekh*), and indeed Pharaoh lavished gifts onto Abraham afterwards (*u-le-Avram hetiv ba-avurah*, 12:16). This additional motivation tainted Abraham's actions. Abraham grew from this error, and in his encounter with Abimelech, Abraham did not think about personal gain anymore. Perhaps for this reason, God stopped

Abimelech before he even touched Sarah. Isaac then improved further on his father's conduct. Abraham preemptively said that Sarah was his sister (12:11-13; 20:1-2), whereas Isaac waited until the Philistines inquired about Rebekah (26:7). Rabbi Bazak suggests that perhaps Isaac was "rewarded" in that Abimelech never even took Rebekah to his home.

Abraham and Isaac both made treaties with Abimelech (chapters 21, 26). However, Abraham accepted the covenant immediately, and gave more than Abimelech wanted. Abimelech had asked for an oath of obligation, but Abraham responded with a mutual covenant. Abraham made this covenant despite the fact that Abimelech had taken Sarah, and took no responsibility for the Philistine seizing of Abraham's wells. One Midrash (*Gen. Rabbah* 54:4) criticizes Abraham for making this covenant, and Rashbam agrees that it was an error. In contrast with Abraham, Isaac did not agree to a treaty until he first voiced his grievances to Abimelech. Abimelech then requested a mutual covenant, but Isaac only swore to him. Fittingly, the Torah records that both treaties led to the naming of the place Beer-sheba (21:31; 26:31-33). However, Abraham's naming was only temporary, whereas Isaac's renaming made it permanent: "therefore the name of the city is Beer-sheba to this day" (26:33).

Through these and other examples, Rabbi Bazak argues that Abraham was the trailblazer, and Isaac emulated him but also improved on his ways. Although the text makes no mention that God "rewarded" Abraham and Isaac for their increased concern for their wives,[8] the overall trends between Abraham and Isaac detected by Rabbi Bazak appear sustained by the text.

Isaac's Marriage and Jacob's Marriage

Isaac and Rebekah sent Jacob to Laban's home both to escape Esau and also to find a wife (27:42-28:5). Similarly, God promised Jacob both progeny and protection in the prophetic ladder dream (28:13-16). Despite the dual-purpose of Jacob's journey to Laban, however, Jacob prayed exclusively for God's protection and sustenance: "If God remains with me, if He protects me on this journey that I am making, and gives me bread to eat and clothing to wear, and if I return safe to my father's house—the Lord shall be my God" (28:20-21). Surprisingly, Jacob did not also pray for a wife or children.

Addressing this omission, Rabbanit Sharon Rimon (315-322) observes that Isaac and Jacob both married family members from Nahor's family in stories involving wells (chapters 24, 29). Despite these external similarities, there are a number of significant contrasts between these narratives that may help explain Jacob's surprising concern only with his safety:

1. When Abraham's servant went, it was for the sole purpose of finding a wife for Isaac. In addition to seeking a wife, Jacob also was fleeing from Esau.
2. The finding of Rebekah is cast explicitly as divine providence. Abraham anticipated God's help (24:7), and his servant set up a divine sign and later thanked God when Rebekah was found worthy. In contrast, Jacob simply saw Rachel and wanted to marry her, and then worked to earn her hand in marriage. There is no explicit mention of divine providence, nor did Jacob pray for divine help.
3. Abraham's servant refused to eat until he discussed marriage with Rebekah's family. In contrast, Jacob did not

mention his desire to marry Rachel until one month later in the context of negotiating his wages. Even then, Jacob did not mention his parents' intention of sending him to Laban in order to find a wife.

4. The moment Rebekah agreed to marry Isaac, Abraham's servant returned her to Israel and she immediately married Isaac. In contrast, Jacob experienced a lengthy delay before marrying Rachel.

The marriage of Isaac to Rebekah is motivated solely by the desire to continue the covenantal family line by ensuring that Isaac not marry a Canaanite. The Torah makes it amply clear that God directly helped in this marriage. In contrast, Jacob fled from Esau and took refuge with Laban's family. He fell in love with Rachel on his own and then worked to marry her. After his ladder vision, Jacob did not petition God for help in finding a wife.

Rabbanit Rimon concludes that there is dual causality in the story, where Jacob acted for his own reasons but simultaneously fulfilled the divine plan for him.[9] God's plan—expressed in the ladder dream—was for Jacob to fulfill his covenantal destiny of building his family and returning to the land of Israel. Jacob's efforts thereby fulfilled the divine purpose of the flight to Laban, even if Jacob himself was concerned primarily about his personal safety.

As a complementary suggestion, it is possible that Jacob's flight, fears, and struggles were consequences of his deception of Isaac.[10] Although he had divine assurances and a covenantal mission to fulfill, Jacob was plagued by fear and doubt after the deception. The Talmud suggests that Jacob no longer felt confident, even after God's explicit promise of protection: "One verse reads: 'And behold, I am with you, and will keep you wherever you go' (28:15), and the other verse reads: 'Then Jacob was greatly afraid' (28:17)! [The answer is that] he thought that some sin might cause [God's promise not to be fulfilled]" (*Berakhot* 4a).

Adopting Complex Positions
to Bridge Clashes in Interpretation

The Torah often presents multifaceted verses that lead commentators to adopt diametrically opposed interpretations. Several writers in this volume adopt complex positions that bridge the views of the earlier commentators by incorporating the best elements from each side of the debate. We will consider the essay of Rabbi Yehuda Rock on the literary significance of Noah's name (63-69).

Lemech names his son Noah, saying: *zeh yenahamenu mi-maʿasenu u-me-itzevon yadenu min ha-adamah asher ererah Hashem*, "This one will provide us relief from our work and from the toil of our hands, out of the very soil which the Lord placed under a curse" (5:29). Presumably, Lemech refers to God's curse to Adam after he ate from the forbidden fruit: *Arurah ha-adamah ba-avurekha be-itzavon tokhalenna kol yemei hayyekha*, "Cursed be the ground because of you; by toil shall you eat of it all the days of your life" (3:17). The literary parallel between the two verses supports this reading, and Rashi adopts this understanding, as well.

After the Flood, Noah brings sacrifices, and God responds positively: *Lo osif le-kallel od et ha-adamah baʾavur ha-adam*, "Never again will I doom the earth because of man, since the devisings of man's mind are evil from his youth; nor will I ever again destroy every living being, as I have done" (8:21). At first blush, this divine reaction illustrates that indeed Noah did eliminate the curse on the earth.

However, 8:21 refers to God's promise never to destroy humanity again, and not to the original curse of agricultural hardship to Adam. There is no furthering of the theme of the elimination of the agricultural curse on Adam in the Torah. If Lemech referred to that curse when he named Noah, why would the Torah mention it at all if it never was eliminated? Rashi fills in this gap by quoting a Midrash (*Tanhuma Bereshit* 11) that suggests that after Noah there was a revolution in the development of agricultural tools. However, there is no mention of this development in the text.

Ibn Ezra therefore concludes that Lemech anticipated the Flood and named Noah to bring the consolation in 8:21. He was not referring to Adam's punishment in 3:17. If Lemech referred to the blotting out of humanity, however, how could he have known about that decree in advance? Ibn Ezra suggests that Lemech must have prophetically anticipated the Flood.

Ibn Ezra gains by creating a connection between Lemech's naming Noah and the furthering of the plot after the Flood. However, Ibn Ezra ignores the literary connection between the curse of the land to Adam and Lemech's naming of Noah. More significantly, his assumption of Lemech's receiving prophecy also is absent from the text. Rashi and Ibn Ezra both identify critical elements in the text, but also both confront serious difficulties with their respective readings.

Rabbi Yehuda Rock adopts a complex reading that incorporates the best elements of the interpretations of Rashi and Ibn Ezra. On the primary level, Lemech's naming of Noah is linked to the curse of Adam, as per Rashi's reading. Lemech could have known about that curse through family tradition, and the literary parallels between 3:17 and 5:29 connect those verses. However, we need a different explanation of the connection to 8:21, which refers to the destruction of humanity.

Rabbi Rock suggests that Lemech's blessing simultaneously relates back to the curse of Adam and also introduces the Flood narrative. At the time of Noah's birth, Lemech prayed for a return to an Eden-like existence, but instead all humanity became corrupt and God decided to destroy them. The reality of human weakness generates different divine reactions in the Flood narrative. God has greater mercy on people: "Never again will I doom the earth because of man, since the devisings of man's mind are evil from his youth; nor will I ever again destroy every living being, as I have done" (8:21). At the same time, God punishes people for their sins: "The Lord saw how great was man's wickedness on earth, and how every plan devised by his mind was nothing but evil all the time" (6:5).

Thus, Lemech's original hope for agricultural relief never was realized. His prayer for Noah was deferred until after the Flood, at which point God had mercy on people as a consequence of their weaknesses. God could not restore the world to an Eden-like state, since people had sinned. Instead, God eliminated the possibility for total despair in humanity, and promised never to wipe them out again.

To summarize, Lemech's naming of Noah refers back to the original curse to Adam, as per Rashi's reading. However, it also anticipates God's complex reaction to human weakness. God punishes humanity for their sins, but acknowledges that they need greater mercy, as per Ibn Ezra's reading that the naming also connects to God's positive reaction in 8:21 after the Flood.

Conclusion

This review is only a sampling of the treasures one may find in the Genesis volume, which itself is only a sampling of the essays found at the Virtual Beit Midrash. And of course there are four other books of the Torah that also have many valuable essays available. Those include many essays on the halakhic sections of the Torah, involving their structure, meaning, and the relationship between the Written and Oral Law.

We live in a blessed age when Israel has become the greatest center of Torah study in the world. Although the Messiah has not yet arrived, one critical aspect of the ideal vision is a palpable reality: "For instruction shall come forth from Zion, The word of the Lord from Jerusalem" (Isa. 2:3). The volumes of *Torat Etzion* ably represent the exceptional vision that has been at the vanguard of religious Tanakh learning over the past half-century.

NOTES

1. See, for example, *Berakhot* 31a, *Yevamot* 71a, and many others.

2. Rabbi Shalom Carmy has written extensively on what he terms this literary-theological approach. See especially "A Room with a View, but a Room of Our Own," in *Modern Scholarship in the Study of Torah: Contributions and Limitations*, ed. Shalom Carmy (Northvale, NJ: Jason Aronson, 1996), pp. 1-38; "To Get the Better

of Words: An Apology for *Yir'at Shamayim* in Academic Jewish Studies," *Torah U-Madda Journal* 2 (1990), pp. 7–24; "Always Connect," in *Where the Yeshiva Meets the University: Traditional and Academic Approaches to Tanakh Study*, ed. Hayyim Angel, *Conversations* 15 (Winter 2013), pp. 1-12.

3. Hayyim Angel, "*Torat Hashem Temima*: The Contributions of Rav Yoel Bin-Nun to Religious Tanakh Study," *Tradition* 40:3 (2007), pp. 5-18; reprinted in this volume. Rabbi Yaakov Beasley, "The Methodology of Creativity: A Review of Rav Yaakov Medan's Contribution to the Modern Study of Tanakh," *Tradition* 45:1 (2012), pp. 61-77. Hayyim Angel, "Review of Rabbi Elhanan Samet, Iyyunim BeParashot HaShavua," in Angel, *Through an Opaque Lens* (New York: Sephardic Publication Foundation, 2006), pp. 21-33; revised second edition (New York: Kodesh Press, 2013), pp. 6-18.

4. My student Avi Friedberg (Yeshiva University) suggests that, in addition to the contents of their dreams, the butler was willing to tell his dream to Joseph immediately. In contrast, the baker seemed more comfortable only once Joseph gave the butler a favorable interpretation (40:16). This distinction also may suggest a positive outcome for the butler and a negative one for the baker.

5. Although Rabbi Granot's observation about this additional detail in Pharaoh's retelling is astute, Joseph specifically interprets this detail in Pharaoh's retelling, that the thin cows were as bad as before: "After them will come seven years of famine, and all the abundance in the land of Egypt will be forgotten. As the land is ravaged by famine, no trace of the abundance will be left in the land because of the famine thereafter, for it will be very severe" (Gen. 41:30-31). Therefore, Rabbi Granot's explanation appears forced.

6. For an exploration of these different facets in the Joseph narratives and analysis of the views of our classical commentators, see Rabbi Elhanan Samet, *Iyyunim be-Parashot ha-Shavua*, vol. 1, third series (Hebrew), ed. Ayal Fishler (Tel-Aviv: Yediot Aharonot, 2012), pp. 172-221.

7. Radak assumes that Abraham must have prayed, but since God did not answer him, the prayer is not recorded. In contrast, Rashi maintains that since the Torah never mentions such a prayer, Abraham really never prayed for Sarah. In Rashi's view, Sarah was angry at Abraham for not praying for her (Rashi on 16:5).

8. In his essay on Genesis 18 (177-182), Rabbi Bazak similarly suggests that the merit of Abraham and Sarah's hospitality is directly linked to the divine promise of the birth of Isaac. However, God also promised Isaac to Abraham and Sarah in the previous chapter, and there is no mention of "reward" for their hospitality. It is plausible that the angels came to Abraham and Sarah to tell them of the future birth of Isaac from the outset.

9. See Hayyim Angel, "Dual Causality and Characters' Knowledge: The Interaction between the Human and the Divine," printed in this volume.

10. See Hayyim Angel, "Morality and Literary Study: What does the Torah Teach about Jacob's Deception of Isaac?" printed in this volume.

TORAT HASHEM TEMIMAH

THE CONTRIBUTIONS OF RAV YOEL BIN-NUN
TO RELIGIOUS TANAKH STUDY[1]

Introduction

The growing popularity of what Rabbi Shalom Carmy calls the "literary-theological" approach to Tanakh study has been transforming the way we approach our most sacred texts. This methodology demands a finely tuned text reading, along with a focus on the religious significance of the passage. The premises of this methodology include: (1) Oral Law and traditional commentary are central to the way we understand the revealed word of God, and (2) it is vital to study biblical passages in their literary and historical context.[1]

The rabbis and scholars at Herzog College (affiliated with Yeshivat Har Etzion), and other contributors to journals such as *Megadim* (first published in 1986), have championed this literary-theological approach. One of the great leaders of this movement is Rabbi Yoel Bin-Nun. Through his articles and

---

1. This article appeared originally in *Tradition* 40:3 (Fall 2007), pp. 5-18; reprinted in Angel, *Revealed Texts, Hidden Meanings: Finding the Religious Significance in Tanakh* (Jersey City, NJ: Ktav-Sephardic Publication Foundation, 2009), pp. 30-47.

editorial policies, he has articulated what he views to be the proper boundaries of religious Tanakh study. Because he is so prominent an editor-contributor to *Megadim*, the story of his work is linked with the story of that journal.

Additionally, Rabbi Bin-Nun presents a more comprehensive approach to Tanakh than many of his colleagues as a result of his unusual ability to address historical and archaeological scholarship on a serious level. He combines expertise in Tanakh, classical commentary, *halakhah*, history, archaeology, linguistics, and theology. His fresh approach to Tanakh inspires, stimulates, and challenges his readers. At the same time, he actively confronts some of the religious challenges of biblical criticism by using its own tools of scholarship. This chapter will consider some of his principal contributions in *Megadim* and beyond.

Defining the Boundaries of Traditional Learning

Since *Megadim* stands at the cutting edge of religious Tanakh learning, it has engendered major policy debates. Perhaps three of the most controversial areas over the past thirty years have been: (1) Rabbi Mordechai Breuer's Theory of Aspects; (2) encounter with non-Orthodox scholarship; and (3) the balance between *hiddush* (original interpretation) and deference to classical interpretations.

Rabbi Mordechai Breuer's Theory of Aspects

One of the most creative—and controversial—figures in contemporary religious Tanakh study is Rabbi Mordechai Breuer. Rabbi Breuer posits that the proposed divisions of the Documentary Hypothesis are correct, and he agrees with the critics that no one person could have composed the Torah.

However, he disagrees fundamentally with the critics by insisting that no *person* wrote the Torah. God revealed it to Moses in its complex form so that the multiple aspects of the infinite Torah could be presented in different sections. Since we are limited as humans, we cannot simultaneously entertain these perspectives, so they appear to us as contradictory. The complete truth emerges only when one takes all facets into account.[2]

Soon after the inception of *Megadim*, Amos Hakham attacked Rabbi Breuer for pushing the limits of traditional learning too far, and implicitly criticized *Megadim* for publishing articles from this school of thought.[3] Among Hakham's chief objections were the following: (1) Fundamentally, Rabbi Breuer's theory is simply biblical criticism with a religious face. It is plausible only if one already believes in *Torah min ha-Shamayim* (divine revelation of the Torah). (2) Rabbi Breuer argues that only God could have written the Torah, since it is incomprehensible to humans—a specious argument about a Torah which is written "according to the language of people." More responsible scholars have demonstrated that the Torah is a great literary work even by human standards, and it is indeed comprehensible.[4]

In response to Amos Hakham, Rabbi Bin-Nun defended Rabbi Breuer.[5] Rabbi Breuer fully believes in *Torah min ha-Shamayim*, so his approach is religiously acceptable.[6] Of course, one may disagree with Rabbi Breuer's methodology and his individual analyses. At the same time, however, Rabbi Bin-Nun fundamentally accepts Rabbi Breuer's view that one cannot learn *peshat* in the Torah without some recourse to a methodology involving the synthesis of different aspects of the Torah.[7]

Non-Orthodox Scholarship

Espousing Rambam's principle of "hear the truth from the one who says it," a number of authors in *Megadim* draw from non-Orthodox scholarship. A serious policy discussion arose, however, when *Megadim* published a review of the inaugural volume of a new secular commentary series, *Mikra LeYisrael: Ruth,* by Yair Zakovitch. In his review, Rabbi Avraham Shamah criticized Zakovitch's non-traditional arguments on scholarly grounds. He also noted several positive features of the commentary, including Zakovitch's literary analysis of the text.[8]

Several readers expressed outrage that *Megadim* would review a non-traditional commentary altogether, let alone favorably. The publication of this review, according to those respondents, implicitly conferred legitimacy onto a commentary that clearly lies outside of tradition. In his response, Rabbi Bin-Nun maintained that printing the review did not lend religious legitimacy to the secular commentary. Rabbi Shamah specifically pinpointed and rejected the religious problems with it. At the same time, there is much to be learned from academic scholarship (and, for that matter, there is much that the academy may learn from the *bet midrash*). Blanket attacks serve only to widen the gap between us.[9]

Hiddush vs. Time-Honored Interpretations

Tanakh is an infinite work, and therefore there is always room for the *perushim ha-mehaddeshim be-khol yom* (new interpretations that develop each day). While Rabbi Bin-Nun's comprehensive methodology fosters many creative interpretations, it also has drawn criticism from those who prefer the time-honored explanations of our predecessors.

An example of healthy debate revolves around the issue of why Joseph, after he rose to power in Egypt, did not contact Jacob. In the inaugural issue of *Megadim*, Rabbi Bin-Nun proposed a novel solution to this problem. We (the "omniscient readers") are informed by the narrative, but Joseph did not know the aftermath of his being sold: Jacob, deceived by Joseph's brothers, mourned inconsolably. Unaware of Jacob's mourning, Joseph began to wonder: Why does Jacob not search for me? Why did he send me to my brothers whom he knew were hostile? Perhaps Jacob was banishing me as a result of my dreams! For years, Joseph mistakenly suspected that Jacob participated in the plot to sell him! Therefore, Joseph never attempted to contact his father. Only when Judah quoted Jacob's belief that Joseph was killed (Gen. 44:28) did Joseph learn what Jacob had been thinking—and what the reader knew—all along. This revelation prompted Joseph to reconcile with his brothers.[10]

In the following issue of *Megadim*, Rabbi Yaakov Medan wrote a lengthy article disagreeing. Is it more likely that Joseph would suspect his father of being a total hypocrite, or that Joseph would blame his brothers who certainly hated him? Moreover, Joseph did not break down when Judah informed him that Jacob was saddened by the loss of Joseph; he revealed his identity only after Judah asserted that Jacob would die if Benjamin did not return. Rabbi Bin-Nun's thesis is therefore uncompelling.

Rabbi Medan adopts the more conventional view that the narrative revolves around repentance, with Joseph orchestrating events to enable his brothers to repent for having sold him. Only after Judah demonstrated full repentance by offering himself in Benjamin's stead did Joseph reveal himself to his brothers. This answer is far more in line with the approaches of earlier commentators, notably that of Ramban.[11]

In response, Rabbi Bin-Nun observes that Rabbi Medan's analysis does not receive textual support from what Joseph said or did. Moreover, Joseph could not have orchestrated this repentance, since he could not have known that his brothers would come to Egypt in the first place: "The assumption that Joseph read the Torah portion each week with Midrash, and knew all future events, is wishful thinking."[12]

On one level, this debate revolves around the Joseph narrative. However, there is an underlying methodological disagreement as well. Finding questions against the views of earlier commentators, Rabbi Bin-Nun develops a new approach. Rabbi Medan, in contrast, attempts to resolve the questions leveled against those earlier commentators. The reason this debate works so effectively is the palpable respect each writer has for the other. This is the sort of pushing and pulling necessary to refine truth within the boundaries of traditional discourse.

Alas, the dialogue is not always so respectful. In a later issue of *Megadim*, Rabbi Bin-Nun explains the existence of Amalekite raiders in 1 Samuel 27 and 30 after Saul ostensibly had wiped Amalek out in chapter 15. He deems Saul's premature plundering of the Amalekites to be central to his failure. This action detained his troops from pursuing Amalek, enabling many to escape. David, in contrast, thoroughly defeated the Amalekites first, and only then returned to plunder their camp.[13]

Rabbi Yisrael Rozen responded with an article of his own, caustically attacking Rabbi Bin-Nun for employing non-midrashic exegesis. Declaring that his method smacks of Karaism, he levels several textual critiques of his hypothesis and presents an alternative solution which he considers "the view of our Sages."[14]

Rabbi Bin-Nun responds that advancing novel interpretations based on careful readings of the text is what classical *pashtanim* have always done, and hardly constitutes Karaism. Additionally, it is misleading to present a "midrashic view" as though the Sages spoke with one unified voice. For each Midrash that Rabbi Rozen quotes, Rabbi Bin-Nun cites several others that present different viewpoints. Whether or not Rabbi Bin-Nun's hypothesis is compelling in his analysis of Amalek, this debate was important to teach the readership not to speak so sharply and dogmatically, nor to reject novel interpretations just because they are new. Each argument must be weighed against the text evidence.

An unfortunate casualty of the foregoing dispute is that the arguments pertaining to the Amalekite issue in the book of Samuel were not sufficiently refined. While the erroneous dogmatic pronouncements of Rabbi Rozen were properly rejected, several of his textual considerations—which remain valid—are left unaddressed as a result of the confrontational nature of this dialogue.

Rabbi Zvi Thau's Criticism and Responses

In 2002, Rabbi Zvi Thau of Yeshivat Har HaMor published a scathing condemnation of Herzog College and similar institutions. That these teachers confront the challenges of biblical criticism was enough for Rabbi Thau to label them "poisoners," to consider their educational methods "the root problem of our generation," and to declare it preferable to forfeit one's life before studying in such institutions (*yehareg ve-al ya'avor*). Rabbi Thau accused these rabbis and scholars of teaching Tanakh as a secular book, accepting heretical premises, and forcing these assumptions upon their students.[15]

The tone and content of this critique are reprehensible. Nevertheless, Rabbi Thau achieved the positive effect of spurring a productive dialogue at Yeshivat Har Etzion promoting further elucidation of the issues. Rabbi Amnon Bazak initiated the dialogue, expressing chagrin over Rabbi Thau's baseless and horrible slander of God-fearing, learned scholars. Although there is much room for debate in the realm of educational policy and method, the teachers at Herzog College reckon with critical issues in Tanakh from a religious perspective. Aside from the need to "answer the heretic" and to train teachers to handle a wide array of questions, there are many positive contributions from academic scholarship that enhance our understanding of Tanakh. Rabbi Thau's proclamation that non-Orthodox Bible scholars have nothing intelligent to say is erroneous. Rabbi Thau stated in his article that he does not know how to respond to critical questions; Rabbi Bazak retorts that this willful ignorance shirks integrity in learning and educational responsibility.[16]

Rabbi Bazak's article elicited a response from Rabbi Mosheh Lichtenstein, who endorses Rabbi Bazak's defense against Rabbi Thau's attacks but then submits that introspection still is necessary. Rabbi Lichtenstein outlines several potential religious hazards of the methodology taught at Herzog College. He raises some of the common critiques of Rabbi Breuer's approach, including his acceptance of the divisions of the Documentary Hypothesis as "science" and his assumption that the Torah is incomprehensible to humans. In addition, Rabbi Lichtenstein believes that Rabbi Breuer's method leads one away from traditional commentary and Oral Law, forging an entirely new approach to learning. While fundamentally accepting the possibility of positive contribution from historical scholarship,

Rabbi Lichtenstein espouses a negative view of the risk/benefit ratio from that confrontation.[17]

Rabbi Lichtenstein's remarks in turn elicited responses from Rabbi Breuer, Rabbi Shamah, and Rabbi Bin-Nun. Rabbi Breuer defends his own methodology, insisting that it is specifically through his theory of aspects that one may fully appreciate the intimate relationship between the Written and Oral Law.[18] Rabbi Shamah adds that Rabbi Lichtenstein cannot escape the fact that there are difficult issues that must be confronted and explained. This does not mean that Rabbi Breuer's approach is the only valid traditional method, but it certainly is one method of achieving the desired ends of interpreting the Torah from a God-fearing perspective. Rabbi Shamah notes that of course there are religious dangers in confrontation, but there also are religious dangers in avoiding careful study of Tanakh.[19]

Rabbi Bin-Nun reiterates the underlying religious assumptions of his school of thought. It is necessary to grapple with literary and historical-critical issues for the sake of learning the word of God. Rabbi Lichtenstein fails to distinguish between secular theories and underlying assumptions which Rabbi Bin-Nun and his colleagues categorically reject; and facts (e.g., contradictions, repeated stories) which they address using methodologies different from those of the critics. Rabbi Bin-Nun concludes:

I reject the restrictive attitudes practiced in religious circles championed by those who never have studied these subjects thoroughly, and who are unqualified to address the essential issues.... One wishing to discuss the underlying assumptions of learning Tanakh first must clarify the depth of the subject matter in Tanakh and linguistics, and then we will be happy to hear his opinion on the important educational issues connected to this subject.[20]

While these rabbis espouse substantially different views, their dialogue is exactly what is needed to clarify the most important issues in religious Tanakh learning and education. Through the give and take in *Megadim* and other forums, Rabbi Bin-Nun has effectively articulated the boundaries of traditional learning and set the tone for respectful discourse. Once inside those boundaries, debates in *peshat*, methodology, and educational policy always will occur, enabling us to refine our understanding of Tanakh and how it should be studied even further.

Comprehensive Approach to Tanakh

In his writings, Rabbi Breuer steers clear of historical criticism, concentrating exclusively on literary issues. Rabbi Bin-Nun, in contrast, believes that these disciplines, when studied responsibly, combine harmoniously and deepen our understanding of Tanakh and other areas of Jewish thought. With his comprehensive approach to Tanakh, it appears that Rabbi Bin-Nun has overcome all of the major critiques leveled against Rabbi Breuer:

1. He is not committed to the divisions of higher criticism and therefore has autonomy in learning.
2. He weaves together all areas of inquiry rather than artificially isolating the literary elements of the text.
3. His approach works just as effectively in *Nakh* (the Prophets

and Holy Writings) as it does in the Torah. The following are a few outstanding examples of his synthesized approach.

Joshua: Text, Archaeology, and Theology

Long before archaeologists began doubting the veracity of Joshua's conquest, the narratives in the book of Joshua presented textual difficulties. Joshua chapters 1-12 convey the impression of Israel's conquest of the entire land, but chapters 13-19 then list many unconquered Canaanite cities.

Fully aware of these discrepancies, classical commentators attempted to harmonize them. For example, Radak (on Josh. 11:23) suggests that Israel captured the borders of the land, creating the wherewithal to conquer the rest of the land over time. Alternatively, Ralbag suggests that since the war had ended, it was considered as though the entire land had been conquered.

With the rise of secular literary and historical scholarship, non-traditional scholars challenged the truth of the narratives, and argued that Joshua 1-12 and 13-19 represented conflicting traditions. Additionally, archaeologists insisted that the total conquest described in Joshua is not corroborated by findings in Israel dated to that period. Rather, the evidence suggests a gradual settlement of the land.

With his expertise in both Tanakh and archaeology, Rabbi Bin-Nun is uniquely qualified to shatter these arguments.[21] According to the book of Joshua, only Jericho, Ai, and Hazor are reported to have been burned to the ground. Contrary to our initial impression of a total conquest, some of the 31 defeated cities listed in Joshua 12 could not be conquered even *after* Joshua's victories (e.g., Jerusalem in 12:10, 15:63; Gezer in 12:12, 16:10). Most of Israel's victories under Joshua likely were battles of armies against other armies, rather than annihilations of those cities. The campaign described in Joshua 1-12, then, simply broke the back of the Canaanite military coalitions.

A comprehensive reading of the book of Joshua suggests a gradual settlement of the land, since most cities remained Canaanite in Joshua's lifetime. Similarly, we should not expect archaeologists to uncover any more than three destroyed cities dated to Joshua's period—Jericho, Ai, and Hazor. Rabbi Bin-Nun argues that archaeological evidence corroborates the destruction of Ai and Hazor in Joshua's time (elsewhere he wrote a full-length article concerning the proper identification of Ai[22]), and we do not have conclusive evidence one way or the other from current findings in Jericho. In sum, the archaeological record is largely consistent with the account in Tanakh, if one only reads the text and considers the archaeological evidence carefully.[23]

Rabbi Bin-Nun's text-archaeology analysis also is significant in his separate treatment of the ethical ramifications of the war against the Canaanites. As is noted above, Joshua likely engaged the Canaanites in a military battle rather than a war of annihilation against men, women, and children. While the war against the Canaanites was a battle against immorality, Israel retained its strong ethical character, fighting only out of necessity.[24] Rabbi Bin-Nun thus has demonstrated a strong link between the text complexities in the book of Joshua, the ethical ramifications of conquest, and the connection to what has and has not been unearthed by contemporary archaeologists.[25]

Ivri-Hapiru **Connections**

> From the beginning of the second millennium B.C.E.
> through the twelfth century B.C.E., cuneiform tablets
> from Sumer, Babylon... as well as hieroglyphic texts
> from Egypt, register the presence of groups of people
> variously referred to as... *hapiru, 'pr(m),* and *'pr(w).*
> The meaning of these terms has long been subject to
> scholarly dispute, but they are all concerned with
> the same class of people.... The people referred to by
> these terms are distinguished not only by extensive
> geographic distribution but also by considerable ethnic
> diversity and linguistic variety. They everywhere
> constitute a recognizable subservient social class....
> They are rootless aliens, deprived of legal rights.... Are
> the 'Apiru and the Hebrews related? (Nahum Sarna)[26]

In approaching this subject, one must examine biblical evidence
and the relevant ancient Near Eastern texts. Moshe Greenberg
believes that the Hapiru referred to in ancient Near Eastern texts
were refugees. Thus the term denotes a class or social status,
not a specific ethnic group. On the biblical side, Greenberg
agrees with Ibn Ezra (on Exod. 21:2) that *Ivri* is an ethnic term
referring specifically and exclusively to Israel.

Having studied the relevant ancient Near Eastern texts
with his mother (herself a scholar[27]), Rabbi Bin-Nun agrees
fundamentally with Greenberg's analysis of Hapiru, that it is a
non-ethnic term in ancient Near Eastern texts. However, based
on a case-by-case presentation, he disagrees with Greenberg's
analysis of Tanakh, and maintains that *Ivri* in Tanakh likewise
is not an ethnic term.

For example, he cites Moses and Aaron's first dialogue with Pharaoh. Moses and Aaron began, "Thus says the Lord, the God of Israel (*Elokei Yisrael*): Let My people go that they may celebrate a festival for Me in the wilderness" (Exod. 5:1). Pharaoh was unimpressed: "Who is the Lord that I should heed Him and let Israel go?" (5:2). Moses and Aaron retorted: "The God of the Hebrews (*Elokei ha-Ivrim*) has manifested Himself to us..." (5:3). Rabbi Bin-Nun observes that farmers typically believed in local gods. In contrast, refugees and slaves could not rely on local gods; they needed a cosmic god who transcends geographical boundaries. As the king of an agrarian society, Pharaoh was unconcerned with *Elokei Yisrael*. Pharaoh lived in Egypt, ostensibly outside the jurisdiction of a God in Israel. Moses and Aaron therefore countered by referring to God as *Elokei ha-Ivrim*, the God Who transcends all boundaries and Who can help the oppressed wherever they live.

In the case of Jonah, many think that the prophet was giving an ethnic description when he proclaimed *Ivri anokhi* ("I am a Hebrew") to the sailors (Jon. 1:9). Rabbi Bin-Nun, however, insists that exactly the opposite is true. The terrified sailors prayed to their local deities and asked Jonah to do the same. Jonah responded that he was an *Ivri*, that is, a refugee who serves the God Who is everywhere. This response shocked the sailors, who now recognized that Jonah was fleeing a God Who controls everything.

Rabbi Bin-Nun concludes that the term *Ivri* in Tanakh has the same basic meaning as *Hapiru*, referring to the Israelites not in an ethnic sense but rather in the sense of their social status and belief in God Who is everywhere. In this instance, he marshals biblical and ancient Near Eastern text evidence to arrive at a plausible hypothesis to a longstanding scholarly inquiry.[28]

The Meaning of God's Name

In his discussion of the meaning of God's Name, Rabbi Bin-Nun sifts through the evidence carefully in a linguistic-semantic study. He concludes that historically there was a transition from a more active meaning in Tanakh (God will appear, will dwell, will save, will rule forever) to a more passive meaning in rabbinic literature (God exists).

He submits two reasons for this transition. First, the Aramaic root "to be" takes a more passive meaning. The Sages, who spoke Aramaic, would have been influenced by their usage of that language. However, there is a theological reason as well. After the destruction of the Temple and the cessation of prophecy and the Davidic dynasty, God no longer revealed Himself to Israel in the same way. The Sages therefore deliberately concealed the active meaning of God's Name, waiting for the time when God would again manifest Himself directly in this world. Implicitly, by writing this article, Rabbi Bin-Nun is reclaiming the active meaning of God's Name as part of the redemption process, that God is actively manifesting Himself to our generation.[29]

Conclusion

In an article discussing Rabbi Mordechai Breuer's methodology and contributions, Rabbi Meir Ekstein observes:

> The title of the journal *Megadim* is from a verse in *Shir haShirim*: "When the plants are blooming and the lover anticipates taking his loved one." The Midrash interprets the verse as referring to the time of the Messiah when the scholars and Rabbis engage in new textual study in order to accept upon themselves the kingdom of God.

These verses and the Midrash are highlighted on the front cover of the journal. There is a passion inspiring these writings, a belief that with the Jewish people's return to the land of Israel we have begun a new era that ought to be reflected in Torah study.[30]

Rabbi Bin-Nun's work is captured perfectly by this depiction. His love of God and desire to know Tanakh with all its dimensions permeate his work. His passion for Israel and his stress on the connections between our ancient roots and the present day similarly are regular themes in his writings.

In an essay on Purim, Rabbi Bin-Nun notes that God's Name does not appear in the Megillah, nor do we find evidence of prayer or other overtly Jewish actions. The Megillah presents a world we have not yet encountered in Tanakh—a totally pagan and secular kingdom. Does God govern even there? The Megillah teaches that He most certainly does. God defeated pagans on their home court, using turnarounds, a lottery, and "coincidence" to win.[31] This conclusion sounds strikingly similar to his idea of the need to defeat secular scholarship on its own court, using the tools of literary analysis and historical scholarship to undermine the critics' false assumptions.

Most importantly, Rabbi Bin-Nun's love for the word of God and intellectual honesty are inspirational to all who study his work. He successfully demonstrates the unity of text, tradition, history, and land in an overarching and untiring effort to serve God and to bring His teachings to life.

NOTES

1. Rabbi Shalom Carmy, "A Room with a View, but a Room of Our Own," in *Modern Scholarship in the Study of Torah: Contributions and Limitations*, ed. Shalom Carmy (Northvale, NJ: Jason Aronson Inc., 1996), pp. 1-38.

2. See the essays in *Modern Scholarship in the Study of Torah: Contributions and Limitations*: Rabbi Shalom Carmy, "Introducing Rabbi Breuer," pp. 147-158; Rabbi Mordechai Breuer, "The Study of Bible and the Primacy of the Fear of Heaven: Compatibility or Contradiction?" pp. 159-180; Prof. Shnayer Z. Leiman, "Response to Rabbi Breuer," pp. 181-187. For analysis of the implications of Rabbi Breuer's method, with many important references for further study, see Rabbi Meir Ekstein, "Rabbi Mordechai Breuer and Modern Orthodox Biblical Commentary," *Tradition* 33:3 (Spring 1999), pp. 6-23; Rabbi Shalom Carmy, "Concepts of Scripture in Mordechai Breuer," in *Jewish Concepts of Scripture: A Comparative Introduction*, ed. Benjamin D. Sommer (New York: New York University Press, 2012), pp. 267-279. For a collection of Rabbi Breuer's articles on his methodology, and some of the important responses to his work, see *The Theory of Aspects of Rabbi Mordechai Breuer* (Hebrew), ed. Yosef Ofer (Alon Shevut: Tevunot, 2005).

3. Amos Hakham, *"Al Heker ha-Mikra, Torat ha-Te'udot ve-Shitat ha-Behinot,"* *Megadim* 3 (1987), pp. 67-71. He was responding to the first three articles published in *Megadim* 2 (1986), pp. 9-44, including one by Rabbi Breuer.

4. Rabbi Shalom Carmy ("Introducing Rabbi Breuer," pp. 156-157) observes further that great human writers also employ multiple

styles. Moreover, one may apply the theory of aspects in *Nakh* as well, whereas Rabbi Breuer insists that the Torah was specifically written in this manner, since it was revealed directly from God.

5. *"Teguvah le-Divrei Amos Hakham be-Inyan Torat ha-Te'udot ve-Shitat ha-Behinot,"* Megadim 4 (1987), p. 91.

6. A few years later, Rabbi Bin-Nun defended an article by Rabbi David Henshke (and therefore the religious integrity of *Megadim*) against similar charges. See Rabbi David Henshke, *"Mi-Mahorat ha-Shabbat—Mabbat Hadash,"* Megadim 14 (1991), pp. 9-26; and Rabbi Bin-Nun's response in *"Teguvot—Shetayim,"* Megadim 15 (1991), pp. 99-101.

7. Rabbi Bin-Nun employs this approach in articles such as *"'Derekh Eretz Pelishtim' Mul 'Derekh ha-Midbar Yam Suf': Mekor ha-Issur la-Shuv Mitzraymah u-Mashma'uto,"* Megadim 3 (1987), pp. 21-32; *"Ha-Yom ha-Shemini ve-Yom ha-Kippurim,"* Megadim 8 (1989), pp. 9-34; *"Zakhor ve-Shamor be-Dibbur Ehad Ne'emru,"* Megadim 9 (1989), pp. 15-26; *"Hametz u-Matzah be-Pesah, be-Shavu'ot u-va-Korbanot ha-Lehem,"* Megadim 13 (1991), pp. 25-45; *"'Ha-Aretz' ve-'Eretz Kena'an' ba-Torah,"* Megadim 17 (1991), pp. 9-46; reprinted in *Pirkei ha-Avot: Iyyunim be-Parshiyot ha-Avot be-Sefer Bereshit* (Alon Shevut: Tevunot, 2003), pp. 29-71.

8. Rabbi Avraham Shamah, Review of *Mikra le-Yisra'el—Perush Hadash la-Mikra (Megillat Rut)*, Megadim 14 (1991), pp. 148-150.

9. *"Teguvot—Shetayim,"* Megadim 15 (1991), pp. 101-102.

10. *"Ha-Pillug ve-ha-Ahdut: Kefel ha-Ta'ut ve-Halom ha-Gillui—Mippenei Ma Lo Shalah Yosef (Shali'ah) el Aviv?"* Megadim 1 (1986),

pp. 20-31; reprinted in *Pirkei ha-Avot*, pp. 165-180. Moshe Pinchuk (*Kankanim: A Multifaceted Approach to Biblical Episodes* [Hebrew] [Jerusalem: Urim, 2009], pp. 114-115, nn. 2, 6) observes that Rabbi Shemuel Shraga ben Shalom Feigenson suggested a similar idea in his marginal notes to the Jerusalem Talmud in 1949.

11. Rabbi Yaakov Medan, "'*Ba-Makom she-Ba'alei Teshuvah Omedim*' (*Parshat Yosef ve-Ehav*)," *Megadim* 2 (1986), pp. 54-78; reprinted in *Pirkei ha-Avot*, pp. 181-214.

12. Rabbi Bin-Nun's response appeared in *Megadim* 2, 109-110, and was reprinted in expanded form in *Pirkei ha-Avot*, pp. 215-222. For further analysis of this debate, see Rabbi Yuval Cherlow, *Yireh la-Levav* (Hebrew) (Tel Aviv: Miskal—Yediot Aharonot Books, 2007), pp. 279-283.

13. "*Masa Agag—Het Shaul ba-Amalek*," *Megadim* 7 (1989), pp. 49-63.

14. Rabbi Yisrael Rozen, "*Al Shaul va-Amalek ve-Al 'Mahafkhanut Hadshanit*," *Megadim* 9 (1989), pp. 81-87. They continued their debate in *Megadim* 9, pp. 88-94.

15. *Tzaddik be-Emunato Yihyeh—Al ha-Yahas le-Bikkoret ha-Mikra, Ibbud Sihot she-Nittenu al Yedei ha-Rav Zvi Yisrael Thau, Shelita*, ed. Netanel Binyamin Elyashiv (Jerusalem, 2002).

16. Rabbi Amnon Bazak, "'*Yesharim Darkei Hashem—Ve-Tzaddikim Yelekhu Bam*," *Daf Kesher* #845, Yeshivat Har Etzion (at www.etzion.org.il/dk/1to899/845mamar.htm).

17. Rabbi Mosheh Lichtenstein, "'*Ahat Dibber Elokim—Shetayim Zu Shamati?*'" *Daf Kesher* #851, Yeshivat Har Etzion (at www. etzion.org.il/dk/1to899/851mamar.htm).

18. Rabbi Mordechai Breuer, "*Bikkoret ha-Mikra ve-ha-Emunah ba-Torah Min ha-Shamayim*," *Daf Kesher* #864, Yeshivat Har Etzion (at www.etzion.org.il/dk/1to899/864mamar.htm).

19. Rabbi Avraham Shamah, "*Teguvah le-Ma'amaro shel ha-Rav Mosheh Lichtenstein*," *Daf Kesher* #866, Yeshivat Har Etzion (at www.etzion.org.il/dk/1to899/866mamar.htm).

20. Rabbi Bin-Nun, "'*Ahat Dibber Elokim—Shetayim Zu Shamati?*'" *Daf Kesher* #863, Yeshivat Har Etzion (at www.etzion.org.il/dk/1to899/863mamar.htm).

21. "*Ha-Mikra be-Mabbat Histori ve-ha-Hitnahlut ha-Yisraelit be-Eretz Kena'an*," in *Ha-Pulmus al ha-Emet ha-Historit ba-Mikra*, ed. Yisrael L. Levin and Amihai Mazar (Yad Yitzhak Ben Zvi, Merkaz Dinur: 2001), pp. 3-16.

22. "'*Ba el Ayit'—Pitaron Hadash le-Zihui ha-Ai*," in *Mehkerei Yehudah ve-Shomeron*: second conference, ed. Zeev H. Ehrlich and Yaakov Eshel (Kedumim-Ariel: Makhon HaMehkar, Mikhlelet Yehudah VeShomeron, 1992), pp. 43-64. For a collection of essays by scholars of archaeology who reach similar conclusions as Rabbi Bin-Nun on textual and archaeological grounds, see *Critical Issues in Early Israelite History*, ed. Richard S. Hess, Gerald A. Klingbeil, and Paul J. Ray Jr. (Winona Lake, IN: Eisenbrauns, 2008). See also Rabbi Amnon Bazak, *Ad ha-Yom ha-Zeh, Until This Day: Fundamental Questions in Bible Teaching*, ed. Yoshi Farajun (Yediot Aharonot-Tevunot, 2013), pp. 247-346.

23. In another article (*"Historiyah u-Mikra—ha-Yelekhu Shenayim Yahdav?: Sefer Bereshit,"* Al Atar 7 [2000], pp. 45-64), Rabbi Bin-Nun undercuts the arguments of those who deny the authenticity of Genesis based on the absence of external corroboration. He summarizes the critics' main arguments and then refutes them one by one using historical and literary arguments.

24. *"Sefer Yehoshua—Peshat ve-Divrei Hazal,"* in *Musar Milhamah ve-Kibbush* (Alon Shevut: Tevunot, 1994), pp. 31-40. Rabbi Bin-Nun elaborates on Israel's ethic of war—the need to retain a fully ethical character while still having the strength to fight evil when necessary—in *"Yedei Esav— Kol Yaakov,"* Shenaton Amit 5758-1998, pp. 13-20; reprinted in *Pirkei ha-Avot*, pp. 154-164. For further elaboration on the ramifications of this position, see Rabbi Shalom Carmy, "The Origin of Nations and the Shadow of Violence: Theological Perspectives on Canaan and Amalek," in *War and Peace in the Jewish Tradition*, ed. Lawrence Schiffman and Joel B. Wolowelsky (New York: Yeshiva University Press, 2007), pp. 163-199.

25. In an article discussing the [possible] altar found at Mount Ebal (*"Ha-Mivneh be-Har Eval ve-Zihuyo ke-Mizbe'ah: Nitu'ah Parshiyot ha-Mizbe'ah ba-Mikra Le'umat Hilkhot Mizbe'ah ba-Talmud,"* in *Lifnei Efrayim u-Binyamin u-Menasheh*, ed. Zeev Ehrlich [Jerusalem: HaMidrashah BeEretz Binyamin, Bet Sefer Sedei Ofra, 1985], pp. 137-162), Rabbi Bin-Nun weaves together Tanakh, *halakhah*, and archaeology. In an article on Benjamin's tribal inheritance, Rabbi Bin-Nun attempts to demonstrate how the geographical location of that tribe has theological ramifications (*"Nahalat Binyamin—Nahalat Shekhinah,"* in *Lifnei Efrayim u-Binyamin u-Menasheh*, pp. 25-46).

26. Nahum Sarna, *The JPS Torah Commentary: Genesis* (Philadelphia: Jewish Publication Society, 1989), pp. 378-379.

27. Both of Rabbi Bin-Nun's parents were Bible scholars, and he cites them periodically in his articles.

28. *"Ha-Ivrim ve-Eretz ha-Ivrim,"* *Megadim* 15 (1991), pp. 9-26.

29. *"Havayah Pe'ilah ve-Kiyumit ba-Mikra—Perusho shel Shem Hashem"* *Megadim* 5 (1988), pp. 7-23. It is worth noting the analogue to the human component of pre-destruction activeness vs. post-destruction passivity in Rabbi Bin-Nun's writings. In an article discussing the nature of prophetic prayer, he argues that from Abraham through Jeremiah, prophets prayed as active partners with God. Ezekiel, living at the beginning of the post-destruction era, inaugurated a new era of prayer characterized by passivity. See *"Nevu'at ha-Tefillah shel Avraham,"* in *Pirkei ha-Avot,* pp. 72-99.

30. Rabbi Meir Ekstein, "Rabbi Mordechai Breuer and Modern Orthodox Biblical Commentary," *Tradition* 33:3 (Spring 1999), p. 15.

31. *"Megillat ha-Hefekh,"* in *Hadassah Hi Esther: Sefer Zikaron le-Hadassah Esther (Dassi) Rabinowitz z"l* (Alon Shevut: Tevunot, 1999), pp. 47-54.

FAITH AND SCHOLARSHIP
CAN WALK TOGETHER

RABBI AMNON BAZAK ON THE
CHALLENGES OF ACADEMIC BIBLE
STUDY IN TRADITIONAL LEARNING[1]

Introduction

As the revealed word of God, the study of Tanakh should lie
at the heart of the learning of religious Jews along with the
Talmud and classical rabbinic thinkers. In Israel, particularly in
the Religious Zionist community, there has been a flourishing
of serious Tanakh learning in recent decades. Thankfully, some
of this excitement has spilled over into America and beyond.

With every positive development, however, there are
accompanying challenges. The scholarly values of the *peshat*
school are espoused, unaccompanied by our religious beliefs,
throughout much of the secular academic establishment.
Academic Bible study offers a wealth of valuable information

---

1. Review Essay of Rabbi Amnon Bazak, *Ad ha-Yom ha-Zeh, Until This Day: Fundamental Questions in Bible Teaching*, ed. Yoshi Farajun (Yediot Aharonot-Tevunot, 2013), 470 pages. This article appeared originally in *Tradition* 47:3 (Fall 2014), pp. 78-88.

and analytic tools. However, it also poses severe challenges to the very heart of traditional faith. The academic consensus asserts that the Torah was composed by different people and schools, all from periods after Moses. Many scholars doubt or deny the historicity of our foundational narratives. The presence of ancient textual witnesses such as the Dead Sea Scrolls and Septuagint lead many to claim that these variant texts are sometimes more reliable than the Masoretic Text.

The ostensible conflicts between tradition and academic scholarship have led many scholars, including several who identify with the Orthodox community, to conclude that traditional faith is incompatible with good scholarship. This supposition has led some to reject traditional belief outright, or to radically redefine faith to make it compatible with their scholarly conclusions, or to reinterpret classical sources in an attempt to justify such radical paradigm shifts as being within tradition. These positions have led to counter-reactions in some Orthodox circles that adopt excessively dogmatic and restrictive positions to prohibit scholarly inquiry or *peshat* learning altogether. Both sides may be motivated by a profound and authentic religious desire to connect to God and the Torah, but they distort aspects of tradition and create dangerous and unnecessary rifts between us.

In *Ad ha-Yom ha-Zeh*, Rabbi Amnon Bazak—one of the bright stars at Yeshivat Har Etzion and its affiliated Herzog College—surveys classical sources, and offers a sophisticated understanding of Tanakh and the axioms of our faith, while simultaneously being fully open to contemporary scholarship. Addressing the fact that many in the Orthodox world disregard contemporary scholarship, Rabbi Bazak offers three reasons why such willful ignorance is inexcusable:

1. These issues are widely publicized and available, and therefore rabbis and religious educators must be able to address them intelligently.
2. Many of the questions from the academy are genuine, and must be taken seriously on scholarly grounds.
3. We often stand to gain a better understanding of Tanakh with the aid of contemporary scholarship.

Rabbi Bazak presents the current state of scholarship and uses sources judiciously, rather than proposing idiosyncratic theories of his own. This book is indispensable for all who engage with the critical issues of learning Tanakh, and particularly for rabbis and educators.[1]

Rabbi Bazak frames his book as focused on the challenges from the secular academy. He explores the following topics: (1) the authorship of the Torah and other biblical books; (2) the reliability of the Masoretic Text; (3) archaeology and the historicity of the narratives in Tanakh and comparative studies between Tanakh and ancient Near Eastern texts; (4) the relationship between *peshat* and *derash*; and (5) the sins of biblical heroes. However, his book also addresses debates within the world of *yeshivot*, especially regarding the extent to which we must reckon with the academic study of Bible.[2] Yeshivat Har Etzion and Herzog College also recently published a collection of essays, entitled *Hi Sihati, My Constant Delight: Contemporary Religious Zionist Perspectives on* Tanakh *Study* (2013), to address areas debated more specifically in the Orthodox world.

Rabbi Bazak's central premise is that we must distinguish between facts and compelling tools of analysis, which must be considered in our learning; and the assumptions of scholars, which we reject when they conflict with traditional beliefs (12). He argues that nothing based on facts forces one to choose between traditional faith and good scholarship. In this essay, we will review his main arguments with a focus on the most fundamental issue: traditional Jewish belief in *Torah min ha-Shamayim* (Torah from Heaven) and its purported clashes with contemporary academic scholarship.

The Early Date of the Torah and Later Glosses

The text of the Torah never states that the Five Books of Moses were all revealed by God to Moses. The word *"torah"* in the Torah generally refers to subsections of what we now call the Torah. Only at the end of the biblical period, in Ezra-Nehemiah and Chronicles, do we find verses that likely refer to the entire Torah as we know it. Critics cite this evidence to suggest that the final form of our Torah hails from the beginning of the Second Temple period (21-29).

Rabbi Bazak rejects this conclusion, countering that other biblical books often refer to verses from the Torah, and there also are many literary parallels between the Torah and other biblical books. At least some of those parallels suggest that the passages in the Prophets and Holy Writings are dependent on the Torah, rather than the other way around (30-34). Additionally, the Patriarchs violate explicit Torah laws. If later authors composed the Torah in a manner that reflected their own beliefs through the narratives, as the critics claim, they would have invented stories in which the Patriarchs were faithful to the Torah (269).[3] The Torah also features a unique vocabulary, which is difficult to explain if it were composed later than other biblical books (103-105). Thus, the textual evidence demonstrates that the Torah is earlier than the other biblical books.

That much of the Torah can be shown to pre-date the Prophets and Holy Writings, however, does not prove that every verse in the Torah dates back to Moses. In fact, the Talmud and several medieval commentators agree that small parts of the Torah may have been added by prophets later than Moses. The starting point is the discussion whether the final eight verses in the Torah—which narrate the death of Moses—were written by Joshua or by Moses (*Bava Batra* 14b-15a).

Medieval figures such as Rabbis Abraham ibn Ezra, Judah the Pious, and Joseph Tov Elem Bonfils (*Tzafenat Pane'ah*) explained several narrative verses or half-verses (and never laws) as additions by later prophets. This position did not interfere with their belief in *Torah min ha-Shamayim* (Torah from Heaven). In their view, God revealed the overwhelming majority of the Torah, including all of its laws, to Moses, and later prophets added these minor narrative glosses through prophetic revelation. In this spirit, Rabbi Bazak submits several additional verses that also appear to have been added by later prophets (49-65).

However, some contemporary scholars extend this argument to its extreme, maintaining that even were one to believe that *all* the Torah was revealed to different prophets after Moses, that position would still be within Jewish tradition. They argue that the academic consensus of dating the entire Torah to after Moses is compatible with traditional Jewish belief, so long as one believes that the authors of the Torah were prophets.[4]

Rabbi Mordechai Breuer emphatically rejected this view. One cannot equate the views of classical commentators who allow for minor later prophetic narrative glosses with the views of those contemporary scholars who insist that most or all of the Torah was written by prophets later than Moses.[5] This view is inconsistent with what Jews have historically believed, namely, that God revealed the Torah to Moses. Rabbi Breuer also insists that this contemporary extension is based on a misunderstanding of *Torah min ha-Shamayim*. That concept does not simply mean "prophetic revelation," and we would not say, for example, that the Book of Isaiah is "from Heaven" in the same sense. *Torah min ha-Shamayim* refers exclusively to the Torah, whose level of divine revelation infinitely transcends that of other prophecy.[6]

Rabbi Bazak adds that those phrases interpreted as later glosses could hypothetically be removed from the Torah and we still would have a full coherent text, which tradition ascribes to God's revelation to Moses (65-69). Even if there were later glosses, those additions do not materially alter the Torah's fundamental messages and teachings. However, were one to say that the entire Torah, or huge chunks of it, were written after Moses, then the remainder would be non-existent or too sparse to be meaningful.

In his book *The Limits of Orthodox Theology*, Professor Marc Shapiro demonstrates that many thinkers before and after Rambam espoused views different from that of Rambam's formulations of the Principles of Faith. In his review of that book, Rabbi Yitzchak Blau cogently observes that Professor Shapiro is correct, but the existence of disagreements over the precise boundaries of Jewish faith does not imply that there are no Jewish beliefs held by all traditional religious thinkers. A wider boundary still must be defined that unites classical Jewish thinkers.[7] Rabbi Bazak's thorough treatment of these critical topics is precisely what was needed in response to Rabbi Blau's challenge.

Documentary Hypothesis

Our Sages and later commentators have long recognized the preponderance of contradictions in both narrative and legal sections of the Torah. Generally, however, they explained each issue individually, rather than asking the more global question of why this phenomenon is so prevalent in the Torah (81-88).

In the 18th and 19th centuries, liberal Protestant scholars began asking this question in a systematic manner. After several generations of scholarly inquiry, Julius Wellhausen proposed the Documentary Hypothesis. It is based on literary considerations such as repetitions and contradictions, and also contains a historical component, as Wellhausen attempted to date the putative documents into an evolutionary history of Israel's religion. This hypothesis dominated the academy for several generations, and continues to hold sway in many academic circles, though it is not as universally accepted as it once was.

Rabbi Bazak summarizes the primary arguments against the Documentary Hypothesis, many of which have been raised by academic scholars as well (94-109).[8] Even granting the weaknesses of the Documentary Hypothesis, however, we still need to explain the genuine literary evidence that led the architects of the Documentary Hypothesis to their conclusions.

Rising to this challenge, Rabbi Mordechai Breuer proposed his Theory of Aspects. He posited that God revealed the Torah to Moses in its complex form so that the multiple aspects of the infinite Torah could be presented in different sections. Since we are limited as humans, we cannot simultaneously entertain these perspectives, so they appear to us as contradictory. The complete truth emerges only when one takes all facets into account. In this manner, Rabbi Breuer accepted the text analysis of the Documentary Hypothesis, while rejecting its underlying beliefs and assumptions.[9]

There are weaknesses in Rabbi Breuer's theory, including several discussed by Rabbi Bazak. Notwithstanding, Rabbis Yoel Bin-Nun[10] and Shalom Carmy[11] maintain that one must use a methodology that understands different sections of the Torah as presenting aspects of a larger picture, regardless of whether one accepts Rabbi Breuer's theory in its entirety. Rabbi Bazak agrees with Rabbis Bin-Nun and Carmy on this point (109-150).

To summarize, regnant academic theories do not force one to choose between traditional faith and scholarship. Contemporary Orthodox scholars address the text evidence and accept that there are contradictions that must be analyzed systematically, while rejecting the underlying assumptions of those scholars who have hypotheses about the origins of the Torah that go beyond the text evidence.

Text Criticism

We stand in awe of the Jewish scribal tradition for its painstaking efforts to transmit the text of Tanakh and particularly the Torah. Nevertheless, it is difficult to insist that our Torah scrolls are letter-perfect versions of the text that God revealed to Moses, and our Sages and later commentators were well aware of this reality. The Masoretic Text differs—sometimes meaningfully— from the text of Tanakh used by our Sages in their Midrashim. Our Sages and commentators acknowledge variants and express uncertainty about a number of elements in the text. There also are significant variants between the most authoritative versions of what we call the Masoretic Text (183-210). From within canonical sources alone, then, one must arrive at the conclusion of Rabbi Yaakov Weinberg:

> The words of the Rambam, "the entire Torah in our possession today [was given to us by the Almighty through Moshe Rabbeinu]," must not be taken literally, implying that all the letters of the present Torah are the exact letters given to Moshe Rabbeinu. Rather, it should be understood in a general sense that the Torah we learn and live by is for all intents and purposes the same Torah that was given to Moshe Rabbeinu.[12]

After surveying the classical sources, Rabbi Bazak then discusses the Dead Sea Scrolls, Septuagint, and other ancient textual witnesses (210-243). These versions often reflect interpretive or ideological changes from the Masoretic Text. However, sometimes it is possible that they reflect genuine ancient versions of the Hebrew text.

Although the Masoretic Text of the Torah may not be a letter-perfect transmission from Moses, we accept it on halakhic grounds for writing Torah scrolls. Additionally, in his introduction to Leviticus, Rabbi David Zvi Hoffmann argues that, since textual emendations cannot be conclusively proven, in practice we treat the Masoretic Text as God's revealed word and interpret that text. Finally, Rabbi Bazak shows several examples where a superficial reading of each passage may have led some to propose emendations, but a more careful reading reveals that the Masoretic Text is preferable.

Archaeology and the Historicity of Tanakh

Archaeology presents a different set of challenges from those discussed above. Many contemporary archaeologists dismiss the historicity of Tanakh's foundational stories, including the existence of the Patriarchs, the exodus from Egypt, and the conquest and settlement of Israel. Rabbi Bazak addresses the most important questions pertaining to each historical period (247-316).

Once again, there are facts that must be taken seriously, and there are assumptions that should be rejected: (1) Many archaeologists rely on the speculative assertions of biblical criticism, which themselves are unproven. (2) Many archaeologists have political and religious agendas, and their interpretations of the data reflect those agendas. (3) Those who deny the historicity of the Torah's narratives often make such arguments based on lack of evidence, but arguments from silence are weak.

Moreover, the Patriarchal narratives reflect the realities of their period and do not reflect the realities of a much later era when critics claim they were written. The same is true of the exodus from Egypt. Rabbi Bazak quotes Rabbi Yoel Bin-Nun, who observes that nobody living many centuries after these events could have invented details that so closely reflect the periods in which the Torah says they occurred.[13] Additionally, many of the ostensible conflicts that archaeologists raise between their findings and the biblical text are based on superficial readings of the biblical text.

One element lacking from Rabbi Bazak's discussion is the extent to which tradition insists that we must accept that every detail in the stories is intended to be understood in a rigidly literal way. He states simply that our faith requires belief in the historicity of the narratives since those events form the basis for mitzvah observance. He then extends this argument by observing that if one begins casting doubt on some of the details, one may come to doubt the historicity of the stories altogether (250).

This is the one occasion in *Ad ha-Yom ha-Zeh* where Rabbi Bazak greatly oversimplifies a complex issue. Not all traditional interpreters accept one hundred percent of the Torah narratives as literal. Talking animals, the appearance of angels, and divine body parts and emotions, among many others, convinced several of our greatest thinkers that if there is a conflict between the literal reading of the Torah and reason/science, then the Torah must be reinterpreted. Rambam stated:

> I believe every possible happening that is supported by a prophetic statement and do not strip it of its plain meaning. I fall back on interpreting a statement only when its literal sense is impossible, like the corporeality of God: the possible however remains as stated (*Treatise on Resurrection*).[14]

Rambam included considerably more than God's corporeality among the impossible, and therefore allegorized many biblical passages.

Citing Rambam, Professor Uriel Simon suggested that a traditionalist should accept the literal reading of Tanakh unless it contradicts genuine archaeological evidence—the position of the "maximalists."[15] To apply this principle to a specific example: Many critics argue that camels were not domesticated until the twelfth century BCE. However, Abraham and Jacob are said to have had camels. Therefore, the critics conclude that Genesis must have been written in a later period, anachronistically inserting camels into its narratives.

As noted above, arguments from silence are weak to begin with, and therefore this hardly could be considered a conflict at the level of fact. In this instance, however, Rabbi Bazak maintains that the archaeological record and the biblical text do not conflict. We have evidence of limited camel domestication considerably earlier than the twelfth century BCE, and that process of domestication became more widespread after the twelfth century. Similarly, the Patriarchs had only a few camels, whereas camels become more prevalent beginning in the book of Judges, which relates events after the twelfth century BCE (260-263). Thus, we may accept the literal reading as historical.

What of the position of Professor Simon, though? Is there room in tradition for the argument that the Torah need not be taken literally on small details if there were to be an apparent factual conflict? A more effective argument for Rabbi Bazak would have been a systematic treatment of the boundaries of tradition regarding taking the Torah's narratives literally, followed by his chapter on archaeology that insists that contemporary scholarship does not in fact conflict with the Torah's narratives.[16]

Conclusion

To some extent, *Ad ha-Yom ha-Zeh* is intended as an inoculation for challenges to faith by arguing that one does not need to choose between faith and scholarship. While understanding that we cannot conclusively answer all questions, Rabbi Bazak espouses the tenets of our faith and forthrightly addresses the major challenges within the realm of contemporary Bible scholarship. It is hoped that rabbis, educators, and all who are interested in serious Tanakh learning will study this book in its entirety.

Rabbi Bazak's approach also fosters a language that speaks to believers and non-believers alike, building bridges and opening dialogue based on traditional faith and scholarship for the sake of Heaven. Religious scholarship benefits from contemporary findings—both information and methodology. On the other side of the equation, the academy stands to benefit from those who are heirs to thousands of years of tradition, who approach every word of Tanakh with awe and reverence, and who care deeply about the intricate relationship between texts. The academy also must become more aware of its own underlying biases. It also is hoped that members of the academic community will read *Ad ha-Yom ha-Zeh* and respond to Rabbi Bazak's learned challenges to some of today's regnant academic theories. In this manner, we may refine the genuine scholarly issues in mutual dialogue.

Finally, and most importantly, as Rabbi Shalom Carmy regularly emphasizes, our primary focus must be the encounter of God's word in Tanakh, rather than the study of ancillary subjects such as history, linguistics, or literature for their own sake. Nor should we become overly distracted by the challenges of Bible Criticism:

> To the extent that we take seriously some of the things noticed by the critics that were previously overlooked, or in the case of the great Jewish exegetes, were noticed

unsystematically, it is the task of contemporary Orthodox students to show how the Torah coheres in the light of our belief in *Torah mi-Sinai*. The goal of those engaged in this activity... is not primarily to refute the Documentary Hypothesis but rather to do justice to worthwhile questions within the larger framework of Torah study.[17]

Our early morning daily liturgy challenges us: "Ever shall a person be God-fearing in secret as in public, who admits the truth and speaks truth in his heart." May we be worthy of pursuing that noble combination in the study of Tanakh.

NOTES

1. The material is translated into English and archived at the Virtual Beit Midrash of Yeshivat Har Etzion, at http://www.vbm-torah. org/Tanakhstudy.html. Rabbi Moshe Sokolow has since published a book in English that addresses several of the same issues and classical sources: *Tanakh: An Owner's Manual: Authorship, Canonization, Masoretic Text, Exegesis, Modern Scholarship and Pedagogy* (Brooklyn, NY: Ktav, 2015).

2. In 2002, this issue became needlessly explosive as a result of an unfortunate condemnation by Rabbi Zvi Thau from Yeshivat Har HaMor. On the positive side, his attack elicited a series of thoughtful responses by teachers at Yeshivat Har Etzion and its affiliated Herzog College, including Rabbi Bazak. For a summary of that discussion, see Hayyim Angel, "*Torat Hashem Temima:* The Contributions of Rav Yoel Bin-Nun to Religious Tanakh Study," *Tradition* 40:3 (Fall 2007), pp. 9-11; reprinted in this volume.

3. See also Rabbi Yoel Bin-Nun, "*Historiyah U-Mikra—Ha-Yelekhu Shenayim Yahdav?: Sefer Bereshit*," *Al Atar* 7 (2000), pp. 45-64. For a survey of medieval commentators who recognized that the Patriarchs did not observe all of the commandments in the Torah, see Uriel Simon, "*Peshat* Exegesis of Biblical History—Between Historicity, Dogmatism, and the Medieval Period" (Hebrew), in *Tehillah le-Moshe: Biblical and Judaic Studies in Honor of Moshe Greenberg*, ed. Mordechai Cogan, Barry L. Eichler, and Jeffrey Tigay (Winona Lake, IN: Eisenbrauns, 1997), Hebrew section, pp. 171*-203*.

4. See, for example, Israel Knohl, "Between Faith and Criticism" (Hebrew), *Megadim* 33 (2001), pp. 123-126.

5. Rabbi Mordechai Breuer, response to Israel Knohl (Hebrew), *Megadim* 33 (2001), pp. 127-132. Already in the 18th century, Rabbi Hayyim ibn Attar (*Or ha-Hayyim* on Deut. 34:5) expressed alarm when he heard about some Jews who extended the talmudic view regarding the final eight verses to lead to denial of faith in the revelation of the Torah to Moses altogether.

6. Rabbi Mordechai Breuer, "On Bible Criticism" (Hebrew), *Megadim* 30 (1999), pp. 97-107.

7. Marc B. Shapiro, *The Limits of Orthodox Theology: Maimonides' Thirteen Principles Reappraised* (Oxford: Littman Library of Jewish Civilization, 2004); Rabbi Yitzchak Blau, "Flexibility with a Firm Foundation: On Maintaining Jewish Dogma," *Torah U-Madda Journal* 12 (2004), pp. 179-191. Shapiro writes as an intellectual historian and not as a theologian, and therefore did not attempt to draw any boundaries from his research. However, that work remained to be done, and Rabbi Bazak has done an admirable job.

8. For a sustained critique of source-criticism and its underlying biases and methodology, see Joshua A. Berman, *Inconsistency in the Torah: Ancient Literary Convention and the Limits of Source Criticism* (Oxford: Oxford University Press, 2017).

9. For analysis of Rabbi Breuer's methodology, see Rabbi Meir Ekstein, "Rabbi Mordechai Breuer and Modern Orthodox Biblical Commentary," *Tradition* 33:3 (Spring 1999), pp. 6-23; Rabbi Shalom Carmy, "Concepts of Scripture in Mordechai Breuer," in *Jewish Concepts of Scripture: A Comparative Introduction*, ed. Benjamin D. Sommer (New York: New York University Press, 2012), pp. 267-279. For a collection of Rabbi Breuer's articles on his methodology, and important responses to his work, see *The Theory of Aspects of Rabbi Mordechai Breuer* (Hebrew), ed. Yosef Ofer (Alon Shevut: Tevunot, 2005).

10. Rabbi Yoel Bin-Nun, "*Teguvah le-Divrei Amos Hakham be-Inyan Torat ha-Te'udot ve-Shitat ha-Behinnot*" (Hebrew), *Megadim* 4 (1987), p. 91.

11. Rabbi Shalom Carmy, "Always Connect," in *Where the Yeshiva Meets the University: Traditional and Academic Approaches to Tanakh Study*, ed. Hayyim Angel, *Conversations* 15 (Winter 2013), pp. 8-9.

12. Rabbi Yaakov Weinberg, *Fundamentals and Faith: Insights into the Rambam's 13 Principles*, ed. Mordechai Blumenfeld (Southfield, MI: Targum-Feldheim, 1991), p. 91. For surveys of the views of classical commentators, see B. Barry Levy, *Fixing God's Torah: The Accuracy of the Hebrew Bible Text in Jewish Law* (Oxford: Oxford University Press, 2001); Yeshayahu Maori, "Rabbinic Midrash as

Evidence for Textual Variants in the Hebrew Bible: History and Practice," trans. Hayyim Angel, in *Modern Scholarship in the Study of Torah: Contributions and Limitations*, ed. Shalom Carmy (Northvale, NJ: Jason Aronson, 1996), pp. 101-129.

13. For a thorough treatment of the different periods that details this argument, see Kenneth A. Kitchen, *On the Reliability of the Old Testament* (Grand Rapids, MI: Eerdmans, 2003).

14. Translation from *Crisis and Leadership: Epistles of Rambam*, Abraham S. Halkin, trans. and D. Hartman (Philadelphia: Jewish Publication Society, 1985), p. 228.

15. Uriel Simon, "Post-Biblical and Post-Zionist Archaeology" (Hebrew), in *Ha-Pulmus al ha-Emet ha-Historit ba-Mikra*, ed. Yisrael L. Levin and Amihai Mazar (Jerusalem: Yad Yitzhak Ben Zvi, 2001), pp. 135-140.

16. For exploration of different areas where traditional commentators debate the extent of taking the biblical text literally, see Hayyim Angel, "Controversies over the Historicity of Biblical Passages in Traditional Commentary," in Angel, *Increasing Peace through Balanced Torah Study, Conversations* 27 (Winter 2017), pp. 10-21; reprinted in this volume. For an effort to define the parameters of what is traditionally acceptable within the allegorization of biblical passages, see Joshua L. Golding, "On the Limits of Non-Literal Interpretation of Scripture from an Orthodox Perspective," *Torah U-Madda Journal* 10 (2001), pp. 37-59.

17. Rabbi Shalom Carmy, "A *Peshat* in the Dark: Reflections on the Age of Cary Grant," *Tradition* 43:1 (Spring 2010), pp. 4-5. See also, for example, "Always Connect"; "Homer and the Bible,"

Tradition 41:4 (Winter 2008), pp. 1-7; "A Room with a View, but a Room of Our Own," in *Modern Scholarship in the Study of Torah: Contributions and Limitations*, ed. Shalom Carmy (Northvale, NJ: Jason Aronson Inc., 1996), pp. 1-38; "To Get the Better of Words: An Apology for *Yir'at Shamayim* in Academic Jewish Studies," *Torah U-Madda Journal* 2 (1990), pp. 7-24.

CLASSICAL COMMENTATORS IN THE CONTEMPORARY CLASSROOM

RABBI YAAKOV BLAU ON TOPICAL STUDIES IN TANAKH AND COMMENTARIES[1]

Introduction

We are privileged to live at a time when there has been a resurgence of intensive religious Tanakh study. There is a growing body of scholarship where the interpretations of our classical commentators play a central role. Additionally, advances in the application of literary theory to Tanakh and *parshanut* scholarship, as well as ancillary areas such as archaeology and linguistics, have enabled several contemporary religious scholars and educators to synthesize the old with the new in their efforts to bring Tanakh to life and foster religious growth through what Rabbi Shalom Carmy has termed the literary-theological approach to Tanakh.[1]

Rabbi Yaakov Blau, a master educator for over two decades, recently published a brief book that addresses several of the

---

1. Review essay of Rabbi Yaakov Blau, *Medieval Commentary in the Modern Era: The Enduring Value of Classical Parshanut* (Self-Published, 2014), 83 pages.

central issues that arise in forging that ideal balance. He first reprints an exchange between himself and Rabbi Yaakov Beasley that originally appeared in the journal *Tradition*.[2] Rabbi Blau then presents several essays on what he terms the "*sugya*" (topical) approach to Tanakh and classical commentaries. In this essay, we first will explore the broader debate, and then turn to Rabbi Blau's essays on individual commentators.

Balancing the Old with the New

Rabbis Blau and Beasley fundamentally agree that classical commentary and contemporary scholarship have value, but disagree over educational emphasis. Rabbi Blau insists that the heart of the dialogue remains within classical commentators, and contemporary scholarship should at most serve as "icing on the cake" (1). In contrast, Rabbi Beasley advocates more extensive application of contemporary scholarship and methodology in the yeshiva classroom.

Our goal is to learn to think with our commentators so that we may creatively engage with Tanakh and grow religiously through this encounter. Educators therefore should model a transparent process whereby students can understand how the commentators reached their conclusions. Rabbi Shalom Carmy stresses the need to work from within Professor Nehama Leibowitz's intensive concentration on classical commentary and from that foundation to work outward toward more recent trends in literary and historical-archaeological scholarship when they benefit our learning.[3]

Several elements distinguish the work of our classical commentators from that of all other Bible scholars. The classical commentators represent the connection to our tradition, they are concerned about the relationship between Written and Oral Law, they show reverence to biblical heroes and do not view them as ordinary people,[4] and, most importantly, they read Tanakh as God's revealed word and central to religious study. Rabbi Shalom Carmy has remarked that Ibn Ezra and Radak have more in common with the Hasidic commentary *Sefat Emet* by Rabbi Yehudah Aryeh Leib Alter of Ger than they do with contemporary secular academic Bible scholars.[5]

Of course, our classical commentators also were first-rate *peshat* scholars whose works belong at the forefront of any scholarly discussion of Tanakh. To this point, Michael V. Fox, a contemporary academic scholar, laments the neglect of classical Jewish commentators in much of contemporary academic discourse:

> Medieval Jewish commentary has largely been neglected in academic Bible scholarship, though a great many of the ideas of modern commentators arose first among the medievals, and many of their brightest insights are absent from later exegesis.[6]

There also is much to gain from contemporary scholarship and methodology. For example, Rabbi Mordechai Breuer was inspired by some of the questions (but not the answers) of contemporary academic scholarship and forged a new path by considering contradictions globally, rather than attempting to "solve" them one at a time as was commonly practiced in earlier generations.[7] The treatment of historical issues by Rabbi Yoel Bin-Nun has fostered a deeper understanding of Tanakh in its real-world setting.[8] Rabbi Shalom Carmy has developed a methodology of exploring profound religious questions through a blend of classical commentary and usage of contemporary scholarship when it contributes to the discussion.

Although most issues in the dialogue between Rabbis Blau and Beasley are essential, there are occasions where the "polemical" nature of the debate sidesteps the fundamental issues. For example, Rabbi Blau criticizes many practitioners of the "new school" methodology, since they do not engage seriously with classical commentary and often make things up and call their shoddy analyses "close readings" (4). Although this criticism might sometimes be true, this caveat cuts both ways, as there are also many educators who use classical commentators but lack even the most basic sense of *peshat*. Good scholars and scholarship of both methodologies can be productive, whereas sloppy scholars and scholarship on either side can be unimpressive and even educationally damaging.

To cite another weakness in the debate, Rabbi Beasley invokes two of the greatest Tanakh scholars and educators of the previous generation: "Finally to paraphrase both Nechama [Leibowitz] and Dr. [Mordechai] Breuer, didn't Rashi study the Humash without commentaries? From an educational point of view, doesn't demonstrating to the students how the *mefarshim* arrived at their conclusions have value" (9)? Although Rabbi Beasley is correct that there is great benefit to demonstrating to students how commentators arrive at their conclusions, Rashi hardly learned without commentaries. He frequently cites and paraphrases Midrash, and draws from whatever medieval commentaries he had available. Similarly, Ibn Ezra, that quintessential *pashtan*, quotes some forty commentators by name, more than any other medieval Jewish commentator.[9]

Rashi may not have learned with *Rashi's* commentary, but if we wish to emulate the learning methodology of Rashi and Ibn Ezra, it is not by opening a Tanakh and interpreting it on our own. Rather, it is through rigorous analysis of the biblical text, careful study of our commentators, and evaluation of every argument against the text.

Professor Nehama Leibowitz combined classical commentary with systematic analysis to bring out religious lessons of the Torah.[10] One potential shortcoming of Nehama's method was her overemphasis on commentaries, which made it difficult for the reader to retrace a commentator's steps to return back to the text itself. Nehama feared this outcome of her work, as well:

> In Elementary and High Schools, we do not study *parshanut* or exegetical methodology for their own sake; rather, we study Torah with the assistance of its interpreters. And if, God forbid, the Torah should be pushed to the side—whether its stories and laws, its teachings and ideas, its guidance and beauty—because of overemphasis on *parshanim*, then any small gain my book achieves will be lost at a greater expense.[11]

This is where her analytical approach to *parshanut*, coupled with the contemporary literary-theological approach, can be particularly valuable.

In the final analysis, we must distinguish between contemporary scholarship that serves as "icing on the cake," and that which significantly enhances learning and religious engagement. Educators must balance their own learning time and classroom time, but they certainly should be conversant with some of the works and methodologies of the scholars at Herzog College, Yeshiva University, and beyond. They also should utilize Rabbi Blau's *sugya* approach to develop more classes to maximize the relevance and impact of our classical commentators.

The *Sugya* Approach to Tanakh and *Parshanut*

Rabbi Blau advocates and exemplifies studies of *sugyot*, in which he presents biblical topics and themes within Ramban, Ibn Ezra, Radak, and Targum. Our classical commentators often utilize their command of all of Tanakh to explicate individual verses. By writing in a lucid, concise, and transparent manner, Rabbi Blau offers lessons and methodology that educators can apply to their classrooms. He also models an approach that educators can use to develop their own classes on topics and trends within Tanakh and the commentaries.

Rabbi Blau devotes two chapters to the *sugya* approach to Tanakh (18-40), in which he presents several topics that require knowledge of passages from multiple places in Tanakh. For example, the process of ascertaining true and false prophets requires study of Deut. 18:21-22, Jer. 18:7-10, and Jeremiah 28. Rabbi Blau explores the approaches of several commentators as they attempt to explain the interrelationship between these biblical passages.

In his essays on Ramban, Ibn Ezra, Radak, and Targum (41-83), Rabbi Blau uses the *sugya* approach to pinpoint important aspects of the thought of these commentators. For example, Ramban (on Gen. 18:1) sharply disagrees with Rambam's position that people perceive angels only in prophetic visions

(*Guide of the Perplexed* 2:32), and insists that sometimes people perceive angels while in a waking state. Rabbi Blau traces Ramban's position about prophecy based on his interpretation of Abraham's feeding angels (Genesis 18), angels encountering Lot and his family (Genesis 19), Jacob's wrestling with an angel (Genesis 32), and Hagar's dialogue with an angel (Genesis 16). By combining the multiple places where Ramban addresses this question, Rabbi Blau demonstrates how one can appreciate Ramban's global approach.

Rabbi Blau similarly shows how Ibn Ezra maintains that several passages are written from the mistaken perspective of the characters in the narrative, and do not reflect objective truth. For example, Josh. 2:7 reports that the king of Jericho's guards chased Joshua's spies. However, Rahab had hidden Joshua's spies, and therefore the guards were not objectively chasing anyone. Thus, the narrative speaks from the perspective of the characters. Similarly, Ibn Ezra (on Exod. 20:3) explains the Torah's calling pagan deities "other gods"—seemingly suggesting that these deities exist—in terms of the misguided perspective of the pagans, who wrongly believe that there are other gods. By citing examples from several biblical books, Rabbi Blau illustrates how this is an essential aspect of Ibn Ezra's interpretive strategy.

Excellent and useful as these examples are, Rabbi Blau does not cite a single secondary study in his endnotes, despite the fact that the commentators he discusses have attracted considerable scholarly attention. While of course one should not expect a comprehensive study, several conclusions of Rabbi Blau are weakened since he does not draw from any systematic studies of our classical commentators.

For example, Rabbi Blau draws a sweeping conclusion that Radak generally acts unbound by narrative interpretations of the Sages, but feels bound in "major" cases, such as with David and Bathsheba, where Radak accepts the position in *Shabbat* 56a that Bathsheba and Uriah could not have been halakhically married (69).[12] Rabbi Blau's conclusion is uncompelling. Radak is bound by the biblical text and also the Oral Law.[13] Like Rashi, Ralbag, and Malbim, perhaps Radak also was concerned with God's approval of David's subsequent marriage to Bathsheba. The Mishnah (*Sotah* 27b) teaches that in the case of adultery, "Just as she is prohibited to the husband so is she prohibited to the paramour." The Sages generally consider that ruling to have the status of Torah law. Within this framework, God would not have sanctioned the marriage of David and Bathsheba if they had committed technical adultery. Therefore, Bathsheba must not have been legally married to Uriah at the time of the affair with David. Radak's acceptance of the position in *Shabbat* 56a, then, does not stem primarily because David's sin with Bathsheba was "major." Rather, there is a concern with the halakhic ruling in *Sotah* 27b and its relationship to *peshat*.

Moreover, it also is important to stress that the position championed in *Shabbat* 56a, that Uriah must have given a *get* (writ of divorce) to Bathsheba before going to war, is not the only position of the Sages. Elsewhere in the Talmud, there are opinions that Bathsheba was possibly a married woman or certainly a married woman[14]; and that Bathsheba's consent still might be viewed halakhically as a form of rape of a married woman since she was not in a position to decline.[15] Even in *Shabbat* 56a where several Sages defend David from technical adultery, Rav dismisses some (Rashi) or all (Abarbanel) of that defense. Therefore, it cannot be said that Radak was bound to "the Sages" in this instance. Rather, Radak adopted one opinion within the Gemara that he believed best accounted for *peshat* in the text and the halakhic concern from *Sotah* 27b.

To cite one other example where Rabbi Blau relies on his intuition rather than on more systematic studies, Rabbi Blau observes that Midrashim often associate known figures with unnamed or obscure figures. However, he extends this midrashic trend to *pashtanim*. For example, some *pashtanim* identify the obscure leader Sheshbazzar (mentioned in Ezra 1:8; 5:16) with the well-known leader Zerubbabel (Rabbi Moshe Kimhi, Ralbag, Ibn Ezra on Dan. 6:29). Rabbi Blau assumes that these commentators are concerned over how a minor figure such as Sheshbazzar be entrusted with the Temple's vessels. Therefore, it must be that Sheshbazzar is another name for the major figure, Zerubbabel (35).

However, Rabbi Blau's explanation does not appear to be the most likely way to account for the identification of Sheshbazzar with Zerubbabel. *Pashtanim* are usually motivated by elements in the biblical text, rather than merely a desire to identify obscure characters. In this instance, these commentators were concerned that Ezra 5:16 reports that Sheshbazzar laid the foundation for the Second Temple, whereas Haggai (Hag. 2:18) and Zechariah (Zech. 4:9) state that Zerubbabel laid its foundation. Ibn Ezra on Dan. 6:29 explicitly makes this point. Ibn Ezra and Ralbag further observe that Ezra 2:1 lists Zerubbabel as the leader of the community, only a few verses after Sheshbazzar was listed as the leader of the community.

Conclusion

Overall, Rabbi Blau's book is an excellent resource for educators both for its content and its usefulness to educators. More importantly, his essays present a transparent methodology that educators can apply to countless other examples within Tanakh and to the approaches of our classical commentators. Through these and related systematic studies of Tanakh and commentary, educators and students stand to gain in their learning, creative engagement, and, most importantly, religious growth through Torah.

NOTES

1. See Rabbi Shalom Carmy, "A Room with a View, but a Room of Our Own," in *Modern Scholarship in the Study of Torah: Contributions and Limitations*, ed. Shalom Carmy (Northvale, NJ: Jason Aronson, 1996), pp. 1-38; Rabbi Yaakov Beasley, "Return of the *Pashtanim*," *Tradition* 42:1 (Spring 2009), pp. 67-83; Hayyim Angel, "The Literary-Theological Study of Tanakh," afterword to Moshe Sokolow, *Tanakh: An Owner's Manual: Authorship, Canonization, Masoretic Text, Exegesis, Modern Scholarship and Pedagogy* (Brooklyn, NY: Ktav, 2015), pp. 192-207; also in Angel, *Peshat Isn't So Simple: Essays on Developing a Religious Methodology to Bible Study* (New York: Kodesh Press, 2014), pp. 118-136.

2. Rabbi Yaakov Blau and Rabbi Yaakov Beasley, "The 'New School' of Bible Study: An Exchange," *Tradition* 42:3 (Fall 2009), pp. 85-93.

3. Rabbi Shalom Carmy, "Always Connect," in *Where the Yeshiva Meets the University: Traditional and Academic Approaches to*

Tanakh Study, ed. Hayyim Angel, *Conversations* 15 (Winter 2013), pp. 1-12.

4. See, for example, Rabbi Aharon Lichtenstein, "A Living Torah" (Hebrew), in *Hi Sihati: Al Derekh Limmud ha-Tanakh*, ed. Yehoshua Reiss (Jerusalem: Maggid, 2013), pp. 17-30; Rabbi Amnon Bazak, *Ad ha-Yom ha-Zeh: Until This Day: Fundamental Questions in Bible Teaching* (Hebrew), ed. Yoshi Farajun (Tel Aviv: Yediot Aharonot, 2013), pp. 432-470; Rabbi Shalom Carmy, "To Get the Better of Words: An Apology for *Yir'at Shamayim* in Academic Jewish Studies," *Torah U-Madda Journal* 2 (1990), pp. 7-24; Rabbi Yaakov Medan, *David u-Bat Sheva: Ha-Het, ha-Onesh, ve-ha-Tikkun* (Hebrew) (Alon Shevut: Tevunot, 2002), pp. 7-24.

5. Rabbi Shalom Carmy, "To Get the Better of Words," pp. 12-13.

6. Michael V. Fox, *Proverbs 1-9*. Anchor Bible 18A (New York: Doubleday, 2000), p. 12.

7. For analysis of Rabbi Breuer's method, see Rabbi Amnon Bazak, *Ad ha-Yom ha-Zeh*, pp. 109-139; Rabbi Shalom Carmy, "Concepts of Scripture in Mordechai Breuer," in *Jewish Concepts of Scripture: A Comparative Introduction*, ed. Benjamin D. Sommer (New York: New York University Press, 2012), pp. 267-279; Rabbi Meir Ekstein, "Rabbi Mordechai Breuer and Modern Orthodox Biblical Commentary," *Tradition* 33:3 (Spring 1999), pp. 6-23.

8. See Hayyim Angel, "*Torat Hashem Temima*: The Contributions of Rav Yoel Bin-Nun to Religious Tanakh Study," *Tradition* 40:3 (Fall 2007), pp. 5-18; reprinted in this volume.

9. Nahum M. Sarna, "Abraham Ibn Ezra as an Exegete," in Sarna, *Studies in Biblical Interpretation* (Philadelphia: Jewish Publication Society, 2000), p. 151.

10. For further discussion of Nehama's methodology and balance between text and commentary, see Hayyim Angel, Review Essay: "The Paradox of *Parshanut*: Are Our Eyes on the Text, or on the Commentators?" *Tradition* 38:4 (Winter 2004), pp. 112-128; reprinted in Angel, *Through an Opaque Lens* (New York: Sephardic Publication Foundation, 2006), pp. 56-76; revised second edition (New York: Kodesh Press, 2013), pp. 39-59; *Peshat Isn't So Simple: Essays on Developing a Religious Methodology to Bible Study* (New York: Kodesh Press, 2014), pp. 36-57.

11. *Limmud Parshanei ha-Torah u-Derakhim le-Hora'atam: Sefer Bereshit* (Hebrew), (Jerusalem: The Joint Authority for Jewish Zionist Education, Department for Torah and Culture in the Diaspora, 1975), introduction, p. 1.

12. For the record, Radak (on 2 Sam. 11:4) first says that Bathsheba was a married woman, and then quotes *Shabbat* 56a that Uriah gave Bathsheba a *get* before going to war. It is not fully clear if Radak accepts the talmudic position or if he is simply quoting it. For argument's sake, we will adopt Rabbi Blau's reading of Radak and explore its underlying methodology.

13. For discussion of Radak's approach to conflicts between *peshat* and halakhic rulings of the Talmud, see Naomi Grunhaus, "'Ve-Af Al Pi she-Razal Kibbelu': Peshat and Halakhah in Radak's Exegesis," in *Between Rashi and Maimonides: Themes in Medieval Jewish Thought, Literature and Exegesis*, ed. Ephraim Kanarfogel

and Moshe Sokolow (New York: Yeshiva University Press, 2010), pp. 343-364. For a fuller treatment of Radak's approach to rabbinic Midrash, see Naomi Grunhaus, *The Challenge of Received Tradition: Dilemmas of Interpretation in Radak's Biblical Commentaries* (Oxford: Oxford University Press, 2013).

14. *Bava Metzia* 59a; *Sanhedrin* 107a; *Midrash Psalms* 3:4.

15. *Ketuvot* 9a.

A PROTO-DEMOCRATIC
VOICE OF HOLINESS

RABBI AVIA HACOHEN ON THE BOOK OF NUMBERS[1]

Introduction

The Torah contains many apparent contradictions. Classical rabbinic interpretation often (but not always) reconciles them. In narratives, this approach leads to an integrated account of what happened. In legal passages, this approach leads either to harmonization, or to the conclusion that each passage refers to different elements of the law.

Pioneering a different approach, Rabbi Mordechai Breuer (1921-2007) proposed his Theory of Aspects, in which he maintained that God revealed the Torah to Moses in its complex form such that the multiple facets of the infinite Torah are presented in different sections. Since we are limited as humans, we cannot simultaneously entertain these perspectives, so they appear to us as contradictory. The complete truth emerges only when one takes all facets into account. In this manner, Rabbi

---

1. Review essay of Rabbi Avia Hacohen, *Penei Adam: The Face of Man: The Philosophy of Man and Nation in the Book of Numbers* (Tel-Aviv: Yediot Aharonot, 2014), 295 pages. This article appeared originally in *Tradition* 48:2-3 (Summer-Fall 2015), pp. 71-81.

Breuer accepted the text analysis of critical scholarship through one version of the Documentary Hypothesis while rejecting its underlying beliefs and assumptions.[1]

Rabbi Breuer's uncritical acceptance of the readings of the Documentary Hypothesis as "science" detracted from his work.[2] However, his fundamental premise, that the divinely revealed Torah presents aspects of truth in different places, has significantly influenced subsequent generations of Orthodox scholars.[3] We have come a long way since the early 1960s, when Rabbi Breuer first published his pioneering studies. Many Orthodox scholars have found productive means of incorporating the positive elements of academic Bible study into the religious learning of Tanakh.[4]

One valuable recent study is that of Rabbi Breuer's son-in-law, Rabbi Avia Hacohen. In his book, *Penei Adam*, he argues that the book of Numbers focuses primarily on the human aspect of the God-Israel relationship, in contrast to the other books of the Torah, which focus more on the divine aspect of that relationship. In the spirit of Rabbi Breuer,[5] Rabbi Hacohen attempts to understand each passage on its own terms in order to appreciate the religious message of each aspect of the Torah.

While Rabbi Hacohen follows the analytical method of Rabbi Breuer, he also frames his thesis within the religious context of Hasidic teachings. The Baal Shem Tov taught that the path to finding God is to look for the divine within each person (11-13). At the conclusion of the study, Rabbi Hacohen again invokes the teachings of the Baal Shem Tov, and states that the book of Numbers also teaches that one finds God by looking inside each person (239-247).[6]

With his thesis that Numbers is a literary unit and reflects a distinctive voice of the Torah, Rabbi Hacohen gains an immense methodological advantage over Rabbi Breuer. After all, the book of Numbers actually exists. In contrast, Rabbi Breuer worked with the readings of a hypothesis involving putative voices spliced together between various passages in the Torah, after having isolated them from their local context, and even from the verse in which they appeared. Rabbi Hacohen offers numerous local insights into passages in Numbers, but his book's greatest contribution is its sustained comparison of Numbers to the other books of the Torah in an effort to demonstrate the unique character of Numbers. This essay will focus on that unique contribution. I then will separately examine Rabbi Hacohen's analysis of *sotah* (the suspected adulteress), where he proposes a novel hypothesis pertaining to the interface between traditional belief in revelation and academic Bible study.

The Entire Israelite Camp is Holy

The Sages debate whether the Israelites marched as a line or in a square formation in their desert travels (JT *Eruvin* 5:1, 22c). It might have been logistically easier to march in a line, but a verse reads, "As they camp, so they shall march, each in position" (Num. 2:17), and Rashi concludes that the nation marched in a square formation. Ibn Ezra agrees that they marched in a square formation, but adds that this formation resembles the Celestial Chariot described by Ezekiel (cf. *Num. Rabbah* 2:10; Ramban on Num. 2:2). Rabbi Hacohen observes that in Exodus and Leviticus, the Tabernacle is described in great detail as an independent entity. In Numbers, however, Israel's entire camp, rather than only the Ark or the Tabernacle, serves as the footstool for God's Presence (58-64).[7] In the words of Rabbi Judah Halevi, "the camp and its divisions are to be compared to the body and its constituent limbs, the Tabernacle being to the camp what the heart is to the body" (*Kuzari* 2:26).

Rabbi Hacohen adduces support for this perspective from the laws of ritual impurity. In Numbers, God commands ritually impure people to leave the camp: "Instruct the Israelites to remove from camp anyone with an eruption or a discharge and anyone defiled by a corpse... so that they do not defile the camp of those in whose midst I dwell" (Num. 5:2-3). In Leviticus chapters 11-15, however, most ritually impure people are prohibited from entering the Tabernacle but are not required to live apart from the community. Rashi (on Num. 5:2) quotes *Pesahim* 67a, which distinguishes between the different impurities listed in Numbers. Only people with the skin affliction *tzara'at* had to leave the entire camp. A man with a discharge (*zav*) could not enter the Tabernacle or the Levite inner circle. One who had been in contact with a corpse was barred only from the Tabernacle.[8]

Rabbi Hacohen explains that this discrepancy reflects the different perspectives of the two books. Leviticus emphasizes the holiness of the Tabernacle, and therefore ritually impure people are excluded from going there. Numbers, however, shifts the emphasis to the sanctity of the entire Israelite camp. Therefore, Numbers formulates the commandment in a manner that suggests that the entire encampment is sacred, and ritually impure people must leave (37-39).

In the above example, Rabbi Hacohen's distinction between the books of the Torah is convincing. In another instance, however, Rabbi Hacohen appears to quote selectively to support his thesis. As the Israelites embarked from Sinai toward Israel, the Ark led the way (Num. 10:33). Wasn't the Ark located at the center of the camp? Following *Sifrei*, Rashi concludes that 10:33 must refer to a different Ark, which carried the broken tablets. The Ark that carried the fixed tablets indeed remained at the center of the camp. Insisting that there was only one Ark, Ibn Ezra suggests that it traveled ahead of the camp only for the first journey from Sinai, as described in Numbers 10. After that, the Ark traveled at the center of the camp.

Based on his understanding of the perspectives of the different books, Rabbi Hacohen suggests that in Exodus, the Ark is where God reveals His Presence (Exod. 25:22; 29:42-43). In human-centered Numbers, the Ark serves the nation. It leads the way when Israel travels (Num. 10:33), and leads them into war (Num. 10:35-36). These passages thereby reflect two perspectives on the Ark, rather than two Arks (29-32).

However, the description of Israel's encampments is *also* found in Numbers, and there the Ark marches in the center. The difference in perspective is not between Exodus and Numbers, but rather between Numbers 10:33-36 and everything else.

For that matter, Rabbi Hacohen never addresses the placement of the laws of the Red Heifer in Numbers rather than with the other laws of ritual impurity in Leviticus chapters 11-15. This question is important in any event,[9] but is particularly significant given Rabbi Hacohen's explanation of ritually impure people discussed above. By not addressing this issue, he weakens his overall thesis regarding the distinctive nature of Numbers.

People Replace Priests at the Center of Holiness

Rabbi Hacohen contends that certain laws and narratives belong in Numbers precisely because of that book's emphasis on the entire nation of Israel being holy. For example, aspects of the dedication of the Tabernacle appear in different books of the Torah. Exodus 40 focuses on God's Presence occupying the Tabernacle, and Leviticus 9 highlights the people's service of God. In Numbers 7, the representatives of each tribe dedicate the Tabernacle.[10]

In a similar vein, the laws of the nazirite (Num. 6:1-21) parallel the laws of the High Priest (Lev. 10:6-9; 21:10-15). Both must refrain from wine and contact with the deceased, and both are called holy. The critical difference is that the High Priest is forbidden to grow his hair long, whereas the nazirite must grow his or her hair. These parallels suggest that anyone can temporarily attain the sanctity of the High Priest. The High Priest's trimmed hair represents the dignity of the establishment, whereas the nazirite's long hair symbolizes spontaneous holiness sprouting from within. It is appropriate for the laws of the nazirite to appear in Numbers, which emphasizes the sanctity of all Israel. Fittingly, the High Priest must not leave the Temple precincts (Lev. 21:12), whereas the "sanctuary" of the nazirite is among the people (43-44).

Another analogy between Israel and the priesthood is found in the laws of *tzitzit* (Num. 15:37-41). Rabbi Hacohen connects *tzitzit* to the High Priest's headpiece called the *tzitz*, frontlet. It is a sacred garment and has a string of *tekhelet* blue (Exod. 28:36-37).[11] Like the rules concerning the nazirite, the commandment of *tzitzit* gives regular Israelites a taste of the holiness of the priesthood. Rabbi Hacohen observes further that this passage also belongs in Numbers, where all Israelites are to be a holy nation like the priests (95-96).

Rabbi Hacohen identifies a different human dimension in the passage about *Pesah Sheni* (Num. 9:1-14). On the one hand, the Passover sacrifice is connected to a particular date. On the other hand, people can become ritually impure or they may be far from the Temple on the fourteenth day of the First Month. The Torah therefore stresses the severity of non-participation in the Passover sacrifice with the threat of excision (*karet*), and simultaneously accommodates human reality by creating a makeup date (47-52).

Rabbi Hacohen contrasts the divine ruling regarding the blasphemer in Leviticus (24:10-23) with the divine rulings regarding *Pesah Sheni* and the daughters of Zelophehad in Numbers (27:1-11; 36:1-12). In the case of the blasphemer, the text does not emphasize the people's question. Instead, God reveals the proper laws to Moses. In contrast, the divine rulings in Numbers emanated from human requests. Rabbi Hacohen argues that this contrast again points to the nature of each book.

Surprisingly, however, Rabbi Hacohen ignores the episode of the gatherer of sticks on Shabbat in this discussion (Num. 15:32-36). Similar to the story of the blasphemer, an individual committed a grave sin of Shabbat desecration, and since Moses was unsure regarding the precise punishment, God Himself responded with a ruling. It appears that the distinction between the cases of divine rulings is not one of a divine-oriented Leviticus versus a human-oriented Numbers, but rather two instances of human-initiated questions and two instances of grave sins with punishments. While many of Rabbi Hacohen's examples are convincing, the occasions where he quotes selectively weaken his overall hypothesis.

Korah and His Democratic Argument

Rabbi Hacohen analyzes the complexity in Korah's rebellion (221-238). On the one hand, Korah and his followers clearly are sinners. On the other hand, the people side with Korah even after he is killed, demonstrating the power of his argument. Rabbi Hacohen maintains that although Korah was a demagogue and failed in his rebellion, there is truth to his battle cry, that all Israel is holy (Num. 16:3). Korah loses in Numbers and God upholds the priestly role of Aaron. In Deuteronomy, in contrast, several laws reflect a more democratic perspective than the attitude in Numbers, thereby echoing the positive aspect within Korah's argument.

For example, in Numbers the tithe goes to Levites (Num. 18:21). In Deuteronomy, however, tithes belong to all Israelites (Deut. 14:22-23). *Halakhah* understands each passage as referring to a different law. Numbers 18 refers to *ma'aser rishon*, the first tithe, whereas Deuteronomy 14 refers to *ma'aser sheni*, the second tithe (see Rashi on Deut. 14:23). At the textual level, however, there is no mention of first or second tithes. Numbers offers the perspective of priests and Levites being separate, whereas Deuteronomy presents all Israel as worthy of receiving tithes.

Similarly, in Numbers, firstborn animals are gifts to the priests (Num. 18:15), whereas in Deuteronomy firstborn animals appear to go to all Israelites who must consume them in the place God chooses (Deut. 15:19-20). Following the harmonization in *Bekhorot* 28a, Rashi explains that Deuteronomy must also refer to priests. Rabbi Hacohen maintains that the two passages again reflect different perspectives, with Deuteronomy focusing on the democratic aspect of holiness.

In Leviticus, only priests are explicitly prohibited from eating carrion (Lev. 22:2-8). It sounds like regular Israelites are permitted to eat it, although touching carrion renders an Israelite impure: "If an animal that you may eat has died, anyone who touches its carcass shall be unclean until evening; anyone who eats of its carcass shall wash his clothes and remain unclean until evening; and anyone who carries its carcass shall wash his clothes and remain unclean until evening" (Lev. 11:39-40). In Deuteronomy, eating carrion is prohibited to all Israel, since all Israel is holy (Deut. 14:21). Following the harmonizing reading of *Niddah* 42b, Rashi (on Lev. 11:40) explains that eating carrion is prohibited, and the formulation in Leviticus teaches an additional law, that just as the size of an olive is required for the Torah prohibition of eating carrion, so, too, the size of an olive is required to render one ritually impure. Rabbi Hacohen again maintains that these passages reflect two perspectives, one that distinguishes the priesthood from Israel, and the other that equates all Israel as a holy nation.

Fittingly, the term *b-h-r*, meaning "choose," appears in Numbers with regard to the priesthood (Num. 16:5, 7; 17:20). In contrast, Deuteronomy emphasizes that God chose all of Israel (Deut. 7:6; 14:2).

Through these examples, Rabbi Hacohen demonstrates that different books of the Torah offer facets of the truth. However, his analysis of the Korah rebellion appears to threaten the overall hypothesis of his book, namely, that Numbers focuses specifically on the sanctity of all Israelites rather than only the priests and Levites. Evidently, Numbers ascribes more distinctiveness to priests and Levites than Rabbi Hacohen had argued.

There is a dialectic running throughout the Torah, with one facet viewing everyone as having equal access to God, and the other accepting a hierarchy. This dialectic traces back to the two revelation narratives in Exodus. In chapters 19-20, God reveals Himself to all of Israel, and charges all Israelites to become "a kingdom of priests and a holy nation" (Exod. 19:6). Although Moses ascends the mountain while the people remain at the base of Sinai, Moses initially receives the same revelation as the nation. In chapter 24, in contrast, there are several gradations of access and visionary experience, where Aaron, his sons, and the seventy elders ascend the mountain in addition to Moses (Exod. 24:9).

Similarly, Leviticus 1-16 focuses on the service of God in the Tabernacle that was performed by the priesthood. However, a significant portion of the second half of Leviticus highlights the holiness of every individual and argues that a holy life is to be pursued everywhere and at all times, rather than only in the House of God.[12]

The same dichotomy holds true in Numbers. On the one hand, Rabbi Hacohen convincingly demonstrates the human emphasis of many passages in Numbers, especially through contrast with related passages in Exodus and Leviticus. On the other hand, Korah and his followers were fatally mistaken in asserting that there is no room for a priesthood. While Rabbi Hacohen focuses on the passages in Numbers that stress the democratic dimension of holiness, it still must be said that the priests and Levites form the inner circle around the Tabernacle and must protect the sanctuary from outsiders (Num. 1:51; 3:10, 38; 18:7). They have a separate census and sacred responsibilities, they receive special gifts in return for their sacred work, and they are called chosen by God.

Rabbi Hacohen's central thesis is that in the book of Numbers, the God-human relationship is more democratic than in other books. To a large extent this is true. However, Numbers also recognizes the centrality of the priesthood, as demonstrated by the fact that Korah, who wishes to highlight the democratic aspect at the expense of the priesthood, committed a fatal error that led to his own demise and the deaths of his followers. Regardless, Rabbi Hacohen has opened an important discussion regarding the possibility of identifying a distinctive perspective for each of the books of the Torah.

We may conclude with the poignant last words of the first generation in the wilderness, who so desperately wanted to approach God but feared it was too dangerous to do so in the wake of Korah's rebellion: "But the Israelites said to Moses, 'Lo, we perish! We are lost, all of us lost! Everyone who so much as ventures near the Lord's Tabernacle must die. Alas, we are doomed to perish'" (Num. 17:27-28). The following chapter exhorts the priests and Levites to guard the sanctuary so that it would be safe for Israelites to approach God (Num. 18:1-7). This divine response to the people's fears perfectly encapsulates the dialectical view of Numbers. Priests and Levites are sanctified and in the center so that all Israelites can safely approach God and attain holiness. In a similar vein, Israel needs its priesthood to serve as conduits of the divine blessing to the entire nation, "Thus they shall link My name with the people of Israel, and I will bless them" (Num. 6:27).

APPENDIX

TRADITION AND BIBLE CRITICISM

WHERE THEY MEET AND WHERE THEY DON'T

As we have discussed, the majority of Rabbi Hacohen's book integrates the approaches of rabbinic tradition and the academy by espousing the methodology of Rabbi Breuer's Theory of Aspects and applying it systematically to the book of Numbers as a literary unit. However, on one occasion he adopts a different component of critical analysis that requires separate attention.

Rabbi Hacohen expresses discomfort over the fact that a significant portion of the passage on the *sotah*, suspected adulteress (Num. 5:11-31), appears to presume that the suspected adulteress is guilty even before she drinks the bitter water. One gets the impression that a husband can merely accuse his wife of adultery and thereby subject her to a terribly humiliating procedure.

The Oral Law drastically reduces the scope of this law, requiring witnesses for the husband to warn his wife not to seclude herself (*edei kinnui*) and witnesses who subsequently saw her secluding herself with another man (*edei setirah*) (*Sotah* 3a). The likelihood of adultery must therefore be high before a husband can subject his wife to the *sotah* procedure. The procedure also prevents the husband and the community from taking the law into their own hands, and can reconcile husband and wife when she did not commit adultery. However, Rabbi Hacohen does not think that the *halakhah* reflects *peshat* in this passage, since there is no explicit reference in the Torah to witnesses for the warning or seclusion. He believes that our Sages were troubled by his moral question and therefore circumscribed the Torah's laws.

In his analysis of the biblical passage, Rabbi Hacohen invokes Rambam's premise (*Guide of the Perplexed* 3:32) that the Torah did not make a complete break with the ancient pagan world when it would have been difficult for the Israelites to give up their conventions. Rather, the Torah adapted several ancient practices into its monotheistic system, most notably the Temple and sacrifices.[13] In this spirit, Rabbi Hacohen suggests that prior to the Torah, there must have been an ancient ritual text ruling that if a husband merely suspected his wife of adultery, he could subject her to a humiliating ordeal and she was presumed guilty. The Torah was unwilling to eliminate this well-entrenched ritual, and therefore incorporated the pagan text. However, since the Torah was uncomfortable with the premise that the woman is presumed guilty, it added several glosses to the original text, suggesting that it was only possible that the woman committed adultery. In the putative original pagan text, the waters served as a punishment for adultery. In the final Torah text, the water tested whether she in fact committed adultery. Rabbi Hacohen further suggests that the Sages in the Oral Law continued this process of legal modification, making it even less likely for social injustice to occur.

Conscious of his acceptance of critical methodology, Rabbi Hacohen defends his position on the grounds that he has the best reading of the text. Therefore, he attempts to build a traditional structure around that analysis, giving God the final voice of the text.

There are several objections one may raise against Rabbi Hacohen's analysis. Whereas the text does not explicitly refer to witnesses of warning or seclusion, our Sages' halakhic reading is consistent with the text, and Rabbi Elhanan Samet adopts their reading.[14] If one is convinced that the Oral Law does not correspond with *peshat*, some critical scholars maintain that the text is unified, in which case Rabbi Hacohen's hypothesis is unnecessary.[15] If one is unconvinced by this unified reading, Rabbi Mordechai Breuer—who essentially espouses Rabbi Hacohen's reading—suggests that the passage contains two aspects. One is the divine perspective, since God already knows if the woman committed adultery or not. From this perspective, the *sotah* procedure punishes the woman. The other aspect presents the human perspective, as people do not know if she committed adultery. From this perspective, the *sotah* procedure ascertains whether she is guilty or not.[16] Thus there are three sound readings consistent with tradition.

However, Rabbi Hacohen is unconvinced by these approaches, and prefers his hypothesis. We then must raise additional questions. First, few extant ancient Near Eastern legal texts govern the case of the suspected adulteress. The Code of Hammurabi does (paragraphs 131-132), but its laws do not resemble Rabbi Hacohen's imagined pre-Torah pagan ceremony. While such a legal text may hypothetically have existed, Rabbi Hacohen's thesis is predicated on pure conjecture. Moreover, Rambam maintains that the Torah adapted pagan practices, but does not suggest that the Torah incorporated actual legal *texts* and then merely added editorial glosses.[17] The novel methodology advanced by Rabbi Hacohen in the case of *sotah* is difficult to accept. It appears that there are several textually sound avenues of analysis that account for the difficulties he raises, and it is unnecessary to posit that the Torah incorporates and modifies an actual pagan text.

NOTES

1. For an analysis of Rabbi Breuer's method, see especially Rabbi Amnon Bazak, *Ad ha-Yom ha-Zeh: Fundamental Questions in Bible Teaching* (Hebrew), ed. Yoshi Farajun (Tel-Aviv: Yediot Aharonot, 2013), pp. 109-139; Rabbi Shalom Carmy, "Concepts of Scripture in Mordechai Breuer," in *Jewish Concepts of Scripture: A Comparative Introduction*, ed. Benjamin D. Sommer (New York: New York University Press, 2012), pp. 267-279; Rabbi Meir Ekstein, "Rabbi Mordechai Breuer and Modern Orthodox Biblical Commentary," *Tradition* 33:3 (Spring 1999), pp. 6-23. For a collection of Rabbi Breuer's articles on his methodology, and important responses to his work, see *The Theory of Aspects of Rabbi Mordechai Breuer* (Hebrew), ed. Yosef Ofer (Alon Shevut: Tevunot, 2005).

2. This criticism is all the more relevant as a growing number of academics have rejected or significantly modified the classical Documentary Hypothesis. See, recently, David M. Carr, "Changes in Pentateuchal Criticism," in *Hebrew Bible/ Old Testament: The History of Its Interpretation, III/2: The Twentieth Century*, ed. Magne Saebo (Gottingen: Vandenhoeck & Ruprecht, 2015), pp. 433-466.

3. See Rabbi Yoel Bin-Nun, *"Teguvah le-Divrei Amos Hakham be-Inyan Torat ha-Te'udot ve-Shitat ha-Behinnot"* (Hebrew), *Megadim* 4 (1987), p. 91; Rabbi Shalom Carmy, "Concepts of Scripture in Mordechai Breuer," *op. cit*; Rabbi Shalom Carmy, "Always Connect," in *Where the Yeshiva Meets the University: Traditional and Academic Approaches to Tanakh Study*, ed. Hayyim Angel, *Conversations* 15 (Winter 2013), pp. 1-12.

4. See the essays in *Modern Scholarship in the Study of Torah: Contributions and Limitations*, ed. Shalom Carmy (Northvale, NJ: Jason Aronson, 1996); Hayyim Angel, "The Literary-Theological Study of Tanakh," afterword to Moshe Sokolow, *Tanakh: An Owner's Manual: Authorship, Canonization, Masoretic Text, Exegesis, Modern Scholarship and Pedagogy* (Brooklyn, NY: Ktav, 2015), pp. 192-207, also in Angel, *Peshat Isn't So Simple: Essays on Developing a Religious Methodology to Bible Study* (New York: Kodesh Press, 2014), pp. 118-136.

5. Rabbi Hacohen explicitly associates his methodology with that of Rabbi Breuer in his introduction, pp. 19-20.

6. Rabbi Hacohen also explains the oftentimes trying relationship between Moses and the Israelites through the framework of the challenges of Hasidism pertaining to the difficulty for individuals to develop their own potential when they have a relationship with an overwhelmingly charismatic *rebbe*.

7. See also Rabbi Elhanan Samet, *Iyyunim be-Parashot ha-Shavua*, third series, vol. 2 (Hebrew) (Tel-Aviv: Yediot Aharonot, 2015), pp. 318-336.

8. Adopting a harmonistic reading, Jacob Milgrom argues that the Numbers passage refers only to the prohibition from entering the Tabernacle, rather than banishment from the entire camp (*The JPS Torah Commentary: Numbers* [Philadelphia: Jewish Publication Society, 1990], p. 33). However, the plain sense of the text reflects the reading of our Sages, Rashi, and Rabbi Hacohen.

9. For example, Rabbi Elhanan Samet suggests that the laws of the Red Heifer, which pertain to impurity resulting from contact with the deceased, are placed in between the last narrative of the first generation and the first narrative of the new generation. This was the Torah's gentle way of saying that the first generation died out (*Iyyunim be-Parashot ha-Shavua*, first series, vol. 2 [Ma'alei Adumim: Ma'aliyot, 2002], p. 218). See also Rabbi Joseph Soloveitchik, *Vision and Leadership: Reflections on Joseph and Moses*, ed. David Shatz, Joel B. Wolowelsky, and Reuven Ziegler (Jersey City, NJ: Ktav-Toras HoRav Foundation, 2013), pp. 207-211. For further explanation of why the laws of the Red Heifer also should not have been included with Leviticus 11-15, see Rabbi Elhanan Samet, *Iyyunim be-Parashot ha-Shavua*, third series, vol. 2, pp. 84-87.

10. Elsewhere, Rabbi Hacohen demonstrates that Numbers 5:1-8:26 is a reverse parallel to Leviticus 6-15. He uses these structural parallels to argue that Leviticus focuses on meeting God in the Tabernacle, whereas Numbers focuses on meeting God where you are (251-253). See also Rabbi Hacohen's more detailed article, "Order and Content in the Book of Numbers" (Hebrew), *Megadim* 9 (1990), pp. 27-39.

11. Rabbi Hacohen further observes that *halakhah* links *tzitzit* to the priesthood by permitting *tzitzit* to be made out of wool and linen (*sha'atnez*). The Sages derive this law from the juxtaposition of the prohibition of *sha'atnez* and the commandment for *tzitzit* (Deut. 22:9-12; see *Yevamot* 4a). Some priestly garments similarly were made of *sha'atnez* but were worn only in the Temple precincts. *Tzitzit* can be worn anywhere.

12. For a recent application of this approach in Leviticus, see Rabbi Shalom Carmy, "From Israelites to Priests: On the Unfolding of *Vayikra*'s Teaching," in *Mitokh Ha-Ohel: Essays on the Weekly Parashah from the Rabbis and Professors of Yeshiva University*, ed. Daniel Z. Feldman & Stuart W. Halpern (New York: Yeshiva University Press, 2010), pp. 297-301.

13. See, for example, Russel J. Hendel, "Maimonides' Attitude toward Sacrifices," *Tradition* 13:4-14:1 [Spring-Summer, 1973], pp. 163-179; Menachem Kellner, "Maimonides on the Nature of Ritual Purity and Impurity," *Da'at* 50-52 [2003], pp. i-xxx; Roy Pinchot, "The Deeper Conflict Between Rambam and Ramban over the Sacrifices," *Tradition* 33:3 (Spring, 1999), pp. 24-33.

14. *Iyyunim be-Parashot ha-Shavua*, second series, vol. 2 (Ma'alei Adumim: Ma'aliyot, 2004), pp. 158-174.

15. See, for example, Herbert C. Brichto, "The Case of the *Sota* and a Reconsideration of Biblical 'Law,'" *Hebrew Union College Annual* 46 (1975), pp. 55-70; Michael Fishbane, "Accusations of Adultery: A Study of Law and Scribal Practice in Numbers 5:11-31," *Hebrew Union College Annual* 45 (1974), pp. 25-45.

16. *Pirkei Mikra'ot* (Alon Shevut: Tevunot, 2009), pp. 229-243.

17. I thank Professors Menachem Kellner and Marc Shapiro for confirming that Rambam does not suggest this possibility in his writings.

IT'S ALL CONNECTED

RABBI DAVID SYKES ON LITERARY PATTERNS IN GENESIS AND THROUGHOUT TANAKH[1]

Introduction

The field of literary analysis of Tanakh has been substantially refined over the past four decades. New scholarly insights continue to illuminate the text and its messages. One person's *peshat* is another person's *derash*, and we can and always will debate the boundaries of what the text does or does not intend to say. Regardless of how one defines those boundaries, the dimensions of *peshat, derash, remez,* and *sod* come together in Rabbi David Sykes' stimulating new work.

As he states in his prefatory remarks, this book took him over forty years to complete. Much of this work refines and expands upon his doctoral dissertation completed at the Bernard Revel Graduate School of Yeshiva University in 1985, *Patterns in Genesis.* Back in the 1970s when Rabbi Sykes embarked on

---

1. Review essay of Rabbi David Sykes, *Patterns in Genesis and Beyond* (Patterns Publications, 2014), 589 pages. This article appeared originally in *Jewish Action* 75:3 (Spring 2015), pp. 96-97. Reprinted with permission from *Jewish Action. Jewish Action* is the magazine of the Orthodox Union.

this pursuit, the literary revolution was just taking off in the academic world. Several prominent scholars began to consider the biblical text as a final product to be analyzed for meaning, rather than dissecting the text or speculating as to its origins. This mode of inquiry often dovetailed substantially (but not entirely) with what Midrash and classical commentators had been doing for millennia. Consequently, there was more room for productive dialogue between the yeshiva and the academy than there had been for generations. Orthodox scholars transformed and channeled this method of analysis into a specifically religious framework.[1]

Rabbi Sykes writes from a traditional perspective. His insights are surrounded by Midrashim and our classical commentators, and he conveys a deep sense of reverence for the God-given biblical text as well as for our great biblical heroes. Because he does not distinguish between the different layers of interpretation, one might question the validity of many of Rabbi Sykes' points. It is often unclear that they are compelling from a *peshat* standpoint, even if many are plausible.[2] Alternatively, one may view his book as an invitation to think about the dazzling spectrum of potential meaning latent in the Torah. This approach requires greater flexibility about drawing lines between *peshat* and other layers of interpretation. In this review, I will adopt the latter approach and briefly present several aspects of this work, with the hope of offering a small taste of the range of interpretation in Rabbi Sykes' style and methodology.

Word Patterns

Rabbi Sykes is at his best when the patterns include compelling linguistic support, thereby demonstrating that two or more passages are in dialogue. For example, he traces the usage of *tov* and *ra* in *Parashat Bereshit*. After God's creations are all *tov*, the Tree of Knowledge contains both *tov* and *ra*. This is the first occurrence of *ra* in the Torah, suggesting that evil is latent in creation. It is up to people to make the right choices.

Eve was tempted to eat from the Tree of Knowledge, wrongly perceiving its goodness to be like that of God's creation. The Torah uses the same expression as when God beheld creation: "**Va-tere** ha-ishah **ki tov** ha-etz le-ma'akhal" (3:6). Through this sin, Adam and Eve gained sexual awareness, realizing that sexuality could be used for negative purposes as well as positive. By the end of the *parashah*, the *benei ha-Elokim* see the *benot ha-adam* as good and take them, just as Eve had done when she beheld the forbidden fruit: "**Va-yiru** benei ha-Elokim et benot ha-adam **ki tovot** hennah va-yik'hu lahem nashim mi-kol asher baharu" (6:2). Eve became sexually aware through eating the fruit, and now the *benei ha-Elokim* acted sinfully on that impulse, multiplying evil in the world. Disobedience to God brings curses instead of blessings (1-14).

Rabbi Sykes routinely perceives meaning in the names of people and places. For example, the ark landed on a mountain in Ararat after the Flood, signifying the undoing of the *arur*, curses, from the sins of Adam and Cain (33). Rabbi Sykes thus considers Ararat and *arur* to be a deliberate wordplay. Similarly, Rabbi Sykes identifies wordplays on Noah's name throughout the Flood narrative. Following the Flood, the ark rested, *va-tanah ha-tevah* (8:4); the dove initially found nowhere to land, *ve-lo matzah ha-yonah mano'ah* (8:9); and God smelled Noah's offering: *va-yarah Hashem et re'ah ha-niho'ah* (8:21) (36).

110

Across Tanakh

Rabbi Sykes frequently traces patterns in Genesis through later biblical narratives. For example, he suggests that the narratives about Benjamin foreshadow the reign of King Saul. Jacob names his son Bin-Yamin, "son of my right hand," symbolizing strength and intimating that his tribe will rise to greatness. However, Rachel names him Ben-Oni, "son of my grief and strength," suggesting that this kingship will be tragic and short-lived. Benjamin also was born en route to Bethlehem, implying that Saul's kingship will be a stop on the way to Bethlehem, that is, David's birthplace (254-256).

In an extended study, Rabbi Sykes explores the narratives of Lot and his descendants (145-176). Rabbi Sykes identifies a considerable number of contrasts between Abraham and Lot in the Torah. He also detects a series of parallels between Lot's rescue from Sodom and the Israelites' redemption from Egypt during the exodus. He then explores parallels to the Ruth narrative, suggesting that Elimelech resembles Lot, who was overly self-concerned, whereas Boaz reflects Abraham and his exemplary quality of *hesed*. This study is a fine example of how extensive the patterns might be within the Torah and beyond.

Character Development

Rabbi Sykes exploits possible parallels to demonstrate how righteous and penitent characters can break out of negative patterns and transform them into blessings. For example, there is a negative dimension in Jacob's deceptive behavior toward Isaac.[3] After Jacob returned to his homeland and confronted Esau and wrestled with an angel, he was renamed Yisrael, suggesting straightness (*yashar*). Rabbi Sykes maintains that

111

there are allusions to Jacob's positive transformation in his purchase of land in Shechem. Jacob bought a parcel of land, **helkat** ha-sadeh (33:19), for 100 kesitah. Rabbi Sykes links this purchase to Jacob's deception of Isaac, where Jacob expressed concern that he was smooth-skinned, ish **halak** (27:11). The unusual form of currency, kesitah, might be a wordplay on the Aramaic kushta, "truth." Now that Jacob has resolved the negativity of the deception, he is again "smooth" and is associated with truth (234).

In a different analysis, Rabbi Sykes adopts the reading of Ramban on Genesis 16 and criticizes Abraham and Sarah for their harsh treatment of Hagar (177-193). Ishmael would become a pere adam, a wild ass of a man, understood by Ramban as a barbaric individual whose descendants would persecute the descendants of Abraham and Sarah as punishment for their mistreatment of Hagar.[4] Rabbi Sykes suggests that when Joseph was brought to Egypt as a slave specifically by Ishmaelites, that is a manifestation of this punishment. Moreover, the angel ordered Hagar to return to her oppression under Sarah, *ve-hitanni* (16:9); and Joseph referred to his suffering *be-eretz onyi,* "in the land of his oppression" (41:52).

To summarize, patterns in the Torah sometimes can be perceived as foreshadowing later events in the Torah and the rest of Tanakh. However, patterns throughout Tanakh also teach that repentance and righteous behavior can break and transform earlier negative patterns into blessings. This message, demonstrated through Rabbi Sykes' careful attention to the tiniest details, is an inspiring theme that runs throughout his work.

We have explored but a tiny sample of the ideas suggested by Rabbi Sykes. His book contains much material to inspire, excite, and challenge. Readers can decide what is or is not compelling to them, but all will experience the multifaceted and eternally relevant glory of the Torah by reading this book.

NOTES

1. See especially Rabbi Aharon Lichtenstein, "Criticism and *Kitvei ha-Kodesh*," in *Rav Shalom Banayikh: Essays Presented to Rabbi Shalom Carmy by Friends and Students in Celebration of Forty Years of Teaching*, ed. Hayyim Angel and Yitzchak Blau (Jersey City, NJ: Ktav, 2012), pp. 15-32; Rabbi Shalom Carmy, "Is Sophocles Literature? Is Anything Not? On the Way to Ramban," *Tradition* 47:3 (Fall 2014), pp. 1-7; Yael Ziegler, *Ruth: From Alienation to Monarchy* (Jerusalem: Maggid, 2015), pp. 3-14.

2. Already concerned with defining scholarly standards of literary analysis in the 1980s, Moshe Garsiel wrote a substantial chapter on methodology. See *The First Book of Samuel: A Literary Study of Comparative Structures, Analogies and Parallels* (Ramat Gan: Bar-Ilan University Press, 1985), pp. 11-57.

3. See, for example, Nehama Leibowitz, *Studies in Bereshit (Genesis)*, trans. Aryeh Newman (Jerusalem: Eliner Library, 2010), pp. 264-274; Hayyim Angel, "Morality and Literary Study: What does the Torah Teach about Jacob's Deception of Isaac?" printed in this volume.

4. For further discussion of the evaluation of the behavior of Sarah and Abraham in that episode, see Hayyim Angel, "Sarah's Treatment of Hagar (Genesis 16): Morals, Messages, and Mesopotamia," *Jewish Bible Quarterly* 41 (2013), pp. 211-218; reprinted in Angel, *Peshat Isn't So Simple: Essays on Developing a Religious Methodology to Bible Study* (New York: Kodesh Press, 2014), pp. 213-222.

CONTROVERSIES OVER THE HISTORICITY OF BIBLICAL PASSAGES IN TRADITIONAL COMMENTARY[1]

Introduction

Tanakh lies at the heart of Jewish faith, and comprises God's revealed word. Tanakh represents the truth for believing Jews. However, must or should every word be understood literally?

Do believing Jews need to insist that the world was created in six 24-hour days? Is all of humanity biologically descended from one couple that lived some 6,000 years ago?

God does not have hands or nostrils, despite many verses whose literal reading suggest otherwise. How are we to understand stories of angels who eat (Genesis 18) or wrestle (Genesis 32)?

Did King David really commit adultery and orchestrate murder as suggested by the literal biblical text (2 Samuel 11), and did King Solomon really worship idols (1 Kings 11)?

Rabbi Saadiah Gaon maintained that biblical texts should be taken literally, unless one of four criteria is met:

---

1. This essay appeared originally in Hayyim Angel, *Increasing Peace Through Balanced Torah Study. Conversations* 27 (New York: Institute for Jewish Ideas and Ideals, 2017), pp. 10-21.

And I so declare, first of all, that it is a well-known fact that every statement in the Bible is to be understood in its literal sense except for those that cannot be so construed for one of the following four reasons: It may, for example, either be rejected by the observation of the senses...Or else the literal sense may be negated by reason.... Again [the literal meaning of a biblical statement may be rendered impossible] by an explicit text of a contradictory nature, in which case it would become necessary to interpret the first statement in a non-literal nature.... Finally, any biblical statement to the meaning of which rabbinical tradition has attached a certain reservation is to be interpreted by us in keeping with this authentic tradition (*Emunot ve-De'ot* Book VII).[1]

If the literal reading of a biblical text contradicts empirical observation, a commentator's sense of reason, another biblical text, or rabbinic tradition, then it must be reinterpreted.

Following in Rabbi Saadiah's footsteps, Rambam agreed that if reason or scientific knowledge contradicts the literal sense of a biblical text, that text must not be taken literally[2]:

I believe every possible happening that is supported by a prophetic statement and do not strip it of its plain meaning. I fall back on interpreting a statement only when its literal sense is impossible, like the corporeality of God: The possible however remains as stated (*Treatise on Resurrection*).[3]

Rambam included considerably more than God's corporeality among the impossible, and therefore allegorized many biblical passages. Other rabbinic thinkers adamantly opposed this method of interpretation, protesting that it imposed foreign ideas onto the biblical text. Additionally, it created a dangerous slippery slope for interpreters to allegorize far too many passages.[4]

This essay will consider several debates as they pertain to the interface between Torah and science, Torah and reason, and Torah and other religious concerns such the sins of biblical heroes. Although the two sides of the debate often vigorously disagree, it is possible to navigate a path that hears the voices of both sides.

Torah and Science

Science states that the world is billions of years old; there was a process of evolution; and it is unlikely in the extreme that all humans biologically descend from the same couple that lived only 6,000 years ago. The literal reading of the early chapters in Genesis does not seem to match the scientific evidence.

However, there need not be any conflict between Torah and science. As noted above, Rabbi Saadiah Gaon and Rambam maintain that whenever the literal reading of the Torah contradicts empirical evidence, the Torah should not be taken literally. In his discussion of Aristotle's theory of the eternality of the world, Rambam rejects it because Aristotle was unable to prove his theory. However, were Aristotle able to prove it, Rambam would reinterpret Genesis chapter 1 (*Guide of the Perplexed* 2:25). Rambam did not believe that the entire creation account was intended as literal, regardless (*Guide of the Perplexed* 2:29).

More recently, Rabbi Samson Raphael Hirsch wrote that as long as one believes that God created the world, the length or process of the creation is not a binding article of faith:

> Judaism is not frightened even by the hundreds of thousands and millions of years which the geological theory of the earth's development bandies about so freely.... The Rabbis have never made the acceptance or rejection of this and similar possibilities an article of faith binding on all Jews. They were willing to live with any theory that did not reject the basic truth that "every beginning is from God" (*The Educational Value of Judaism*, in *Collected Writings*, vol. VII, p. 265).[5]

Rabbi Abraham Isaac Kook made a similar point regarding the Theory of Evolution:

> Even if it were to become clear to us that the world came into being by way of the evolution of the species, still there would be no contradiction, for our count follows the plain sense of the biblical verses, which is far more relevant to us than knowledge about the past, which carries little value for us. Without question, the Torah concealed much about creation, speaking in allusions and parables. For everyone knows that the creation story is included among the secrets of the Torah, and if everything followed the plain sense [of the verses], what secret would there be here? ...The main thing is what arises from the entire story—knowing God and [living] a truly moral life (*Iggerot Ra'ayah* I, letters 91, p. 105).[6]

Instead of reinterpreting the Torah to match science, one could argue that the Torah does not teach scientific truth, but rather religious truth. From this perspective, a believing Jew accepts the religious messages of the Torah, while accepting science from scientists. Samuel David Luzzatto espoused this position:

> Intelligent people understand that the goal of the Torah is not to inform us about natural sciences; rather it was given in order to create a straight path for people in the way of righteousness and law, to sustain in their minds the belief in the Unity of God and His Providence (introduction to commentary on the Torah).

Commenting on Psalm 19:6–7, which describes the sun moving across the sky, Rabbi Samson Raphael Hirsch similarly remarks:

> David, as do all the Holy Scriptures, talks in the language of men. His language is the same as that of Copernicus, Kepler and Newton, and as that which we use today.... This language will remain the same even when the assumption that the sun is static and that the earth revolves around it—and not the sun around the earth—will have been proven to be irrefutable certainty. For it is not the aim of the Holy Scriptures to teach us astronomy, cosmogony or physics, but only to guide man to the fulfillment of his life's task within the framework of the constellation of his existence. For this purpose it is quite irrelevant whether the course of days and years is determined by the earth's revolution around the sun, or by the latter's orbit around the former.[7]

To summarize, there is ample room within tradition to avoid faith-science conflicts. One may reinterpret passages in the Torah, or one may study the Torah for its religious messages while accepting science as science. In an age where science is vastly more empirical than it was in the times of Rabbi Saadiah Gaon and Rambam, it is particularly valuable that these medieval rabbinic thinkers paved a path for belief in the Torah without any conflict with scientific knowledge. Their guidance helps us focus on what truly matters—the religious messages that the Torah wishes to teach.

TORAH AND REASON[8]

Angelic Encounters

Rambam maintained that all angelic encounters were experienced in prophetic visions, not in actual reality (*Guide of the Perplexed* 2:41–42). There are occasions where this principle helps explain difficult texts. For example, when Joshua encountered an angel "in Jericho" (Josh. 5:13–15), that city had yet to be captured. Rambam's assumption, that Joshua was experiencing a prophetic vision, eliminates this difficulty. In a prophetic vision, Joshua *could* have been standing inside of Jericho.[9]

On other occasions, however, Rambam's assumption appears to contradict or stretch the simple reading of the biblical text. For example, Rambam maintained that Abraham's encounter with the three angels in Genesis 18 must have occurred in a prophetic vision (*Guide of the Perplexed* 2:32). Ramban (on Gen. 18:1) censured this position. If this were only a vision, why does the Torah provide so many details with regard to

Sarah's preparation of food? Did Lot and the wicked people of Sodom experience prophetic revelation when they encountered the angels in Genesis 19? If they were experiencing prophecy, then Lot would still have remained in Sodom, since the entire destruction was experienced only in prophecy! After bringing these arguments, Ramban concludes that Rambam's position is incompatible with the Torah.[10]

Rambam's premise about angels also became a potentially dangerous precedent. Abarbanel (on Gen. 22:13) expressed chagrin that some writers applied Rambam's principle to argue that the Binding of Isaac occurred only in Abraham's prophetic vision, since an angel stopped Abraham from sacrificing Isaac.[11] Abarbanel considered this view a terrible misapplication of Rambam's teachings, and stated that it was wrong and heretical to deny the historicity of the Binding of Isaac.

God's Unusual Instructions to Prophets

Throughout Tanakh, God ordered prophets to perform symbolic actions, including several that appear shocking. For example, God instructed Hosea to marry an *eshet zenunim* (commonly translated as "prostitute"[12]) to illustrate Israel's infidelity to God. The ensuing narrative reports that Hosea married a woman named Gomer, and fathered three children with her (Hos. 1:2–9). Similarly, God commanded Isaiah to "untie the sackcloth from his loins" to foretell that the Assyrians would lead the Egyptians and Ethiopians away as naked captives. Isaiah faithfully obeyed, and walked around *arom* (literally, "naked") and barefoot (Isa. 20:2–6).

Rambam insisted that God never would order a prophet to do anything foolish or irrational. Therefore, Hosea and Isaiah performed these actions only in prophetic visions:

God is too exalted than that He should turn His prophets into a laughingstock and a mockery for fools by ordering them to commit acts of disobedience. In the same way when He says, *Like as My servant Isaiah hath walked naked and barefoot*, this only happened *in the visions of God.* The position is similar with regard to the words addressed to Hosea: *Take unto thee a wife of harlotry and children of harlotry.* All this story concerning the birth of the children and their having been named so and so happened in its entirety *in a vision of prophecy.* This is a thing that can only be doubted or not known by him who confuses the possible things with the impossible ones (*Guide of the Perplexed* 2:46).[13]

According to Rambam, Hosea did not actually marry a prostitute,[14] nor did Isaiah walk around naked in public.[15] When a conflict arises between the personal perfection of a prophet and his mission to the people, Rambam favored the element of personal perfection.

Abarbanel criticized Rambam (and Ibn Ezra) for contradicting biblical texts, which state explicitly that Hosea and Isaiah performed these actions:

One must be extremely astonished at these learned authors (i.e., Ibn Ezra and Rambam)—how could they advance this kind of sweeping principle in prophetic narrative? If the text testifies that the action occurred, we have no right to depart from its plain sense, lest we interpret the verses incorrectly. Indeed, it is infidelity and a grave sin (*zimmah va-avon pelili*) to contradict the plain sense of the verses; if this is what we do to them, this disease (*tzara'at*) will spread over all verses and reveal interpretations that contradict their veracity (commentary on Hos. 1).

Abarbanel insisted that a prophet's mission to the people is more important than the prophet's personal perfection and dignity. Therefore, according to Abarbanel, if God decides that these shocking symbolic actions could have a positive religious effect on the people, God will order prophets to perform them.

Messianic Visions

The wolf shall dwell with the lamb, the leopard lie down with the kid. In all of My sacred mount nothing evil or vile shall be done; for the land shall be filled with devotion to the Lord as water covers the sea (Isa. 11:6, 9).

Believing that the natural order will not be altered in the messianic era, Rambam adopted Ibn Ezra's reading of this prophecy and interpreted it as a poetic way to express that all nations will live together in peace (*Hilkhot Melakhim* 12:1; *Guide of the Perplexed* 2:29).

Unlike the previous examples, however, Rambam entertained the literal reading as well:

You must realize that I am not at all positive that all the promises and the like of them are metaphorical. No revelation from God has come to teach me they are parables. I will only explain to you what impels

123

me to speak this way. I try to reconcile the Law and reason, and wherever possible consider all things as of the natural order. Only when something is explicitly identified as a miracle, and reinterpretation of it cannot be accommodated, only then I feel forced to grant that this is a miracle (*Treatise on Resurrection*).[16]

Although there were issues that Rambam considered irrational and impossible, there were others where he allegorized because he thought this to be the most plausible way of explaining a text. In those latter instances, he was willing to entertain the more literal reading.

TORAH AND TALMUDIC VALUES[17]

In the above cases, literalism is associated with piety and non-literalism with rationalism. But sometimes it goes the other way. Some, following one strand of talmudic thinking, maintain that King David didn't really commit adultery and orchestrate murder, in spite of the literal biblical text (2 Samuel 11), or that King Solomon didn't really worship idols (1 Kings 11).

In 2 Samuel chapter 11, David commits adultery with Bathsheba, and then has her husband Uriah killed off so that David can marry Bathsheba. The prophet Nathan excoriates him in chapter 12, and David expresses profound remorse for his sins before embarking on a remarkable process of repentance.[18]

Adopting the literal reading of the text, Abarbanel enumerates five sins committed by David: (1) adultery; (2) being prepared to abandon his biological child by asking Uriah to return to Bathsheba; (3) having Uriah—a loyal subject—killed;

(4) having Uriah killed specifically by enemies; (5) insensitively marrying Bathsheba soon after Uriah's demise.

Abarbanel then cites the talmudic passage "whoever says that David sinned is merely erring" (*Shabbat* 56a). That talmudic passage suggests that Uriah had given a bill of divorce to Bathsheba prior to going to battle, and therefore David did not commit technical adultery. Uriah should be deemed a rebel against David for slighting the king, and therefore David was halakhically justified in having him killed (within this talmudic reading, commentators debate what the precise problem was). Although David's actions were unbecoming, he is not guilty of the most egregious sins according to this passage.

However, retorts Abarbanel, the textual proofs adduced in David's defense are uncompelling, whereas the prophet Nathan explicitly accuses David of sinning—and David confesses and repents. Moreover, Rav, the leading disciple of Rabbi Judah the Prince (known simply as "Rabbi"), dismisses his teacher's defense of David on the spot: "Rabbi, who is descended from David, seeks to defend him and expounds [the verse] in David's favor." Therefore, concludes Abarbanel, "these words of our Sages are the ways of *derash*, and I have no need to respond to them.... I prefer to say that [David] sinned greatly and confessed greatly and repented fully and accepted his punishment, and in this manner he attained atonement for his sins."[19]

Although Abarbanel presents himself as an independent interpreter in this instance, he has not broken with rabbinic tradition. A number of rabbinic sources do not exonerate David. For example, there are opinions that Bathsheba was possibly a married woman or certainly a married woman;[20] that Bathsheba's consent still might be viewed halakhically as a form of rape of a married woman since she was not in a position to decline;[21] that David was culpable for the death of Uriah;[22] that Joab bears guilt for failing to defy David's immoral orders regarding Uriah.[23] The unambiguous textual evidence against David, including his own admission of guilt and wholehearted repentance, seems to have convinced Abarbanel that it was unnecessary to cite additional sources beyond Rav's dismissal of his teacher's defense of David.[24]

Despite these protests, many other commentators, including Rashi, Ralbag, and Malbim, accept the talmudic defense of David in *Shabbat* 56a. Similarly, many classical commentators accept the talmudic defense of King Solomon, and conclude that Solomon permitted idolatrous shrines to his wives, but did not worship idols himself.

NAVIGATING A PATH THAT
HEARS BOTH SIDES OF THE DEBATE

Once we recognize that the most critical component of learning Tanakh is to hear God's revealed word and learn the prophetic messages of the text, we can address the issue of taking each text literally.

If we take the texts literally but not as dogmatically literal when there are conflicts, we can make much headway in navigating the debates. For example, the Sages debate whether the story in the book of Job occurred. Rambam believed that the story did not occur, but stressed that we must focus on the religious messages of the narrative:

> To sum up: *whether he has existed or not*, with regard to cases like his, which always exist, all reflecting people become perplexed; and in consequence such things as I have already mentioned to you are said about God's knowledge and His providence (*Guide of the Perplexed* 3:22).[25]

Similarly, the Torah states that God created the world in seven days, thereby teaching that God created the world, and that Shabbat is of vital importance in the God-Israel relationship. If the world is billions of years old, this scientific reality in no way detracts from the religious values of God as Creator above nature or in the importance of Shabbat.

The Torah teaches that all of humanity is descended from one couple, and therefore there is no room for bigotry (*Sanhedrin* 37a). If geneticists demonstrate the extreme unlikelihood of all people descending from one couple that lived 6,000 years ago, this would in no way diminish God's message in the Torah against bigotry.

The sins of King David teach the dangers of lust (Rabbi Judah the Pious), the power of repentance (Abarbanel), and the incredible integrity of prophecy in its condemnation of Israel's most beloved leader when he violates the Torah. If Uriah gave Bathsheba a bill of divorce, that would in no way compromise the prophetic messages of the text.

Tanakh is not a systematic theology, science, or history. We treat nearly all of the narratives in Tanakh as historical, but God did not reveal prophecies in order to teach science or history. God is speaking to us, and it is our religious obligation to hear, understand, and listen to that voice. We take all of the texts seriously, even if some of them may be understood as non-literal. Where there are debates among our commentators, we may navigate the path of taking the texts literally to learn their prophetic messages, while remaining open to science, reason, and other religious values from within tradition.[26]

NOTES

1. Translation from Rabbi Natan Slifkin, *The Challenge of Creation: Judaism's Encounter with Science, Cosmology, and Evolution* (Brooklyn, NY: Yashar, 2006), p. 107.

2. See Menachem Kellner, "Maimonides' Commentary on Mishnah Hagigah II.1, Translation and Commentary," in *From Strength to Strength*, ed. Marc D. Angel (Brooklyn: Sefer Hermon Press, 1998), pp. 101–111.

3. Translation from *Crisis and Leadership: Epistles of Rambam*, Abraham S. Halkin, trans. and D. Hartman (Philadelphia: Jewish Publication Society, 1985), p. 228.

4. See Rabbi Natan Slifkin, *The Challenge of Creation*, pp. 116–119, for discussion of the opposition of Ralbag and Abarbanel to over-allegorization.

5. In Rabbi Natan Slifkin, *The Challenge of Creation*, p. 119.

6. In Rabbi Chaim Navon, *Genesis and Jewish Thought*, trans. David Strauss (Jersey City, NJ: Ktav, 2008), pp. 36–37.

7. *The Hirsch Tehillim, Extensively Revised Edition,* originally translated by Gertrude Hirschler (Jerusalem: Feldheim, 2014), p. 167.

8. Some of this section is adapted from Hayyim Angel, "Rambam's Continued Impact on Underlying Issues in *Tanakh* Study," in *The Legacy of Maimonides: Religion, Reason and Community,* ed. Yamin Levy and Shalom Carmy (Brooklyn: Yashar Books, 2006), pp. 148–164; reprinted in Angel, *Through an Opaque Lens* (New York: Sephardic Publication Foundation, 2006), pp. 35–55; revised second edition (New York: Kodesh Press, 2013), pp. 19–38; *Peshat Isn't So Simple: Essays on Developing a Religious Methodology to Bible Study* (New York: Kodesh Press, 2014), pp. 58–79.

9. Ralbag adopted Rambam's view on these verses. Alternatively, Joshua may have been standing in the Jericho area, not inside the walled city (Rashi, Radak).

10. See further discussion of this debate in Shalom Rosenberg, "On Biblical Exegesis in the *Guide*" (Hebrew), *Jerusalem Studies in Jewish Thought* 1 (1981), pp. 113–120.

11. See discussion in Abraham Nuriel, "Parables Not Designated Parables in the *Guide of the Perplexed*" (Hebrew), *Da'at* 25 (1990), pp. 85–91.

12. See, for example, *Pesahim* 87a–b, Kara, Ibn Ezra, Radak, Abarbanel, Malbim. Yehudah Kiel (*Da'at Mikra: Twelve Prophets vol. 1* [Jerusalem: Mosad HaRav Kook, 1990], p. 3, n. 6) suggests the alternative that the woman was not yet promiscuous, but would cheat on Hosea after they were married.

13. Translation from *The Guide of the Perplexed*, Shlomo Pines, second edition (Chicago: University of Chicago Press, 1963), pp. 404–406.

14. On this issue, Rambam followed Ibn Ezra (Hos. 1:1). Radak accepted Rambam's view in both cases.

15. Several commentators who understood Isaiah's actions as having occurred in a waking state explained that "*arom*" can mean "with torn clothing," or "scantily clad," rather than outright "naked." See, for example, Targum, Rashi, Rabbi Eliezer of Beaugency, Ibn Caspi. For further discussion of classical rabbinic views, and the meaning of Isaiah's symbolic action in light of his historical setting, see Shemuel Vargon, "Isaiah's Prophecy Against the Background of Ashdod's Revolt Against Sargon II and Its Suppression" (Hebrew), in Vargon, *Be-Artzot ha-Mikra: Mehkarim bi-Neuvah, be-Historiah, u-ve-Historigrafiah Nevuit* (Ramat-Gan: Bar-Ilan University, 2015), pp. 104–122.

16. Translation from *Crisis and Leadership*, Abraham S. Halkin, p. 223.

17. Some of this section is adapted from Hayyim Angel, "Abarbanel: Commentator and Teacher: Celebrating 500 Years of his Influence on Tanakh Study," *Tradition* 42:3 (Fall 2009), pp. 9–26; reprinted in Angel, *Creating Space between Peshat and Derash: A Collection of Studies on Tanakh* (Jersey City, NJ: Ktav-Sephardic Publication Foundation, 2011), pp. 1–24; *Peshat Isn't So Simple: Essays on Developing a Religious Methodology to Bible Study* (New York: Kodesh Press, 2014), pp. 80–104.

18. See further in Hayyim Angel, "The Yoke of Repentance: David's Post-Sin Conduct in the Book of Samuel and Psalm 51," at http://www.yutorah.org/lectures/lecture.cfm/818982/Rabbi_Hayyim_Angel/The_Yoke_of_Repentance:_David%E2%80%99s_Post-Sin_Conduct_in_Sefer_Shemuel_and_Tehillim_51.

19. Commentary on Samuel (Jerusalem: Torah VeDa'at, 1955), pp. 342–343.

20. *Bava Metzia* 59a; *Sanhedrin* 107a; *Midrash Psalms* 3:4.

21. *Ketuvot* 9a.

22. *Yoma* 22b; *Kiddushin* 43a.

23. *Sanhedrin* 49a.

24. Abarbanel was not the first medieval interpreter to assert David's guilt, either. Rabbi Judah b. Natan (Rashi's son-in-law, in *Teshuvot Hakhmei Provencia*, vol. 1 no. 71), Rabbi Isaiah of Trani (on Ps. 51:1), and Ibn Caspi (on II Sam. 11:6) preceded him. For a survey of rabbinic sources, see Rabbi Yaakov Medan, *David u-Bat Sheva* (Hebrew) (Alon Shevut: Tevunot, 2002), especially pp. 7–26.

25. Translation from *The Guide of the Perplexed*, Shlomo Pines, p. 486.

26. For an effort to define the parameters of what is traditionally acceptable within the allegorization of biblical passages, see Joshua L. Golding, "On the Limits of Non-Literal Interpretation of Scripture from an Orthodox Perspective," *Torah U-Madda Journal* 10 (2001), pp. 37–59.

EXTREMELY RELIGIOUS
WITHOUT RELIGIOUS EXTREMISM

THE BINDING OF ISAAC AS A
TEST CASE FOR THE LIMITS OF DEVOTION[1]

Introduction

The *Akedah*, or binding of Isaac (Gen. 22:1–19),[1] is a foundational narrative in Jewish tradition. It plays a prominent role on Rosh Hashanah, and many communities include it in their daily morning liturgy.

The *Akedah* is a religiously and morally challenging story. What should we learn from it with regard to faith and religious life? Perhaps more than any other narrative in the Torah, the *Akedah* teaches how one can and should be extremely religious, but also teaches how to avoid the dangers of religious extremism. This essay will consider the ideas of several modern thinkers who explore the religious and moral implications of the *Akedah*.

---

1. This article appeared originally in *Conversations* 24 (Winter 2016), pp. 58-65; reprinted in Angel, *Increasing Peace Through Balanced Torah Study. Conversations* 27 (New York: Institute for Jewish Ideas and Ideals, 2017), pp. 83-90.

Why Did Abraham Not Protest?

Although the idea of child sacrifice is abhorrent to us, it made sense in Abraham's historical context. Many of Israel's neighbors practiced child sacrifice. When God commanded Abraham to sacrifice his son, Abraham may have surmised that perhaps God required this of him. Of course, God stopped Abraham and went on to outlaw such practices as a capital offense (Lev. 18:21; 20:2–5). We find child sacrifice abhorrent precisely because the Torah and the prophets broke rank with large segments of the pagan world and transformed human values for the better.[2]

In its original context, then, the *Akedah* highlights Abraham's exemplary faithfulness. He followed God's command even when the basis of the divine promise for progeny through Isaac was threatened.[3]

The German philosopher Immanuel Kant (1724–1804) was deeply troubled by the *Akedah*. He maintained that nobody is certain that he or she is receiving prophecy, whereas everyone knows with certainty that murder is immoral and against God's will. Therefore, Abraham failed God's test by acquiescing to sacrifice Isaac. According to Kant, Abraham should have refused, or at least protested.[4]

However, the biblical narrative runs flatly against Kant's reading. After the angel stops Abraham from slaughtering Isaac, the angel proclaims to Abraham, "For now I know that you fear God, since you have not withheld your son, your favored one, from Me" (Gen. 22:12). God thereby praises Abraham's exceptional faith and commitment.[5]

Adopting a reading consistent with the thrust of the biblical narrative, Rambam draws the opposite conclusion from that of Kant. The fact that Abraham obeyed God demonstrates his absolute certainty that he had received true prophecy. Otherwise, he never would have proceeded:

> [Abraham] hastened to slaughter, as he had been commanded, his son, his only son, whom he loved.... For if a dream of prophecy had been obscure for the prophets, or if they had doubts or incertitude concerning what they apprehended in a vision of prophecy, they would not have hastened to do that which is repugnant to nature, and [Abraham's] soul would not have consented to accomplish an act of so great an importance if there had been a doubt about it (*Guide of the Perplexed* 3:24).[6]

Although Rambam correctly assesses the biblical narrative, there is still room for a different moral question. After God informs Abraham about the impending destruction of Sodom, Abraham pleads courageously on behalf of the righteous people who potentially lived in the wicked city, appealing to God's attribute of justice (Gen. 18:23–33).[7] How could Abraham stand idly by and not challenge God when God commanded him to sacrifice his beloved son?

By considering the Abraham narratives as a whole, we may resolve this dilemma. Abraham's actions in Genesis chapters 12–25 may be divided into three general categories: (1) responses to direct commands from God; (2) responses to promises or other information from God; and (3) responses to situations during which God does not communicate directly with Abraham.

Whenever God commands an action, Abraham obeys without as much as a word of protest or questioning. When

Abraham receives promises or other information from God, Abraham praises God when gratitude is in order, and he questions or challenges God when he deems it appropriate. Therefore, Abraham's silence when following God's commandment to sacrifice Isaac is to be expected. And so are Abraham's concerns about God's promises of progeny or information about the destruction of Sodom. The Torah thereby teaches that it is appropriate to question God, while simultaneously demanding faithfulness to God's commandments as an essential aspect of the mutual covenant between God and Israel.[8]

The Pinnacle of Religious Faith

Professor Yeshayahu Leibowitz suggests that Abraham and Job confronted the same religious test. Do they serve God because God provides all of their needs, or do they serve God under all conditions? Both were God-fearing individuals prior to their trials, but they demonstrated their unwavering commitment to God through their trials.[9]

Professor Moshe Halbertal derives a different lesson from the *Akedah*. God wishes to be loved by us, but pure love of God is almost impossible, since we are utterly dependent on God for all of our needs. We generally express love through absolute giving. When sacrificing to God, however, we always can hold out hope that God will give us more. Cain and Abel could offer produce or sheep to God, but they likely were at least partially motivated to appeal to God for better crops and flocks next year. What can we possibly offer God that demonstrates our true love?

Through the *Akedah*, God gives Abraham the opportunity to offer a gift outside of the realm of exchange. Nothing can replace Isaac, since his value to Abraham is absolute. As soon as Abraham demonstrates willingness to offer his own son to God, he has proven his total love and commitment. As the angel tells Abraham, "For now I know that you fear God, since you have not withheld your son, your favored one, from Me" (Gen. 22:12)

Halbertal explains that Abraham's offering a ram in place of Isaac becomes the paradigm for later sacrifice. Inherent in all sacrifice in the Torah is the idea is that we love God to the point where we are prepared to sacrifice ourselves or our children to God. The animal serves as a substitution. The *Akedah* thereby represents the supreme act of giving to God.[10]

The ideas explored by Professors Leibowitz and Halbertal lie at the heart of being extremely religious. Abraham is a model of pure, dedicated service and love of God. Such religious commitment is ideal, but it also comes with the lurking danger of religious extremism. We turn now to this critical issue.

Extremely Religious Without Religious Extremism

The Danish philosopher Søren Kierkegaard (1813–1855) composed a classic work on the *Akedah*, entitled *Fear and Trembling*. He argued that if one believes in religion because it appears reasonable, that is a secular distortion. True religion, maintains Kierkegaard, means being able to suspend reason and moral conscience when God demands it. Kierkegaard calls Abraham a knight of faith for his willingness to obey God and sacrifice his son.

Although Kierkegaard did not advocate violence in the name of religion, his view is vulnerable to that horrific outcome. In his philosophy, serving God must take precedence over all moral or rational concerns. A fatal problem arises when the representatives of any religion claim that God demands violence or other forms of immorality.

In a powerful article written in the wake of the terrorist attack on New York City on September 11, 2001, Professor David Shatz addresses this urgent question.[11] He observes that in general, one must create a system that balances competing ideals in order to eliminate ideological extremism. For example, one may place law against liberty, self-respect against respect for others, and discipline against love. In religion, however, there is a fundamental problem: Placing any value against religion, especially if that competing value can prevail over religion, defeats religious commitment.

Professor Shatz suggests a way to have passion for God tempered by morality and rationality without requiring any religious compromise. One must embrace morality and rationality as *part* of the religion. The religion itself must balance and integrate competing values as part of the religion. This debate traces back to Rabbi Saadiah Gaon, who insisted that God chooses moral things to command. In contrast, the medieval Islamic philosophical school of *Ash'ariyya* maintained that whatever God commands is by definition good.[12]

Kierkegaard's reading of the *Akedah* fails Professor Shatz's solution to religious extremism and is therefore vulnerable to the dangers of immorality in the name of God. In fact, Kierkegaard's reading of the *Akedah* fails the Torah itself: God stops Abraham, and then repudiates child sacrifice in the Torah. Whereas Kierkegaard focuses on Abraham's willingness to suspend morality to serve God, God rejects immorality as part of the Torah's religion. The expression of religious commitment in the Torah is the fear of God, which by definition includes the highest form of morality.[13] There must never be a disconnect between religious commitment and moral behavior, and Israel's prophets constantly remind the people of this critical message.[14] Thus, the Torah incorporates morality and rationality as essential components of its religious system.

In a similar spirit, Rabbi Shalom Carmy maintains that the *Akedah* teaches religious passion without fanaticism, and that even when a God-fearing individual keeps God's commandments, he or she remains responsive to the validity of the ethical.[15]

It also is important to stress that people who act violently in the name of religion generally are *not* crazy. Rather, they are following their religious system as they understand it and as their clerics teach it. Such manifestations of religion themselves are evil and immoral. Postmodernism thinks it can relativize all religion and thereby protect against the violence generated by religious extremism. In reality, however, postmodernism achieves the opposite effect as its adherents no longer have the resolve to refer to evil as evil and to battle against it. Instead, they try to rationalize evil away. This position empowers the religious extremists.[16]

Professor Shatz acknowledges that, lamentably, there are negative extremist elements among some Jews who identify themselves as religious. However, their attempts to justify their immorality with Torah sources in fact do violence to our sacred texts.[17] Such Jews are *not* extremely religious, but rather pervert the Torah and desecrate God's Name. Similarly, all religions must build morality and rationality into their systems so that they can pursue a relationship with God while avoiding the catastrophic consequences of religious extremism. As Rabbi

Jonathan Sacks has remarked, "the cure of bad religion is good religion, not no religion."[18]

Conclusion

The *Akedah* teaches several vital religious lessons. Ideal religion is about serving God, and is not self-serving. We aspire to be extremely religious, and Abraham serves as a paragon of the ideal connection to God. The *Akedah* also teaches the key to avoid what is rightly condemned as religious extremism. Morality and rationality must be built into every religious system, or else its adherents risk lapsing into immorality in the name of their religion.

One of the best means of promoting our vision is to understand and teach the underlying messages of the *Akedah*. We pray that all faith communities will join in affirming morality and rationality as being integral to their faiths. It is imperative for us to serve as emissaries of a different vision to what the world too often experiences in the name of religion, to model the ideal fear of Heaven that the Torah demands, and ultimately to sanctify God's Name.

NOTES

1. The Hebrew root for *Akedah* appears in Gen. 22:9, and refers to binding one's hands to one's feet. This is the only time that this root appears in the entire Bible.

2. Samuel David Luzzatto suggests that this legislation was in part an anti-pagan polemic, demonstrating that the Torah's idea of love of God does not involve the immoral sacrifice of one's child.

3. Cf. *Lev. Rabbah* (Margaliot) 29:9.

4. Kant was not the first person troubled by the moral implications of the *Akedah*. In the second century BCE, the author of the non-canonical book of Jubilees (17:16) ascribed the command to sacrifice Isaac to a "satanic" angel named Mastemah, rather than God Himself as presented in the Torah. Adopting a different tactic, Rabbi Eleazar Ashkenazi b. Nathan Habavli (fourteenth century) maintains that the *Akedah* must have occurred in a prophetic vision. Had the *Akedah* occurred in waking state, he argued, Abraham surely would have protested as he did regarding Sodom (in Marc Shapiro, *Changing the Immutable: How Orthodox Judaism Rewrites Its History* [Oxford: Littman Library of Jewish Civilization, 2015, p. 70]).

5. See Rabbi Yonatan Grossman, *Avraham: Sippuro shel Massa* (Hebrew) (Tel-Aviv: Yediot Aharonot, 2014), pp. 300–301.

6. Translation from *The Guide of the Perplexed*, Shlomo Pines, second edition (Chicago: University of Chicago Press, 1963), pp. 501–502.

7. See especially Rabbi Aharon Lichtenstein, "Does Jewish Tradition Recognize an Ethic Independent of Halakha?" in *Modern Jewish Ethics: Theory and Practice*, ed. Marvin Fox (Columbus, OH: Ohio State University Press, 1975), pp. 62–88.

8. See further discussion in Hayyim Angel, "Learning Faith from the Text, or Text from Faith: The Challenges of Teaching (and Learning) the Abraham Narratives and Commentary," in *Wisdom From All My Teachers: Challenges and Initiatives in Contemporary*

Torah Education, ed. Jeffrey Saks and Susan Handelman (Jerusalem: Urim, 2003), pp. 192–212; reprinted in Angel, *Through an Opaque Lens* (New York: Sephardic Publication Foundation, 2006), pp. 127–154; revised second edition (New York: Kodesh Press, 2013), pp. 99–122.

9. Yeshayahu Leibowitz, *Judaism, Human Values, and the Jewish State*, ed. Eliezer Goldman (Cambridge, MA: Harvard University Press, 1992), pp. 48–49, 259. Cf. Michael V. Fox, "Job the Pious," *Zeitschrift fur die Alttestamentliche Wissenschaft* 117 (2005), pp. 351–366.

10. Moshe Halbertal, *On Sacrifice* (Princeton, NJ: Princeton University Press, 2012), pp. 22–25.

11. David Shatz, "'From the Depths I Have Called to You': Jewish Reflections on September 11th and Contemporary Terrorism," in *Contending with Catastrophe: Jewish Perspectives on September 11th*, ed. Michael J. Broyde (New York: Beth Din of America and K'hal Publishing, 2011), pp. 197–233. See also Marvin Fox, "Kierkegaard and Rabbinic Judaism," in *Collected Essays on Philosophy and on Judaism*, vol. 2, ed. Jacob Neusner (Lanham, MD: University Press of America, 2003), pp. 29–43.

12. See Howard Kreisel, *Prophecy: The History of an Idea in Medieval Jewish Philosophy* (Dordrecht: Kluwer Academic Publishers, 2001), p. 38.

13. See, for example, Gen. 20:11; 42:18; Exod. 1:17, 21; Deut. 25:18.

14. See, for example, Isa. 1:10–17; Jer. 7:9–11; Hos. 6:6; Amos 5:21–25; Mic. 6:4–8.

15. Rabbi Shalom Carmy, "Passion, Paradigm, and the Birth of Inwardness: On Rabbi Kook and the *Akeda*," in *Hazon Nahum: Studies in Jewish Law, Thought, and History Presented to Dr. Norman Lamm on the Occasion of His Seventieth Birthday*, ed. Yaakov Elman and Jeffrey S. Gurock (New York: Yeshiva University Press, 1997), pp. 459–478.

16. For a chilling study of the virtual elimination of the very concept of sin and evil from much of Western literature, see Andrew Delbanco, *The Death of Satan: How Americans Have Lost the Sense of Evil* (New York: Farrar, Straus, and Giroux, 1995).

17. See Rabbi Yitzchak Blau, "Ploughshares into Swords: Contemporary Religious Zionists and Moral Constraints," *Tradition* 34:4 (Winter 2000), pp. 39–60.

18. Rabbi Jonathan Sacks, *The Great Partnership: God, Science, and the Search for Meaning* (London: Hodder & Stoughton, 2011), p. 11.

MORALITY AND LITERARY STUDY

WHAT DOES THE TORAH TEACH
ABOUT JACOB'S DECEPTION OF ISAAC?

Introduction

What lesson does the Torah teach about Jacob's deception of Isaac? The story itself is straightforward. Rebekah, who received prophecy that appears to mean that Jacob would prevail (Gen. 25:23),[1] wants Jacob to obtain Isaac's blessing of the birthright. Jacob previously purchased that right from Esau (Gen. 25:29-34). Rather than engage in direct dialogue or confrontation with Isaac, Rebekah arranges a ruse for Jacob to deceive Isaac, and it succeeds. The Torah does not pass explicit judgment on Rebekah or Jacob for their actions. Can we determine the Torah's moral evaluation of the deception from within the text?

Jacob is the divinely chosen successor of Isaac who becomes a prophet and the progenitor of God's chosen nation. He also purchased the birthright from Esau. Esau demonstrates that he is unworthy of the blessings, as he sells and despises his birthright even after being sated (25:29-34, cf. Rashi, Radak, Sforno), and marries Canaanites (26:34-35). The narrative criticizes Esau in these cases, but never explicitly criticizes Jacob.

143

Esau also dishonestly withholds from Isaac the fact that he had sold the birthright, blurting this fact out only after Isaac already had blessed Jacob (27:36). Isaac also upholds his blessing to Jacob even after he knows that he was deceived (27:33; 28:1-5).[2] These factors all support the conclusion that Rebekah and Jacob needed to do what they did to gain what was destined for Jacob.

And yet, Jacob lied to his father. Additionally, the deception of the old, blind, frail Isaac who trembles with shock (27:33), and Esau's pitiable screaming and crying (27:34-38) are sympathetic. It is difficult to conclude that there was *nothing* negative in the deception.

The complexity of the narrative led to significant debates among commentators. In the medieval period, the Jewish-Christian polemic played a role in interpretation, as Christians accused Jews of being deceitful like their ancestor Jacob. In the modern period, scholars debate the extent to which the Torah's values are similar to or different from the values of the surrounding ancient Near Eastern world at that time. They also debate the literary boundaries of the narrative, which have direct bearing on the moral evaluation of the story. In this essay, we will consider these debates, and then turn to a survey of Midrashim. The Sages of the Midrash were keenly sensitive to every detail of the narrative, producing a wide spectrum of approaches that collectively reflect the nuanced values of the Torah.

Medieval Period

Following several midrashic leads, Rashi attempts to erase all deception from Jacob's conduct. He rereads Jacob's comment, "I am Esau, your firstborn" (27:19) as, "I am [the one who brings you the food, and] Esau is your firstborn." He also translates Isaac's comment, "Your brother came with guile" (*ba ahikha be-mirmah*) to mean "your brother came with wisdom [*hokhmah*]."

Rashi's reading does not reflect the plain sense of the text. In the generation following Rashi, Rabbi Menahem b. Shelomo (*Sekhel Tov*) wrote facetiously that were one to accept Rashi's reading here, a dualist would be able to support the existence of two deities from the Ten Commandments by reading its first verse, "*Anokhi. Hashem Elokekha*" (It is I. The Lord is your God)! Professor Avraham Grossman[3] maintains that Rashi knew very well that he was deviating from *peshat* in this instance. He did so, in all likelihood, because Christians regularly accused Jews of being deceitful, emulating their ancestor Jacob. By writing that Jacob did not use deceit, Rashi deflated the Christian indictment at its roots.[4]

Ibn Ezra (on 27:19) dismisses Rashi's and related forced readings that maintain that Jacob did not lie. Instead, Ibn Ezra argues that Jacob lied, and that the ends justify the means. Ibn Ezra cites other examples of prophets lying for legitimate purposes. For example, Ibn Ezra assumes that David lied to Ahimelech the Priest about the ritual purity of his men in order to obtain consecrated food (1 Sam. 21:6). Similarly, Abraham told his servants that he and Isaac would return to them after serving God, even though he expected to sacrifice Isaac (Gen. 22:5). Many other commentators similarly justify the conduct of Rebekah and Jacob.

At the opposite extreme, Rabbi Yitzhak Arama maintains that Jacob's conduct was immoral, and further laments the Christian persecution of the Jews of his time in the wake of this narrative:

> Where is Jacob's purity, about which is it written, "Jacob was a mild man [*Yaakov ish tam*]" (Gen. 25:27)? ... Where is the cleanliness of his hands when he dressed himself with goat skins? Where is the purity of his heart when he said "I am Esau, your firstborn"? ... This criticism and disgrace is not only Jacob's, but is on all of us, we who derive from Jacob's stock (*Akedat Yitzhak*, chapter 23).

Even though many medieval commentators had Christian polemics on their minds, it is unproductive to ascribe all medieval interpretation—whether to justify Jacob, or to criticize him—to responses to medieval Christian accusations and persecutions. The text has to mean and teach something, and both sides can find ample textual support for their respective positions.[5]

Ancient Near Eastern Context

Moving into the modern period, scholarship has gained and refined additional tools from comparative ancient Near Eastern studies, and from advances in systematic literary analysis. Yet, scholars continue to debate how to apply these tools to the story of Jacob obtaining the birthright.

Cyrus Gordon and Gary Rendsburg observe that in the ancient Near East, deception of this variety would have been praiseworthy and admired, not scorned or condemned.[6] Several leading contemporary Orthodox scholars, including Rabbi Mordechai Breuer,[7] Rabbi Elhanan Samet,[8] and Rabbi Yaakov Medan,[9] accept the position that deception was a legitimate means for less powerful people to obtain what was rightfully theirs from more powerful people. In their view, the Torah fully supports the deception by Rebekah and Jacob.

One may ask, however, whether the Torah shares this value *in this case*. The Torah occasionally shares widespread ancient values, but very often rejects or modifies the prevailing values of its time. Literary analysis is required to ascertain the values of the Torah.

Literary Analysis

Rabbi Elhanan Samet maintains that the Torah's word choices, the literary boundaries of the narrative, and Jacob's perspective within the story all demonstrate that the deception was fully justified.

The narrative in chapter 27 repeatedly calls Esau "the elder son" (27:1, 15, 42), and never "firstborn." Objectively, Esau is no longer the firstborn, since he sold his birthright to Jacob. Thus, the Torah views the earlier sale as valid, and Jacob simply is obtaining what he purchased.

Rabbi Samet defines the literary boundaries of the unit as spanning from Esau's marriage to Canaanites (26:34-35) to Esau's penitent act of marrying Ishmael's daughter (28:6-9).[10] Esau is unworthy of the blessing, something Isaac and Rebekah know full well. Even though Isaac is unaware of the original sale of the birthright, he is morally blind to bless Esau at this point (cf. Abarbanel, Sforno).[11] Rabbi Samet bolsters his argument by noting that Jacob did not object morally to the deception; he was worried only that he might get caught (27:11-13). In a separate study, Rabbi Samet adds that the earlier narrative of 25:19-34—where Rebekah receives prophecy that Jacob would prevail and Esau sells the birthright—further supports Jacob and Rebekah in their deception.[12]

Professor Nehama Leibowitz strongly disagrees with this analysis.[13] The story of Jacob does not end with the literary unit about the deception, but continues to the end of the book of Genesis. Despite Jacob's worthiness and Esau's unworthiness, and that Jacob bought the birthright, Jacob is also punished measure for measure by being deceived repeatedly in the aftermath of his deception.

When Jacob reached Haran and wanted to marry Rachel, Laban deceived him by substituting Leah on the wedding night. Laban was aided in his deceit by Jacob's "blindness" in the dark, just as Jacob's father Isaac was blind:

> When morning came, there was Leah! So he said to Laban, "What is this you have done to me? I was in your service for Rachel! Why did you deceive me?" Laban said, "It is not the practice in our place to marry off the younger before the older" (Gen. 29:25-26).

Although Laban is likely unaware of Jacob's deceit of Isaac, there is little doubt that the reader of the Torah, and even Jacob himself, should hear the measure-for-measure punishment in Laban's words.

Later, in Genesis chapter 37, Jacob's sons have Joseph sold into slavery. To deceive Jacob, the brothers take Joseph's coat and kill a goat to use its blood on the coat. Once again, Jacob is deceived, suffers greatly, and the deception itself resembles Jacob's method of using a goat to deceive Isaac.

These deceptions suggest the Torah's implicit criticism of his deception of Isaac. In Professor Leibowitz's view, the means do not justify the ends. Although Jacob deserved the blessing,

Rebekah and Jacob acted immorally through their deception, and paid a heavy price.

Responding to this evidence, Rabbi Elhanan Samet maintains that Rebekah and Jacob were justified. However, Jacob still pays a price for the deception. Rabbi Samet makes an analogy with King David, who fought legitimate wars against Israel's enemies, yet his being a warrior disqualified him from building the Temple (1 Chron. 22:8; 28:2).

However, Laban's deceiving Jacob with Leah, and Jacob's sons' deceiving Jacob regarding Joseph's apparent death, are not automatic consequences of Jacob's deception. Rather, they sound like a form of divine retribution to Jacob, measure for measure. Therefore, Professor Leibowitz appears to have the better reading of the evidence. Jacob deserves the birthright and Abraham's legacy, and Esau is unworthy. Simultaneously, however, the ends do not justify the means of deception, and the Torah subtly criticizes Jacob through narrative "punishment." There is a complex outcome for a complex story.

The debate between Professor Leibowitz and Rabbi Samet revolves fundamentally around the question of how far one must read in the Torah to determine its evaluation of Jacob's deception. Professor Leibowitz insists that the entire Torah must be brought to bear in this discussion, whereas Rabbi Samet focuses on the primary narrative of the deception to arrive at his conclusion. Rabbi Yonatan Grossman takes this literary analysis to a different level by proposing that the dynamic literary boundaries of the birthright narrative shape our perceptions of the story. He maintains that the primary narrative itself presents a complex evaluation of Jacob's actions.[14]

One may define the literary boundaries of the unit as Stephen Langton[15] set off chapter 27. In this reading, the story is "The deception of Isaac." The unit ends with Rebekah asking Isaac to send Jacob away, in order to enable him to flee from Esau (27:46). According to Langton, chapter 28 begins a new theme, "Jacob's leaving home to find a wife." Taking chapter 27 as a unit, the trembling Isaac and the crying Esau are sympathetic characters, whereas Rebekah and Jacob are deceitful and suffer the consequences of the deception as Jacob flees for his life. Additionally, there is no reason given in chapter 27 for the deception, whereas Esau appears as a faithful son who is then swindled of his father's blessings.

However, 28:1 directly connects to 27:46, suggesting different literary boundaries for the narrative:

Rebekah said to Isaac, "I am disgusted with my life because of the Hittite women. If Jacob marries a Hittite woman like these, from among the native women, what good will life be to me?" So Isaac sent for Jacob and blessed him. He instructed him, saying, "You shall not take a wife from among the Canaanite women."

It appears that the narrative continues through 28:9, where Esau marries Ishmael's daughter to appease his parents after his initial marriage to Canaanites in 26:34-35. From this perspective, the boundaries of the narrative are from Esau's marriage to Canaanite wives until he marries Ishmael's daughter. With these boundaries, Esau was unworthy of the covenantal blessings. Jacob merits them, leaves home to continue the covenantal family, and receives Abraham's blessing. Moreover,

Isaac's blindness contains an element of moral blindness, since despite Esau's marriages to Canaanites, Isaac still wanted to bless him. Rebekah and Jacob do what must be done to obtain the covenantal blessing. Rebekah also uses her disgust with Esau's marriage to Canaanites to justify sending Jacob (27:46), directly connecting these elements.

There is a third way of drawing the boundaries of this narrative. If one includes the broader framework of 25:19-34, then one also must take into account Rebekah's prophecy that "the older will serve the younger" (25:23), and that Jacob legitimately bought the birthright. Esau refers to the sale in 27:36, suggesting a direct literary connection to the prior narrative. Esau is cast in a negative light as he fails to mention the sale to his father until after the deception has taken place. In this reading, God already told Rebekah that Jacob would prevail, and Jacob legitimately purchased the birthright. Their deception enables Jacob to receive what he deserves.

Rabbi Grossman maintains that each of these three readings has validity, suggesting a complex moral evaluation of Jacob's deception of Isaac. Jacob deserves the blessing and is the divine choice, but there still remains some negativity in his use of deception.

To summarize: comparative ancient Near Eastern studies are inconclusive for determining the Torah's evaluation of Jacob's deception of Isaac, since one needs to determine whether the Torah espouses or rejects the values of its surrounding culture on this issue. From literary studies, there are different layers of meaning that derive from a justification of Jacob's worthiness and Esau's unworthiness on one side, and simultaneously a negative aspect of the deception with a sympathetic picture of a trembling Isaac and a wailing Esau. This negative dimension finds further support in Jacob's suffering further deceptions, evidently as divine payback measure for measure for his deception of Isaac.

Midrashim

Midrashim capture every moral aspect of the story. One must read them collectively to appreciate their overall effect. Each Midrash focuses on a different aspect of the complex moral issue in the narrative.

The Talmud condemns Esau for spurning his birthright: "Rabbi Johanan said: That wicked [Esau] committed five sins on that day...and he spurned the birthright" (*Bava Batra* 16b). This passage focuses on Esau's willingness to sell the birthright for a bowl of porridge, based on the narrative conclusion, "Thus did Esau spurn the birthright" (Gen. 25:34). On this level, Esau was unworthy.

Some Midrashim (*Gen. Rabbah* 65:5; *Tanhuma Toledot* 8) criticize Isaac for wanting to bless Esau even after Esau had married Canaanites. Esau's bribery of meat "blinded" Isaac. These Midrashim play off the juxtaposition of Esau's intermarriages and Isaac's blindness coupled with his calling Esau to be blessed:

> When Esau was forty years old, he took to wife Judith daughter of Beeri the Hittite, and Basemath daughter of Elon the Hittite; and they were a source of bitterness to Isaac and Rebekah. When Isaac was old and his eyes were too dim to see, he called his older son Esau and said to him, "My son." He answered, "Here I am" (Gen. 26:34-27:1).

While most Midrashim focus on Esau's wickedness and unworthiness, some point to the payback to Jacob and even to his descendants. One detects the measure for measure payback in Laban's deception of Jacob:

> Said Jacob to [Leah]: Daughter of a deceiver! Why have you deceived me? She said to him: And you, why did you deceive your father? (*Tanhuma Vayetzei* 11).

The *Zohar* (*Toledot* 144b) adds that Jacob experienced *haradah* (trembling) when he believed that Joseph was dead, in exchange for the trembling he caused to his father through his deceit (Gen. 27:33).[16]

One Midrash condemns Jacob for causing Esau to cry (Gen. 27:34). As a consequence, Jacob's descendants would cry many centuries later during the Purim story, at the hands of a descendant of Esau—Haman:

> Jacob made Esau cry once, as it is written, "He burst into wild and bitter sobbing [*va-yitzak tze'akah gedolah u-marah*]" (Gen. 27:34). And where was [Jacob] punished for this? In Shushan the capital, as it is written, "And he [Mordecai] cried with a loud and bitter cry [*va-yizak ze'akah gedolah u-marah*]" (Est. 4:1) (*Gen. Rabbah* 67:4).

This Midrash plays off of the literary parallel between the two stories, and interprets it as measure for measure punishment to Jacob for the pain he caused Esau.

To summarize, several Midrashim highlight Esau's unworthiness and criticize Isaac's erroneous desire to bless Esau despite Esau's unworthiness. Other Midrashim focus on the suffering Jacob experienced from Laban and later his sons in deceiving him. One Midrash even reaches across to the Purim story to find payback for Jacob's causing Esau to weep.

Jacob rightly prevails and becomes the prophetic founder of the chosen people. God chooses him, and he obtains the birthright that already belonged to him. At the same time, the negative aspects of his deception haunt him throughout his life and beyond.

NOTES

1. Hebrew, *ve-rav ya'avod tza'ir*. Although the above translation reflects the conventional way of understanding the prophecy, it can be understood as ambiguous, possibly also suggesting, "the elder, shall the younger serve" (*Gen. Rabbah* 63:7, Radak, Abarbanel). It also is possible that Rebekah understood the prophecy in the conventional sense and therefore favored Jacob from the outset (Rashbam), whereas God intentionally left the outcome more ambiguous.

2. Bekhor Shor and Ramban maintain that since Isaac had given Jacob a prophetic blessing, it was not in his power to retract it. Alternatively, Ralbag and Abarbanel suggest that Isaac concluded that since Jacob succeeded, it must be God's will. Rashi proposes that Isaac upheld his blessing only *after* hearing Esau's confession that he had sold birthright years earlier (v. 36).

3. Avraham Grossman, "Religious Polemic and Educational Purpose in Rashi's Commentary on the Torah" (Hebrew), in *Pirkei Nehama: Nehama Leibowitz Memorial Volume*, ed. Moshe Ahrend, Ruth Ben-

Meir and Gavriel H. Cohn (Jerusalem: Eliner Library, 2001), pp. 187-205.

4. For further discussion of Jacob's deception in medieval polemics, see David Berger, "On the Morality of the Patriarchs in Jewish Polemic and Exegesis," in *Modern Scholarship in the Study of Torah: Contributions and Limitations*, ed. Shalom Carmy (New Jersey: Jason Aronson Inc., 1996), pp. 131-146.

5. See further discussion in Hayyim Angel, Review Essay: "*Pirkei Nehama: Nehama Leibowitz Memorial Volume*: The Paradox of *Parshanut*: Are Our Eyes on the Text, or on the Commentators?" *Tradition* 38:4 (Winter 2004), pp. 112-128; reprinted in Angel, *Through an Opaque Lens* (New York: Sephardic Publication Foundation, 2006), pp. 56-76; revised second edition (New York: Kodesh Press, 2013), pp. 39-59; *Peshat Isn't So Simple: Essays on Developing a Religious Methodology to Bible Study* (New York: Kodesh Press, 2014), pp. 36-57.

6. See, for example, Cyrus Gordon and Gary Rendsburg, *The Bible and the Ancient Near East* (New York: W.W. Norton, 1997), pp. 122-123.

7. Rabbi Mordechai Breuer, *Pirkei Bereshit* vol. 2 (Hebrew) (Alon Shevut: Tevunot, 1999), pp. 496-502.

8. Rabbi Elhanan Samet, *Iyyunim be-Parashot ha-Shavua* first series, vol. 1 (Hebrew) ed. Ayal Fishler (Ma'aleh Adumim: Ma'aliyot, 2002), pp. 62-74.

9. Rabbi Yaakov Medan, *Ki Karov Elekha: Leshon Mikra u-Leshon Hakhamim: Bereshit* (Hebrew) (Tel-Aviv: Yediot Aharonot, 2014), pp. 214-219.

10. The Sages of the Midrash (*Gen. Rabbah* 67:13) debate whether Esau's act of penitence was genuine, or whether it was worthless since he continued to be married to Canaanites. Rabbi Samet favors the view that the Torah casts Esau's actions as positive.

11. Attempting to defend Isaac's surprising decision to bless Esau, Rabbi Abraham son of Rambam suggests that Isaac hoped that keeping Esau closer through the blessings would be a positive influence on his son.

12. Rabbi Elhanan Samet, *Iyyunim be-Parashot ha-Shavua* second series, vol. 1 (Hebrew) ed. Ayal Fishler (Ma'aleh Adumim: Ma'aliyot, 2004), pp. 102-121.

13. Nehama Leibowitz, *Studies in Bereshit (Genesis)*, trans. Aryeh Newman (Jerusalem: Eliner Library), pp. 264-270.

14. Rabbi Yonatan Grossman, lecture at the Yeshivat Har Etzion Virtual Beit Midrash, at http://www.etzion.org.il/en/narrative-demarcation-part-iv-dynamic-boundaries.

15. Stephen Langton was the Archbishop of Canterbury, and divided the chapters in 1205.

16. This would have been a more compelling *peshat* argument had the narrative in Genesis 37 stated that Jacob trembled also. No doubt Jacob trembled while he absorbed the shock of Joseph's ostensible death, but the text moves immediately to his inconsolable mourning.

"HEELING" IN THE TORAH

A PSYCHOLOGICAL-SPIRITUAL READING OF THE SNAKE IN EDEN AND JACOB'S WRESTLING MATCH[1]

Introduction

Although one might not generally connect the snake in the Garden of Eden with Jacob, they do share a connection with heels. When God metes out punishment following the sin of the Tree of Knowledge, He decrees antagonism between humans and snakes: "I will put enmity between you and the woman, and between your offspring and hers; they shall strike at your head, and you shall strike at their heel [*ve-attah teshufennu akev*]" (Gen. 3:15). While these two species are forever at war, God delineates their modes of combat. People attempt a frontal attack at the snake's head, whereas the wily snake strikes at the person's heel.

Similarly, Jacob is named after a heel because he tried to catch up with the firstborn Esau: "Then his brother emerged, holding on to the heel of Esau [*ve-yado ohezet ba-akev Esav*];

---

1. This article appeared originally in *Jewish Bible Quarterly* 42:3 (2014), pp. 178-184.

so they named him Jacob" (Gen. 25:26). Following Jacob's deception of Isaac, Esau makes a pun on Jacob's name, giving it the sense of "shifty, underhanded." "[Esau] said, 'Was he, then, named Jacob that he might supplant me these two times [*va-yakeveni zeh pa'amayim*]? First he took away my birthright and now he has taken away my blessing!'" (Gen. 27:36). That is to say, he Jacob-ed me twice!

Significantly, each story also contains mythical aspects in the Torah's efforts to demythologize the world by employing these imageries to convey religious-ethical teachings. In this essay, we will explore the talking snake in the Garden of Eden and Jacob's wrestling match with an angel. Through an analysis of the texts and midrashic insight, common threads emerge. Both episodes reflect psychological-spiritual dimensions of the characters in the text and their development as people.

The Talking Snake

How could a snake speak a language that Eve could comprehend? The Torah does not refer to the snake's communicating with her as a miracle, unlike Balaam's talking donkey when "God opened its mouth" (Num. 22:28). Several commentators therefore insist that this story be read as non-literal.[1] Those who retain a literal reading offer creative interpretations to explain how a snake could communicate with Eve. For example, Hizkuni suggests that the snake accidentally ate from the Tree of Knowledge and consequently attained special powers. For his explanation to work, however, one must assume that the tree had supernatural properties, which is not necessarily the case. Alternatively, S.D. Luzzatto proposes that the snake wiggled in a manner that Eve could understand. In his commentary on Numbers 22, Luzzatto suggests a similar explanation for Balaam's talking donkey.

Perhaps the most intriguing and compelling answer is submitted by the *Zohar* (*Bereshit* 1:35b), as well as by Radak and Sforno. The snake should be understood as a personification of Eve's "evil inclination." In this reading, Eve was struggling with herself and temptation. Prior to her sin, the snake personified sin and temptation outside of Eve. Once Eve sinned, however, sin became an integral part of her personality and this, ultimately, is the "knowledge" she and Adam acquired. From this vantage point, the Torah employs the mythical image of a talking snake to convey a deeper psychological truth that applies to all people.

M.D. Cassuto adduces further textual support of this interpretation. "The man named his wife Eve [Havvah], because she was the mother of all the living [*em kol hai*]" (Gen. 3:20). The name Havvah carries the additional wordplay with the Aramaic word for snake, *hivya*.[2] One Midrash similarly makes this association: "She was given to him for an adviser [*havveh da'at*, "give an opinion"], but she played the eavesdropper like the serpent [*hivya*]" (*Gen. Rabbah* 20:11). Thus, by using snake imagery in particular, the Torah depicts the external personification of Eve's temptation that became internalized through sin. It was enshrined as part of Eve's name and essence. The ongoing battle between humans and snakes (Gen. 3:15) represents this never-ending struggle of the application of free will for the good. One's ideal strategy is to frontally attack the snake with his or her heel. People must likewise confront their inclination to sin if they wish to prevail.

Wrestling with Angels

From the moment he deceived his father, Jacob became a refugee. He suffered the trickery from his father-in-law Laban, which appears to be retribution for his own deceitful act.[3] Jacob also lived in fear after running away from home, despite repeated promises of divine protection (Gen. 31:3; 32:7-13). Why should Jacob have doubted God's explicit assurances? The Talmud suggests that Jacob was concerned that he had perhaps sinned, thereby forfeiting God's promises (*Berakhot* 4a).[4]

Alternatively, perhaps Jacob was worried about the ultimate fulfillment of such long-term promises, and God deemed his questions to be reasonable. One Midrash states that "the righteous have no assurance in this world" (*Gen. Rabbah* 76:2). In fact, Jacob suffered considerably throughout his life, despite God's repeated assurances of protection. He was threatened by Esau and cheated by Laban; his daughter Dinah was raped; his wife Rachel died in childbirth; his son Reuben acted inappropriately toward Bilhah; and his sons sold Joseph to Egypt.

Jacob prepared for his confrontation with Esau by dividing his camp, praying to God, and attempting to appease Esau with gifts. During the night, Jacob wrestled with a being generally assumed to be an angel:

> That same night he arose, and taking his two wives, his two maidservants, and his eleven children, he crossed the ford of the Jabbok ... Jacob was left alone. And a man wrestled [*va-ye'avek*] with him until the break of dawn. When he saw that he had not prevailed against

him, he wrenched Jacob's hip at its socket, so that the socket of his hip was strained as he wrestled with him. Then he said, "Let me go, for dawn is breaking." But he answered, "I will not let you go, unless you bless me" … Said he, "Your name shall no longer be Jacob, but Israel, for you have striven with beings divine and human, and have prevailed" (Gen. 32:23-29).

Who was this angel? "Rabbi Hama b. Rabbi Hanina said: It was the tutelary prince [guardian angel] of Esau" (*Gen. Rabbah* 77:3). Within this interpretation, the struggle with the angel represents Jacob's struggle with his brother. After prevailing over Esau's guardian angel, Jacob obtains forgiveness and a blessing from Esau when they encounter one another. Thus the mythical encounter with an angel is paralleled by Jacob's real-life experience.[5]

When Jacob and Esau subsequently meet, Jacob tells his brother that seeing him is like seeing the face of God. This is an unusual compliment, but Jacob knows that he has battled an angel representing physical and metaphysical Esau. Jacob wants Esau to accept his gift as atonement for past wrongs and refers to it as a *berakhah* (blessing):

> But Jacob said, "No, I pray you; if you would do me this favor, accept from me this gift; for to see your face is like seeing the face of God, and you have received me favorably. Please accept my present [*berakhah*] which has been brought to you, for God has favored me and I have plenty." And when he urged him, he accepted (Gen. 33:10-11).

A second midrashic opinion suggests that "he appeared to him in the guise of a shepherd" (*Gen. Rabbah* 77:2). This Midrash apparently refers to Jacob's struggle with himself. The angel resorts to a sly, underhanded move during the struggle, reminiscent of Jacob's deceitful action and also parallel to the snake's efforts to strike at a person's heel. The angel thus represents that element in Jacob, whereas the latter defeats his adversary with a frontal attack. Jacob ultimately needed to confront himself if he was to prevail over the old ghosts of his deception. The angel therefore blessed him, declaring that he would no longer be called Jacob, referring to that former deception, but rather Israel, a symbol of straightness (*yashar*).

Jacob and Israel

The interpretations in both cases are similar: the snake was an external personification of Eve's inner consciousness, and Jacob wrestled with the personification of an aspect of his inner consciousness. In contrast to Jacob, however, Adam and Eve never took personal responsibility for their sin, shifting the blame onto others instead. Therefore, Adam and Eve incurred banishment for their unwillingness to take responsibility for their actions, whereas Jacob was finally able to return home after this confrontation.

Remarkably, God subsequently renames Jacob (Gen. 35:9-10). Similar to the angel's blessing in chapter 32, God's blessing does not have a permanent effect. Despite this name change, Jacob is called "Jacob" forty-five times up to the end of Genesis, and "Israel" only thirty-four times.[6] Jacob subdued his trait of deception, but he and his descendants as a nation continued to manifest both names and traits. Not only is Jacob regularly called Jacob, but at the end of his life he blesses the firstborns of Bilhah and Zilpah with heel imagery: "Dan shall be a serpent by the road, a viper by the path, that bites the horse's heels [*ha-noshekh ikkevei sus*] so that his rider is thrown backward.... Gad shall be raided by raiders, but he shall raid at their heels [*ve-hu yagud akev*]" (Gen. 49:17, 19).

Later prophets also express the dichotomy of the Israelites being children of Jacob and children of Israel. Hosea offers a critical reading of the Genesis story to rebuke the Northern Kingdom shortly before its demise:

> Ephraim surrounds Me with deceit, the House of Israel with guile [*uv-mirmah*] ... The Lord once indicted Judah, and punished Jacob for his conduct, requited him for his deeds. In the womb he tried to supplant his brother [*ba-beten akav et ahiv*]; grown to manhood, he strove with a divine being (Hos. 12:1-4).

Jeremiah also alludes to Jacob's deceitfulness when he rebukes Jerusalem shortly before its downfall:

> Beware, every man of his friend! Trust not even a brother! For every brother takes advantage [*ki kol ah akov ya'kov*], every friend is base in his dealings. One man cheats the other, they will not speak truth; they have trained their tongues to speak falsely; they wear themselves out working iniquity. You dwell in the midst of deceit [*mirmah*]. In their deceit [*be-mirmah*], they refuse to heed Me—declares the Lord (Jer. 9:3-5).

Both Hosea and Jeremiah invoke the term *mirmah*, used earlier by Isaac in regard to Jacob's trickery: *ba ahiha be-mirmah*, "your brother came with guile" (Gen. 27:35).

On the positive side, Isaiah's prophecy of redemption speaks of a future transformation from Jacob to Israel when the crooked will become straight: "Let every valley be raised, every hill and mount made low. Let the rugged ground become level and the ridges become a plain [*ve-hayah he-akov le-mishor*]" (Isa. 40:4).

Unlike the permanent transformations of Abraham and Sarah with their name changes, Jacob never can fully become Israel. Abraham and Sarah went from being childless to having a child and beginning to build their covenantal nation. Their name changes reflect a one-time transformational event. For Jacob to become Israel, however, an ongoing process is required. Jacob received his blessing from God and the angel when he was willing to confront himself and begin that transformation, but character change is a life-long process rather than a one-time event.

On a personal and national level, Jacob must constantly strive to become Israel. Israel reflects honesty, uprightness, willingness to confront adversity, and taking personal responsibility. The internal struggle between the Israel and the Jacob continues through history on a national plane and also within every individual.

Conclusion

We have considered the relationship between the Garden of Eden and Jacob narratives. Both employ mythical imageries—a talking snake, a wrestling match with an angel. Both use these imageries to explore deep spiritual and psychological realities pertaining to the universal human condition.

Eve's dialogue with the snake is best understood as the inner voice that leads her to sin. The narrative's conclusion, that people and snakes always will battle, reflects the ongoing internal struggle of using free will to choose the good. The snake guilefully attacks a person's heel, but people can use their heels to vanquish the snake in direct confrontation, thereby overcoming their inner urge to sin.

Jacob's wrestling with the angel is a spiritualized expression of his struggle with Esau and with himself over deceiving his father. By confronting the angel head-on, Jacob was able to face his brother and himself, and initiate the process of becoming Israel.

The Torah further teaches that neither battle is ever won. People will never completely vanquish the inner snake driving them to sin, and Jacob will never fully become Israel. Yet by forthrightly addressing internal and external conflicts and challenges, one may steadily move in the right direction.

NOTES

1. For discussion of Rambam's view on reading certain texts non-literally, see Hayyim Angel, "Rambam's Continued Impact on Underlying Issues in *Tanakh* Study," in *The Legacy of Maimonides: Religion, Reason and Community*, ed. Yamin Levy and Shalom Carmy (Brooklyn: Yashar Books, 2006), pp. 153-157; reprinted in

Angel, *Through an Opaque Lens* (New York: Sephardic Publication Foundation, 2006), pp. 41-47; revised second edition (New York: Kodesh Press, 2013), pp. 24-29. For a general overview of traditional views on reading biblical texts non-literally, see Joshua L. Golding, "On the Limits of Non-Literal Interpretation of Scripture from an Orthodox Perspective," *Torah U-Madda Journal* 10 (2001), pp. 37-59; Hayyim Angel, "Controversies over the Historicity of Biblical Passages in Traditional Commentary," in Angel, *Increasing Peace Through Balanced Torah Study. Conversations* 27 (New York: Institute for Jewish Ideas and Ideals, 2017), pp. 10-21; reprinted in this volume.

2. Moshe D. Cassuto, *Commentary on the Book of Genesis* (Hebrew) (Jerusalem: Magnes Press, 1987), p. 114.

3. See Nehama Leibowitz, *New Studies in Bereshit-Genesis*, trans. Aryeh Newman (Jerusalem: Eliner Library), pp. 264-270; Hayyim Angel, "Morality and Literary Study: What does the Torah Teach about Jacob's Deception of Isaac?" printed in this volume.

4. For further discussion of rabbinic approaches to this question, see Hayyim Angel, "Learning Faith from the Text, or Text from Faith: The Challenges of Teaching (and Learning) the Avraham Narratives and Commentary," in *Wisdom from All My Teachers: Challenges and Initiatives in Contemporary Torah Education*, ed. Jeffrey Saks and Susan Handelman (Jerusalem: Urim Publications-ATID, 2003), pp. 201-204; reprinted in Angel, *Through an Opaque Lens* (New York: Sephardic Publication Foundation, 2006), pp. 136-139; revised second edition (New York: Kodesh Press, 2013), pp. 107-109.

5. Rabbi Elhanan Samet, *Iyyunim be-Parashot ha-Shavua* first series, vol. 1, ed. Ayal Fishler (Hebrew) (Ma'aleh Adumim: Ma'aliyot Press, 2002), pp. 89-104.

6. Rabbi Elhanan Samet explains that the biblical Hebrew "*lo X ki im Y*" often means, "not *primarily* X, but rather Y." In Jacob's name changes (Gen. 32:29; 35:10), the angel and God bless Jacob, "You will not primarily be called Jacob anymore, but rather Israel will be your preferred name." Contrast Jacob's name change with Abraham's, where God has the new name negate his previous name Abram: "And you shall no longer be called Abram, but your name shall be Abraham" (Gen. 17:5) (*Iyyunim be-Parashot ha-Shavua* second series, vol. 2, ed. Ayal Fishler [Hebrew] [Ma'aleh Adumim: Ma'aliyot Press, 2004], pp. 361-362).

DUAL CAUSALITY AND CHARACTERS' KNOWLEDGE

THE INTERACTION BETWEEN THE HUMAN AND THE DIVINE

Introduction

Professor Yehezkel Kaufmann is credited with coining the term "dual causality," or *sibbatiyut kefulah*.[1] One of the central axioms of Tanakh is that people have free will and are accountable for their actions. At the same time, prophecy often reveals God's foreknowledge of events. Dual causality is a means of describing how both of these planes simultaneously coexist. People are able to act freely without being controlled by God, while God still supervises people and His will is fulfilled. This effect is achieved by giving the majority of the narrative space to human actions.[2]

Thus, for example, Samson had poor taste by wanting to marry a Philistine woman. His parents rightly attempted to dissuade him, but Samson stubbornly ignored them and married her anyway. On the human level, Samson simply was in love, and later reacted to circumstances by killing Philistines out of personal grudges. However, from the divine perspective, Samson was helping Israel against its mighty foe, the Philistines:

168

His father and mother said to him, "Is there no one among the daughters of your own kinsmen and among all our people, that you must go and take a wife from the uncircumcised Philistines?" But Samson answered his father, "Get me that one, for she is the one that pleases me." His father and mother did not realize that this was the Lord's doing: He was seeking a pretext against the Philistines, for the Philistines were ruling over Israel at that time (Jud. 14:3-4).

On most occasions, the characters in the narratives are unaware of the divine plan or foreknowledge. Readers, and sometimes also prophets in the narratives, are privy to the divine dimensions. Some of the more interesting cases of dual causality occur when some of the characters are aware of or learn of the divine dimension within the narrative itself. This knowledge may significantly affect their thinking and actions. In this essay, we will consider several examples where most characters are unaware of the divine knowledge, but some characters may know or learn about the divine dimension over the course of the narrative.

The Downfall of Eli's Family

At the beginning of the book of Samuel, Eli's sons Hophni and Phinehas are wicked, and Eli does not rebuke them adequately.[3] Consequently, an anonymous prophet (1 Sam. 2:27-36) and Samuel (1 Sam. 3:11-18) prophesy the downfall of Eli's family to Eli. They will die young, and the family will lose the High Priesthood. Aside from the prophets and Eli, the characters are unaware of the divine decree. Readers do know, and therefore are able to see God's hand as well as the characters' freely willed actions as Eli's family steadily declines and eventually loses the High Priesthood.

Before the announcement of the prophetic decree, Hophni and Phinehas persist in their wicked ways despite Eli's rebuke. The narrator adds that God has decreed their fate:

> Now Eli was very old. When he heard all that his sons were doing to all Israel, and how they lay with the women who performed tasks at the entrance of the Tent of Meeting, he said to them, "Why do you do such things? I get evil reports about you from the people on all hands. Don't, my sons!..." But they ignored their father's plea; for the Lord was resolved that they should die (1 Sam. 2:22-25).

Radak and Abarbanel interpret the expression, "for the Lord was resolved that they should die," as one of the exceptional cases where God deprives wicked people of their free will as they already have warranted severe punishment from their previous sins. This interpretation is similar to Rambam's understanding of God's hardening Pharaoh's heart (*Hilkhot Teshuvah* 6:3).

Others, however, maintain that these expressions do not mean that God actively interferes with a person's free will. Rather, they are "superhumanly stubborn" in the face of a rationally obvious decision to repent (Ibn Caspi and S.D. Luzzatto on Exod. 7:3). Within this approach, Hophni and Phinehas refused to listen to their father because they were stubbornly wicked.

The prophetic narrator then reveals the divine foreknowledge that God intended to punish them for their sins. However, God did not manipulate them to persist in their evil.

After Eli's failed rebuke, an anonymous prophet tells Eli that his family will be removed from the High Priesthood and replaced with a different dynasty, and that his descendants will die young. As a sign that the long-term prophecy will be fulfilled, Hophni and Phinehas will die on the same day:

Assuredly—declares the Lord, the God of Israel—I intended for you and your father's house to remain in My service forever. But now—declares the Lord—far be it from Me! For I honor those who honor Me, but those who spurn Me shall be dishonored. A time is coming when I will break your power and that of your father's house, and there shall be no elder in your house...And this shall be a sign for you: The fate of your two sons Hophni and Phinehas—they shall both die on the same day. And I will raise up for Myself a faithful priest, who will act in accordance with My wishes and My purposes. I will build for him an enduring house, and he shall walk before My anointed evermore (1 Sam. 2:30-35).

This prophecy plays out over several generations. Soon after this prophecy, the Philistines kill Hophni and Phinehas in battle (1 Sam. 4:11). The characters in the narrative are unaware of the prophecies. Hophni and Phinehas brought the Ark to the battlefront because the people wrongly believed that the mere presence of the Ark would guarantee victory. The Philistines and Israelites were battling for their own reasons. However, the reader understands that the circumstances leading to the deaths of Eli's sons *also* fulfill the short-term sign predicted by the anonymous prophet in chapter 2.

Unlike all the other characters in the narrative, Eli is aware of the prophecies known to the reader. When he learns of the tragic news and falls backwards to his death (4:18), he must be conscious that the death of his sons is partially his fault. This added dimension of consciousness contributes to one character's experience, even as everyone else in the narrative is unaware.

The remainder of the downfall of Eli's family occurs without the knowledge of the characters. Only readers (and the prophet Samuel) are aware of the divine dimension of the events. In 1 Samuel 21-22, the priestly city of Nob assists David as he flees Saul. Outraged, Saul orders the massacre of the priests. The narrative pertains to Saul's paranoid pursuit of David. However, the High Priest Ahimelech son of Ahitub is also the great-grandson of Eli, likely the brother of Ahijah who appeared in an earlier narrative: "Ahijah son of Ahitub brother of Ichabod son of Phinehas son of Eli, the priest of the Lord at Shiloh, was there bearing an ephod..." (1 Sam. 14:3).

Although the text does not explicitly connect the massacre of the priests of Nob to the prophecy that Eli's descendants would die young, it appears to be an aspect of the divine dimension of the story. Josephus already made this connection (*Ant.* 5.350).

The final stage of the decline of Eli's family occurs with Ahimelech's surviving son Abiathar (1 Sam. 22:20). Abiathar joins David, and later appears to function as a High Priest. However, he joins David's son Adonijah (1 Kings 1:7), leading to his eventual dismissal by Solomon:

To the priest Abiathar, the king said, "Go to your estate at Anathoth! You deserve to die, but I shall not put you to death at this time, because you carried the Ark of my Lord God before my father David and because you shared all the hardships that my father endured." So Solomon dismissed Abiathar from his office of priest of the Lord—thus fulfilling what the Lord had spoken at Shiloh regarding the house of Eli (1 Kings 2:26-27).

Abarbanel notes that Solomon's banishment of Abiathar fulfills the prophecy against Eli's family, but the characters were unaware that it was being fulfilled. Abiathar joined Adonijah for his own reasons, and Solomon now removed him from his post for joining his rival brother.

To summarize, dual causality occurs at four[4] junctions of the Eli narrative:

- Hophni and Phinehas are stubbornly wicked, and their persistence in evil behavior fulfills a divine dimension as God wishes to punish them.
- Hophni and Phinehas die on the same day, as predicted by the anonymous prophet.
- Saul's massacre of the priests of Nob fulfills the decree that Eli's descendants would die young.
- Abiathar was banished from the High Priesthood, thereby ending Eli's dynasty.

The only character aware of the divine decree was Eli, who died with that knowledge when he learned of the death of his sons.

When Characters Learn the
Divine Dimension During the Narrative

On occasion, characters learn the divine dimension of events over the course of the narrative. Their newfound knowledge may influence aspects of the story. We will consider Jacob and Joseph's knowledge of their descent to Egypt as a fulfillment of the covenant with Abraham in Genesis chapter 15, and Rehoboam's learning that the secession of the Northern Kingdom was divinely willed.

Descent to Egypt

Jacob favors Joseph, the brothers have Joseph sold into slavery, Joseph rises to the top in Egypt, and Jacob brings his family to Egypt to reconnect with Joseph. In addition to these human dimensions of the narrative, readers also are conscious of God's promise to Abraham:

> And He said to Abram, "Know well that your offspring shall be strangers in a land not theirs, and they shall be enslaved and oppressed four hundred years; but I will execute judgment on the nation they shall serve, and in the end they shall go free with great wealth. As for you, you shall go to your fathers in peace; you shall be buried at a ripe old age. And they shall return here in the fourth generation, for the iniquity of the Amorites is not yet complete" (Gen. 15:13-16).

This is a classic example of dual causality. Jacob and his family members descend to Egypt to obtain food and to reconcile with

Joseph, and the wicked Pharaoh later enslaves the Israelites because of his paranoia. Simultaneously, these actions fulfill the divine foreknowledge in the story.

In this instance, we may ask an additional question: was Jacob aware of God's promise to Abraham? Perhaps there was a family tradition passed down to him through Abraham and Isaac. Even if Jacob was aware, did he know that this descent to Egypt was the beginning of the promised exile?

Rabbi Elhanan Samet[5] points to God's prophecy to Jacob as he went to Egypt as containing a possible clue:

> God called to Israel in a vision by night: "Jacob! Jacob!" He answered, "Here." And He said, "I am God, the God of your father. Fear not to go down to Egypt, for I will make you there into a great nation. I Myself will go down with you to Egypt, and I Myself will also bring you back; and Joseph's hand shall close your eyes" (Gen. 46:2-4).

Why was Jacob afraid to go to Egypt? Radak suggests that Jacob was concerned, since God had stopped Isaac from going to Egypt during a famine. However, there is no *fear* in this concern, and Jacob had been away from Israel before during his sojourn with Laban. Ramban therefore posits that Jacob sensed the beginning of the exile promised to Abraham. However, it is unclear how Jacob could have known. He was going to Egypt because of the famine and to see Joseph.

Adopting a modified position that captures the dual causality of the moment, Hizkuni suggests that Jacob *suspected* that it might be the beginning of the exile. This approach seems most plausible. In the prophecy, God tells Jacob that he will become a great nation while in Egypt. This prophecy confirms Jacob's suspicion of a prolonged stay, since he could not grow into a great nation during the remaining five years of famine.

From the duration of the narrative, it appears that Jacob is conscious that the nation will be in Egypt for some time, and that God will take them out one day: "Then Israel said to Joseph, 'I am about to die; but God will be with you and bring you back to the land of your fathers...'" (Gen. 48:21).

It is unclear when Joseph understands the full implications of Jacob's message. Immediately following Jacob's death, Joseph recognizes God's providence behind his being sold to save his family and Egypt. However, he does not mention the covenant with Abraham:

> But Joseph said to them, "Have no fear! Am I a substitute for God? Besides, although you intended me harm, God intended it for good, so as to bring about the present result—the survival of many people. And so, fear not. I will sustain you and your children." Thus he reassured them, speaking kindly to them (Gen. 50:19-21).

Some seventy years later, at the end of his life, Joseph appears to understand that the nation will endure a prolonged stay in Egypt and require God to take them out:

> At length, Joseph said to his brothers, "I am about to die. God will surely take notice of you and bring you

up from this land to the land that He promised on oath to Abraham, to Isaac, and to Jacob." So Joseph made the sons of Israel swear, saying, "When God has taken notice of you, you shall carry up my bones from here" (Gen. 50:24-25).

Thus, it appears that Jacob, and later Joseph and his family, gain awareness that their sojourn in Egypt to survive a famine would fulfill the divine covenant with Abraham. Joseph uses this knowledge to instruct his brothers to bring his bones out, and his oath contains the words that would trigger hope in redemption during the slavery:

Go and assemble the elders of Israel and say to them: the Lord, the God of your fathers, the God of Abraham, Isaac, and Jacob, has appeared to me and said, 'I have taken note of you [*pakod pakadti*] and of what is being done to you in Egypt, and I have declared: I will take you out of the misery of Egypt to the land of the Canaanites, the Hittites, the Amorites, the Perizzites, the Hivites, and the Jebusites, to a land flowing with milk and honey.' They will listen to you… (Exod. 3:16-18).

Following a Midrash (*Exod. Rabbah* 3:8), Rashi explains that the elders would believe Moses, specifically because he used the key phrase, *pakod yifkod*, passed down from Joseph. The phrase is repeated when Moses fulfills Joseph's oath and takes his bones out during the exodus:

> And Moses took with him the bones of Joseph, who had exacted an oath from the children of Israel, saying, "God will be sure to take notice of you [*pakod yifkod*]: then you shall carry up my bones from here with you" (Exod. 13:19).

Additionally, Rabbi Samet suggests that Joseph's family chose to remain in Egypt after the famine because they were comfortable. Perhaps, however, Jacob chose to remain silent about returning to Israel, since he was aware of the fulfillment of the divine plan.

The Division of the Monarchy

Another example of a character gaining awareness of dual causality is Rehoboam, shortly after the Northern Kingdom seceded. In the book of Kings, the splitting of the kingdom occurred on the human plane by Rehoboam's foolish decision to continue his father Solomon's difficult work policies (1 Kings 12:1-15). On the divine plane, Solomon's turning to idols caused the split of the kingdom (1 Kings 11:1-13, 29-40). The summary verse at the conclusion of the two narratives spells out the dual causality:

> The king did not listen to the people; for the Lord had brought it about in order to fulfill the promise that the Lord had made through Ahijah the Shilonite to Jeroboam son of Nebat (1 Kings 12:15).

Thus far, Rehoboam acted freely and the results of his foolish decision dovetailed the divine punishment to Solomon.[6] In the ensuing narrative, however, God is "forced" to inform Rehoboam of the divine plane. After the secession of the Northern Kingdom, Rehoboam musters a vast army to attack. Left to his uninformed free will, there would be much bloodshed in Israel. Therefore, God intervenes through the prophet Shemaiah to avoid this war:

> On his return to Jerusalem, Rehoboam mustered all the House of Judah and the tribe of Benjamin, 180,000 picked warriors, to fight against the House of Israel, in order to restore the kingship to Rehoboam son of Solomon. But the word of God came to Shemaiah, the man of God: "Say to King Rehoboam son of Solomon of Judah, and to all the House of Judah and Benjamin and the rest of the people: Thus said the Lord: You shall not set out to make war on your kinsmen the Israelites. Let every man return to his home, for this thing has been brought about by Me." They heeded the word of the Lord and turned back, in accordance with the word of the Lord (1 Kings 12:21-24).

God had to inform Rehoboam of the divine layer to avoid disaster. Thankfully, Rehoboam listened to God's word and accepted the divided monarchy.

Complete Knowledge of the Divine Dimension

One of the most fascinating, and painful, examples of dual causality in Tanakh is when David is as aware of the divine decree as readers are. Following David's sins with Uriah and Bathsheba, the prophet Nathan pronounces the divine decree to David:

"Therefore the sword shall never depart from your House—because you spurned Me by taking the wife of Uriah the Hittite and making her your wife." Thus said the Lord: "I will make a calamity rise against you from within your own house; I will take your wives and give them to another man before your very eyes and he shall sleep with your wives under this very sun. You acted in secret, but I will make this happen in the sight of all Israel and in broad daylight" (2 Sam. 12:10-12).

The death of David's infant son (chapter 12), Amnon's rape of Tamar and murder by Absalom (chapter 13), Absalom's rebellion, his rape of David's concubines, and his death at the hands of Joab (chapters 15-18) are presented as divine retribution for David's sins. Aside from David, the other characters in the narrative were unaware of the divine decree, and acted freely. David, in contrast, was aware of the divine decree from the beginning. In the following essay, we will explore the impact of this divine knowledge on David.

Conclusion

Tanakh sometimes gives us glimpses of divine knowledge. At all times, characters have complete personal responsibility. Occasionally, we are told that their freely-willed actions also fulfill divine knowledge or a decree. On most occasions, the characters are unaware of the divine dimension, and act out of their personal motivations.

Dual causality becomes more fascinating when some of the characters are aware of the divine dimension within the plot.

Eli's knowledge that Hophni and Phinehas would die offers the reader a deeper angle into his final thoughts and emotions as he died from the catastrophic news. Jacob and Joseph learn that the descent to Egypt is the beginning of the fulfillment of God's covenant with Abraham. Joseph's oath to his brothers carries through the exodus narratives. Perhaps Jacob's knowledge of the divine dimension of the descent to Egypt also encouraged him to remain silent. In the case of the division of the monarchy, God revealed the decree to Rehoboam in order to avoid civil war. Finally, David's knowledge of the divine decree throughout the woes in 2 Samuel chapters 13-20 significantly altered his actions, encouraging him to repent and also paralyzing him as he understood that the various disasters were consequences of his sin, on the divine plane.

It always is important to bear in mind what we know and what the characters may know. This viewpoint helps us understand the characters in the narrative, and occasionally also gives us glimpses into the world of the divine.

NOTES

1. *The Book of Joshua* (Hebrew), (Jerusalem: Kiryat Sefer, 1970), p. 128.

2. Yairah Amit, "The Dual Causality Principle and Its Effects on Biblical Literature," *Vetus Testamentum* 37 (1987), pp. 390-391.

3. He did rebuke them, however, in 1 Sam. 2:22-25. Yehudah Kiel maintains that it was weak and confused, and therefore

ineffective (*Daat Mikra: 1 Samuel* [Hebrew] [Jerusalem: Mossad HaRav Kook,1981], p. 27). Radak (on 3:13) criticizes Eli for waiting until he was old, rather than rebuking them immediately. Rashi (on 3:13) suggests that since Eli did not remove them from office, Eli is held accountable for their evils even if Eli verbally rebuked them.

4. Following *Seder Olam Rabbah* 14, Rashi suggests a fifth example. When David flees Jerusalem, the priests Zadok and Abiathar bring the Ark, and David sends them back to Jerusalem (2 Sam. 15:23-29). This is Zadok's introduction to the narrative (except on a general roster of David's officials in 2 Sam. 8:17), and he is listed before Abiathar, suggesting his priority. Rashi views this as evidence of another stage in Abiathar's descent from the High Priesthood.

5. Rabbi Elhanan Samet, *Iyyunim be-Parashot ha-Shavua* (third series), vol. 1 (Hebrew) ed. Ayal Fishler (Tel-Aviv: Yediot Aharonot, 2012), pp. 222-239.

6. Jeroboam, on the other hand, was conscious of the dual causality prior to the rebellion because Ahijah the Shilonite informed him of the prophecy. This knowledge no doubt affected his actions, even as his northern followers may not have known what he knew. He could have been confident that God was on his side, emboldening him to speak brazenly to Rehoboam and subsequently to revolt. On the other hand, it was the people of the north who appointed him king, without any knowledge of a divine dimension (1 Kings 12:20).

DOING EVERYTHING HALFWAY

DAVID AFTER HIS SIN
WITH URIAH AND BATHSHEBA

Introduction

David's sin with Bathsheba and Uriah was severe, and tore David's family and the nation apart. It is also one of the most honest moments in Tanakh. The book of Samuel's straightforward presentation of Nathan's integrity, David's repentance, and sin-aftermath are peerless. Nobody, not even the most beloved figure in Tanakh, is beyond prophetic rebuke when he violates God's word.

Nathan prophesies to David that although David will not die immediately, there will be catastrophes within his own family and the nation:

> Thus said the Lord: I will make a calamity rise against you from within your own house; I will take your wives and give them to another man before your very eyes and he shall sleep with your wives under this very sun. You acted in secret, but I will make this happen in the sight of all Israel and in broad daylight (2 Sam. 12:10-12).

The narratives in 2 Samuel chapters 13-20 are cast in the biblical model of dual causality, where characters act freely but simultaneously fulfill a divinely predicted future.[1] Unlike the other characters, David is conscious of the divine decree that disaster will come from within his family. This awareness led David to a process of repentance and the acknowledgement of God's role.[2]

At the same time, this awareness also paralyzed David so that he was able to do only half of what was needed for the duration of his life. In this essay, we will consider a few examples of this recurring phenomenon. David's sin tears apart his family and the nation, but his actions also contribute directly to this downfall.

Amnon

In 2 Samuel 13, David's oldest son Amnon lusts after his half-sister Tamar, and orchestrates her rape. In 13:21, David learns of this horrific act, and is angry. Yet, he does not punish Amnon, and the text does not explain his inaction. Likely following the prophetic criticism of David's spoiling of Adonijah later on (1 Kings 1:6), the Septuagint and Josephus suggest that David exhibited favoritism toward Amnon because he loved him as his firstborn son.

No doubt paternal favoritism played a role in the human dimension of David's behavior. However, Yehudah Elitzur cogently maintains that unlike the other characters who acted on their own, David also understood that Amnon's rape of Tamar was in part divine retribution for David's sins. This knowledge paralyzed David from meting out justice when his son Amnon committed a similar crime.[3]

David's non-punishment of Amnon outraged Absalom, who waited two years until killing Amnon in retribution for the rape of Tamar. Abarbanel observes that when Absalom rebelled against his father David, his battle cry was that David is unjust whereas Absalom would be just (2 Sam 15:1-6). Although Absalom was a demagogue, his argument rings true after David's failure to punish Amnon. David's earlier career is characterized by his just rule: "David reigned over all Israel, and David executed true justice among all his people" (2 Sam. 8:15). This injustice with Amnon undermined David's throne.

To summarize, David was angry over Amnon's rape of Tamar, but failed to punish him. This inaction likely stemmed from a combination of paternal bias and knowledge that on the divine plane this act was retribution for David's own sins. David's inability to do what was necessary contributed to Absalom's killing of Amnon, and later formed the ideological basis for Absalom's rebellion against David.

Absalom

From the moment Absalom kills Amnon until Absalom's death during his rebellion, David consistently acts halfway with his son. As with Amnon, David's paternal love of his son biased him, and David also was plagued by his sin and consciousness that Absalom's actions were in part divine retribution.

After Absalom kills Amnon, he flees to Geshur. Three years later, David misses him, "King David was pining away for Absalom, for [the king] had gotten over Amnon's death" (2 Sam. 13:39). Despite David's longing for Absalom, however, he does not invite him back to Jerusalem.

Joab therefore sends a wise woman from Tekoa to convince David to reconcile with Absalom (14:1-20). After she succeeds, David sends for Absalom, but then refuses to see him:

> Then the king said to Joab, "I will do this thing. Go and bring back my boy Absalom."… And Joab went at once to Geshur and brought Absalom to Jerusalem. But the king said, "Let him go directly to his house and not present himself to me." So Absalom went directly to his house and did not present himself to the king (2 Sam. 14:21-24).

After two years of living in Jerusalem without seeing David (14:28), the furious Absalom forces Joab to gain him an audience with David (14:29-32). David summons Absalom, but then gives him a cold reception:

> Joab went to the king and reported to him; whereupon he summoned Absalom. He came to the king and flung himself face down to the ground before the king. And the king kissed Absalom [*va-yishak ha-melekh le-Avshalom*] (14:33).

David kissed *le-Avshalom*, not *et Avshalom*. Ralbag explains that this kiss was more distant, on the hand or shoulder. David is called "king" four times in this one verse, supporting Ralbag's reading. It is a cold royal kiss, not an affectionate fatherly kiss.

One may read human dimensions into David's actions: He loves Absalom, but cannot forgive Absalom's murder of

Amnon. Additionally, David wants to avoid showing favor to Absalom, since that might suggest that Absalom is pardoned and now can become the next king.[4] On the divine plane, David also is paralyzed by his own sins, and cannot bring himself to punish Absalom when David knows that Absalom's actions are in part divine retribution.

Once again, David's halfway actions lead to further injustice in the kingdom, and no doubt also contribute to Absalom's sense that he should revolt against David.

When Absalom subsequently revolts (2 Sam. 15:1-12), David does not react to Absalom's taking a chariot and having fifty runners before him. David does nothing until the rebellion breaks out, and then immediately flees Jerusalem. It is as though David allowed himself to lose (2 Sam. 15:13-14).

Once he leaves Jerusalem, however, David suddenly transforms back into a brilliant strategist determined to protect his throne. He remains conscious of God's decree and accepts God's will, but also does whatever he can to triumph over Absalom.

David's different layers of motivation are expressed poignantly in his reaction to Zadok and Abiathar when they bring the Ark and David orders them to return it to Jerusalem:

> But the king said to Zadok, "Take the Ark of God back to the city. If I find favor with the Lord, He will bring me back and let me see it and its abode. And if He should say, 'I do not want you,' I am ready; let Him do with me as He pleases." And the king said to the priest Zadok, "Do you understand? You return to the safety

of the city with your two sons, your own son Ahimaaz and Abiathar's son Jonathan. Look, I shall linger in the steppes of the wilderness until word comes from you to inform me" (2 Sam. 15:25-28).

David humbly expresses that he is entirely in God's hands. Simultaneously, David will gain loyal spies in Jerusalem by having the priests remain. David combines a high level of faith and strategy into one act.

David continues his strategy by asking Hushai to infiltrate Absalom's inner circle to thwart Ahithophel:

When David reached the top, where people would prostrate themselves to God, Hushai the Archite was there to meet him, with his robe torn and with earth on his head. David said to him, "If you march on with me, you will be a burden to me. But if you go back to the city and say to Absalom, 'I will be your servant, O king; I was your father's servant formerly, and now I will be yours,' then you can nullify Ahithophel's counsel for me. You will have the priests Zadok and Abiathar there, and you can report everything that you hear in the king's palace to the priests Zadok and Abiathar. Also, their two sons are there with them, Zadok's son Ahimaaz and Abiathar's son Jonathan; and through them you can report to me everything you hear" (2 Sam 15:32-36).

The priests and Hushai become vital players in David's victory strategy.

David had helped stoke Absalom's rebellion, and then passively allowed it to develop to the point where David had to flee Jerusalem. Once out of the city, however, David suddenly developed strategies to thwart Absalom and to win his throne back. Only at the moment of truth, when David was prepared to win it all, he gave the command to his army:

> The king gave orders to Joab, Abishai, and Ittai: "Deal gently with my boy Absalom, for my sake." All the troops heard the king give the order about Absalom to all the officers (2 Sam. 18:5).

Of course, this command undermined the very purpose of the war, and could have led to the needless deaths of countless soldiers. Joab defied David, had Absalom killed, and ended the war. He then rebuked and even threatened David for his public mourning over Absalom:

> The king was shaken. He went up to the upper chamber of the gateway and wept, moaning these words as he went, "My son Absalom! O my son, my son Absalom! If only I had died instead of you! O Absalom, my son, my son!"...Joab came to the king in his quarters and said, "Today you have humiliated all your followers, who this day saved your life, and the lives of your sons and daughters, and the lives of your wives and concubines, by showing love for those who hate you and hate for those who love you. For you have made clear today that the officers and men mean nothing to you. I am sure

that if Absalom were alive today and the rest of us dead, you would have preferred it. Now arise, come out and placate your followers! For I swear by the Lord that if you do not come out, not a single man will remain with you overnight; and that would be a greater disaster for you than any disaster that has befallen you from your youth until now." So the king arose and sat down in the gateway; and when all the troops were told that the king was sitting in the gateway, all the troops presented themselves to the king... (2 Sam. 19:1-9).

Yehudah Elitzur again maintains that David does not appear to be acting merely out of parental favoritism. David understood that Absalom's rebellion was also in part divine retribution for sin of Bathsheba and Uriah. The weight of his sin and his acceptance of the divine decree paralyzed David.[5] Malbim suggests an additional dimension of this conflict from David's exclamation, "If only I had died instead of you!" (19:1). Perhaps David wishes that he had died as a punishment for Bathsheba and Uriah, rather than enduring this catastrophic consequence from Absalom.

David acted halfway throughout the Absalom conflict. His inability to act decisively contributed directly to every stage of the disaster.

Mephibosheth and Ziba

One other saga in the post-sin narrative of David is that of Mephibosheth and Ziba. In chapter 9, David seeks living relatives of Jonathan so that he can care for them. He learns of Jonathan's lame son Mephibosheth. In the process, David unwittingly enters a thorny situation. Saul's servant Ziba occupies Jonathan's mansion, living like royalty with fifteen sons and twenty slaves of his own (9:10). Mephibosheth, on the other hand, lives across the Jordan River with a generous man named Machir (9:4).

David immediately rights this wrong:

The king summoned Ziba, Saul's steward, and said to him, "I give to your master's grandson everything that belonged to Saul and to his entire family. You and your sons and your slaves shall farm the land for him and shall bring in [its yield] to provide food for your master's grandson to live on; but Mephibosheth, your master's grandson, shall always eat at my table."—Ziba had fifteen sons and twenty slaves.—Ziba said to the king, "Your servant will do just as my lord the king has commanded him." "Mephibosheth shall eat at my table like one of the king's sons." Mephibosheth had a young son named Mica; and all the members of Ziba's household worked for Mephibosheth (2 Sam. 9:9-12).

It is unclear whether Ziba actually stole the house from Mephibosheth by driving him out, or whether Mephibosheth simply fled from David, fearing that David might exterminate Saul's family line. Regardless, Ziba wanted that mansion. He obeyed David, but waited for the right moment to regain his newfound life of luxury. Absalom's rebellion provided that moment.

As David fled Jerusalem during Absalom's rebellion, Ziba came to greet him:

> David had passed a little beyond the summit when Ziba the servant of Mephibosheth came toward him with a pair of saddled asses carrying two hundred loaves of bread, one hundred cakes of raisin, one hundred cakes of figs, and a jar of wine. The king asked Ziba, "What are you doing with these?" Ziba answered, "The asses are for Your Majesty's family to ride on, the bread and figs are for the attendants to eat, and the wine is to be drunk by any who are exhausted in the wilderness." "And where is your master's son?" the king asked. "He is staying in Jerusalem," Ziba replied to the king, "for he thinks that the House of Israel will now give him back the throne of his grandfather." The king said to Ziba, "Then all that belongs to Mephibosheth is now yours!" And Ziba replied, "I bow low. Your Majesty is most gracious to me" (2 Sam. 16:1-4).

Ziba feeds David generously, and accuses Mephibosheth of desiring the return of the monarchy to him. David accepts the food and the accusation, and declares that the house now belongs to Ziba.

David's ruling is surprising. Ziba already had a track record of usurping the house, and David rightly restored it to Mephibosheth. Was it plausible that Mephibosheth wanted the throne? He was lame, and of course Absalom himself was interested in becoming king, and would not crown

Mephibosheth. Yet, David accepts Ziba's story. Presumably, the food bribe during David's time of distress helped Ziba. In the Talmud, Rav expresses disappointment with David:

> Rav said, David paid heed to slander...[David] saw that he [Ziba] was a liar; then when he slandered him a second time, why did he pay heed thereto? (*Shabbat* 56a).

At the end of the war, the narrative closes the various circles, including that of Mephibosheth:

> Mephibosheth, the grandson of Saul, also came down to meet the king. He had not pared his toenails, or trimmed his mustache, or washed his clothes from the day that the king left until the day he returned safe. When he came [from] Jerusalem to meet the king, the king asked him, "Why didn't you come with me, Mephibosheth?" He replied, "My lord the king, my own servant deceived me. Your servant planned to saddle his ass and ride on it and go with Your Majesty—for your servant is lame. [Ziba] has slandered your servant to my lord the king. But my lord the king is like an angel of the Lord; do as you see fit. For all the members of my father's family deserved only death from my lord the king; yet you set your servant among those who ate at your table. What right have I to appeal further to Your Majesty?" (2 Sam. 19:25-29).

The narrator describes the unkempt appearance of Mephibosheth. He was mourning for David during Absalom's rebellion (Radak, Ralbag), and certainly did not aspire to having the kingdom returned to him, as per Ziba's accusation.

Yehudah Kiel reconstructs Mephibosheth's story: When David's loyal followers fled Jerusalem, Mephibosheth ordered Ziba to take him on a donkey to leave the city to join David. Ziba instead rode off with the donkey, so lame Mephibosheth had no way to leave the city. Ziba had slandered him.

Mephibosheth is grateful to David, and humbly states that he has no rights. Mephibosheth is unkempt, his story is plausible, Ziba previously had usurped the house, and Ziba's gift to David during Absalom's rebellion now seems like a flat-out bribe. David could apologize to Mephibosheth for his error, and return the estate to him. Instead, David does not want to be bothered any further:

> The king said to him, "You need not speak further. I decree that you and Ziba shall divide the property." And Mephibosheth said to the king, "Let him take it all, as long as my lord the king has come home safe" (2 Sam. 19:30-31).

It is astonishing that David gives Ziba half of the estate. This appears to be a miscarriage of justice. One talmudic passage considers this ruling to be the root cause of the subsequent division of the kingdom, and Israel's turning to idolatry as a result of Jeroboam's policies:

Rabbi Judah said in Rav's name: When David said to Mephibosheth, 'You and Ziba divide the land,' a Heavenly Echo came forth and declared to him, Rehoboam and Jeroboam shall divide the kingdom. Rabbi Judah said in Rav's name: Had not David paid heed to slander, the kingdom of the House of David would not have been divided, Israel had not engaged in idolatry, and we would not have been exiled from our country (*Shabbat* 56b).

This talmudic passage has its finger on the entire post-sin narrative of David. It is not merely David's ruling with the house, but a symptom of everything where David acts halfway, bringing damage and injustice onto his family and tearing apart the nation.

On a different level, David's sin tore David himself in half. His half-paralysis crippled his ability to act decisively, and his halfway actions often helped bring about further demise.

Conscious of the divine dimension of the story, David's soul was torn in half. He failed in the critical area of justice. David's injustices with Amnon, Absalom, and Ziba ultimately split the nation in half as well.

David also engaged in a lengthy process of repentance after his sin. In the following essay, we will consider aspects of his remarkable efforts to repair his relationship with God after the rupture from his sin.

NOTES

1. See Hayyim Angel, "Dual Causality and Characters' Knowledge: The Interaction between the Human and the Divine," printed in this volume.

2. See Hayyim Angel, "The Yoke of Repentance: David's Post-Sin Conduct in the Book of Samuel and Psalm 51," at http://www. yutorah.org/lectures/lecture.cfm/818982/Rabbi_Hayyim_Angel/ The_Yoke_of_Repentance:_David%E2%80%99s_Post-Sin_ Conduct_in_Sefer_Shemuel_and_Tehillim_51; Hayyim Angel, "Mizmor 51: David as Model of Repentance," in *MiTokh Ha-Ohel, From Within the Tent: The Festival Prayers*, ed. Daniel Z. Feldman and Stuart W. Halpern (Jerusalem: Maggid, 2017), pp. 19-27; reprinted in this volume.

3. Yehudah Elitzur, "David Son of Jesse—A Model for Penitents," in *Yisrael ve-ha-Mikra: Mehkarim Geografi'im Histori'im ve-Hagoti'im* (Hebrew), ed. Yoel Elitzur and Amos Frisch (Ramat Gan: Bar Ilan University Press, 1999), pp. 144-149. Cf. Yehudah Kiel, *Da'at Mikra: 2 Samuel* (Hebrew) (Jerusalem: Mosad HaRav Kook, 1981), p. 435.

4. Cf. Yehudah Kiel, *Da'at Mikra: 2 Samuel*, p. 446.

5. Yehudah Elitzur, "David Son of Jesse—A Model for Penitents."

PSALM 51

DAVID AS MODEL OF REPENTANCE[1]

Introduction

One of the most beloved figures in Israel's history, King David continues to inspire through the Psalms and the narratives about his spectacular faith and kingship. We pray for his descendant to herald the messianic era. The painful episode of Bathsheba and Uriah, involving grave sins pertaining to adultery and murder, is all the more wrenching coming from David.

The simple reading of David's sins yields several significant lessons. Rabbi Judah the Pious observes that this story warns of the immense power of lust (*Sefer Hasidim* 619). Ralbag further suggests that a leader must identify with his nation's suffering; David's problems began when he remained at home instead of leading Israel to war against Ammon (*To'elet* 42, at the end of 2 Samuel 21).[1] More broadly, Rabbi Amnon Bazak observes that this story exemplifies the absolute honesty and integrity of

---

1. This article appeared originally in *MiTokh Ha-Ohel, From Within the Tent: The Festival Prayers*, ed. Daniel Z. Feldman and Stuart W. Halpern (Jerusalem: Maggid, 2017), pp. 19-27.

Tanakh. Prophecy shows no favoritism and judges all people—even the beloved David—by the standards of the Torah.[2]

In addition to these lessons to be derived from David's sins, Abarbanel focuses on David's repentance. Similarly, the Talmud views this narrative as the ultimate model for individual repentance:

> Rabbi Johanan said in the name of Rabbi Simeon b. Yohai: David was not the kind of man to do that act [the Bathsheba incident], nor was Israel the kind of people to do that act [the Golden Calf incident]…Why, then, did they act thus? [God predestined it so] in order to teach that if an individual has sinned [and hesitates about the effect of repentance] he could be referred to the individual [David], and if a community commits a sin they should be told: Go to the community [to appreciate the effect of repentance] (*Avodah Zarah* 4b-5a).

In this essay, we will follow the lead of this passage and Abarbanel, and explore aspects of David's exemplary process of repentance in the narratives in Psalm 51.

Confronted by Nathan's scathing prophetic rebuke in chapter 12, David responds with two of the most poignant words in all Tanakh: *hattati la-Hashem*, "I have sinned to God." With these words, David embarks on a profound process of repentance.[3]

After Nathan's rebuke, David composed Psalm 51. Offering a penetrating psychological dimension into the connection between David's confession in the book of Samuel and Psalm 51, Rabbi Haskel Lookstein quoted his teacher Rabbi Joseph Soloveitchik, who noted the open gap (*parashah setumah*) in the middle of the verse after David confessed his sin (2 Sam. 12:13):

וַיֹּאמֶר דָּוִד אֶל־נָתָן חָטָאתִי לַה' ס וַיֹּאמֶר נָתָן אֶל־דָּוִד גַּם
ה' הֶעֱבִיר חַטָּאתְךָ לֹא תָמוּת.

David said to Nathan, "I stand guilty before the Lord!" [open gap in the text] And Nathan replied to David, "The Lord has remitted your sin; you shall not die."

Rabbi Soloveitchik interpreted this open gap as reflecting the raw, unexpressed emotions that accompanied David's admission of guilt to the prophet.[4]

Psalm 51 poignantly fills that gap by using words to express his grief. It universalizes David's process of repentance, enabling all penitents to derive inspiration from David.

Psalm 51

[1]For the leader. A psalm of David, [2]when Nathan the prophet came to him after he had come to Bathsheba.

Based on the introductory verses of the Psalm, it appears that David composed this prayer while Nathan still stood before David. However, Radak maintains that David composed this prayer after Nathan left the palace. This interpretation appears logistically preferable, since it may have been difficult for David to compose this heart-wrenching petition in the middle of his conversation with the prophet.[5] Alternatively, Amos Hakham suggests the possibility that David did compose the Psalm in Nathan's presence.[6]

> [3]Have mercy upon me, O God, as befits Your faithfulness; in keeping with Your abundant compassion, blot out my transgressions. [4]Wash me thoroughly of my iniquity, and purify me of my sin; [5]for I recognize my transgressions, and am ever conscious of my sin. [6]Against You alone have I sinned, and done what is evil in Your sight; so You are just in Your sentence, and right in Your judgment.

David petitions God to wash away his sins,[7] and reflects on how his sin constantly plagues him. In verse 6, David surprisingly remarks, "against You alone have I sinned." Didn't he also sin against Bathsheba and Uriah?

Rashi explains that of course David wronged people as well. However, every sin against another human being also is a sin against God. While David sinned against people, this prayer focuses on repairing David's broken relationship with God.

Radak adds that although David was conscious of his sins, the other characters could not have known that David's intent was sinful since David had successfully covered up the affair. Therefore, David proclaims that only God knows of David's sinful intent, and David honestly faces up to his sins before God.

> [7]Indeed I was born with iniquity; with sin my mother conceived me.

Needless to say, David was not really born with iniquity. Rashi offers two explanations of this surprising verse:

"Indeed I was born with iniquity": So how can I not sin? I was created through a sexual act, through which many sins occur. Alternatively, I was created from a man and woman, who are filled with sin.

Perhaps David is expressing a basic fact of human nature. Since we are all created out of a sexual act, the sexual urge is deeply ingrained into our nature.[8] Alternatively, David states that since he is human, he is naturally fallible from birth.[9]

Adopting a different approach, Meiri explains that David is poetically exaggerating his sin:

Indeed I was born with iniquity: In my opinion, this means that throughout all of my days, from birth, I have done only evil, from my very conception. This is poetic exaggeration, similar to "you were called a rebel from birth" (Isa. 48:8).

David is so devastated that he feels as though he has sinned his entire life. It is unlikely that David is making any excuses to mitigate the magnitude of his sin. Meiri's reading captures the power of David's prayer, as the penitent king is completely overwhelmed by his guilt.[10]

[8]Indeed You desire truth about that which is hidden; teach me wisdom about secret things. [9]Purge me with

hyssop till I am pure; wash me till I am whiter than snow. [10]Let me hear tidings of joy and gladness; let the bones You have crushed exult. [11]Hide Your face from my sins; blot out all my iniquities.

Following *Midrash Psalms* 51:2, Rashi and Ibn Ezra observe that hyssop is used in the purification process of one who has healed from the skin affliction *tzara'at* and one defiled by a corpse (Lev. 14:4; Num. 19:6). David feels banished from God, and pleads that God reinstate their relationship.

[12]Fashion a pure heart for me, O God; create in me a steadfast spirit. [13]Do not cast me out of Your presence, or take Your holy spirit away from me. [14]Let me again rejoice in Your help; let a vigorous spirit sustain me.

David's prayer for a new, pure heart and spirit includes a request that he should never sin again (Rashi, Ibn Ezra, Radak). David wants to reset his relationship with God and emerge with a new state of purity and perfection.

On a deeper level, David asks for God to create for him a new heart and spirit, instead of asking God to repair his old heart. This petition touches on a fascinating divergence between the prophecies of Jeremiah and Ezekiel. The Torah, followed by Jeremiah, speaks of repentance in terms of "circumcision" of the heart (Deut. 30:6, 16; Jer. 4:4). This imagery suggests that Israel began with a pure heart, then their sin created blockage in their relationship with God. Repentance functions as spiritual heart surgery to remove that blockage, restoring the original pristine state of purity.

In contrast, Ezekiel prophesies that Israel's repentance requires a God-initiated spiritual heart transplant. Israel's old heart is dead, made of stone. God therefore must remove Israel's lifeless heart and replace it with a heart of flesh (Ezek. 11:19; 36:23-27).

By pleading with God to create for him a pure heart and new spirit, David expresses the anguished feeling that his sin has caused him to "die" inside. Within this analysis, we may extend Rashi and Ibn Ezra's explanation of the hyssop discussed above in verse 9. Not only does David feel alienated from God like one who is impure, but he feels dead inside, and therefore wants the hyssop purification of the one with the skin affliction *tzara'at*—who is likened to one who is dead[11]—and one who came into contact with a corpse.

> [15]I will teach transgressors Your ways, that sinners may return to You. [16]Save me from bloodguilt, O God, God, my deliverer, that I may sing forth Your beneficence.

After focusing on his own guilt and repentance in verses 3-14, David looks beyond himself and views his sin and repentance as an opportunity to teach other penitents. He now can inspire all future generations to repent since God's forgiveness of David's grave sins would demonstrate that the gates of repentance are always open.

> [17]O Lord, open my lips, and let my mouth declare Your praise. [18]You do not want me to bring sacrifices; You do not desire burnt offerings; [19]True sacrifice to God is a

contrite spirit; God, You will not despise a contrite and crushed heart.

We preface every Amidah with verse 17.[12] Although it is the supreme privilege to be invited to stand before God, we begin by petitioning God to help us pray. This introductory verse becomes all the more poignant when we understand its context in Psalm 51. Before we stand before God, we should feel humbled and unworthy, as David felt after his sin.

Because David sinned intentionally, he understands that sacrifices do not atone for his sins, but that he must repent directly to God (Rashi, Ibn Ezra). David also reflects the spirit of the prophets, who regularly teach that sincere righteousness and repentance are the ideal means of building and rebuilding a relationship with God. Sacrifices without repentance are worthless and offensive.[13]

[20]May it please You to make Zion prosper; rebuild the walls of Jerusalem. [21]Then You will want sacrifices offered in righteousness, burnt and whole offerings; then bulls will be offered on Your altar.

We often find movement in the book of Psalms from personal prayers to those for the entire community. Therefore, it is unsurprising to find a prayer for national forgiveness at the end of a prayer for the penitent individual. However, the last two verses appear to reflect a reality from a time different from that of David. Why would David pray for the rebuilding of the walls of Jerusalem? In his time, Jerusalem's walls were standing. One

also gains the impression that nobody could bring sacrifices—
"*then* bulls will be offered"—but David certainly could and did
offer sacrifices in his time![14]

Rashi follows the lead of *Lev. Rabbah* (7:2) and suggests that
David is praying for the Temple to be built by his son Solomon.
However, *homot Yerushalayim* refers to the walls of Jerusalem,
not the Temple. Additionally, David was able to bring sacrifices,
whereas these final two verses suggest that people were unable
to do so.

Offering a different interpretation, Ibn Ezra quotes an
anonymous rabbi from Spain who maintained that these verses
were added by someone living in the Babylonian exile centuries
after David:

> One Spanish sage said that these two verses were added
> by a righteous individual in Babylonia who beseeched
> God and prayed with this Psalm, for it was not yet
> known [in David's time] that Zion was God's chosen
> place until David's old age. It also is possible that this
> Psalm was composed through divine inspiration.

These two verses reflect the reality of the Babylonian exile. They
either were composed then and added to David's Psalm, as per
the comments of the Spanish sage, or else David prophetically
anticipated the period of the exile. Radak and Meiri agree with
the notion of prophetic anticipation of the Babylonian exile.[15]

Within this reading, the Jews in the Babylonian exile plead
to God: just as You forgave David for the sin of Bathsheba,
please forgive us now and rebuild the walls of Jerusalem and

the Temple so that we may again bring sacrifices in Jerusalem. David's prayer in verse 15, that he should become a model for repentance, is fulfilled within this Psalm.

Conclusion

David powerfully expresses his feelings of being overwhelmed by sin, and pleads to God to help restore their relationship. He then looks outward, hoping that God will forgive him so that he may become a model for penitents for all time:

> Rabbi Samuel b. Nahmani citing Rabbi Jonathan explained: The saying of David the son of Jesse and the saying of the man raised on high (2 Sam. 23:1), [this means, it is] the saying of David the son of Jesse who established firmly the yoke [discipline] of repentance (*Mo'ed Katan* 16b).

The conclusion of the Psalm shifts from the sin and repentance of the individual to that of the community.

There is no more suitable prayer than Psalm 51 for us to learn and internalize to trigger the deepest process of repentance, religious growth, and connection to God and the community of Israel.

NOTES

1. This point may be disputed. Kings did not go into every battle, since their death would be devastating. See, especially, 2 Sam. 21:16-17 where David's troops insisted that David was more valuable

to them if he were to remain safe in Jerusalem: "It was then that David's men declared to him on oath, 'You shall not go with us into battle any more, lest you extinguish the lamp of Israel!'"

2. Rabbi Amnon Bazak, *Ad ha-Yom ha-Zeh, Until This Day: Fundamental Questions in Bible Teaching*, ed. Yoshi Farajun (Yediot Aharonot-Tevunot, 2013), p. 469. Scholars have observed that there is no known analogy to this honest, critical stance toward one's own heroes in ancient Near Eastern literature. See, for example, George Mendenhall, *Ancient Israel's Faith and History: An Introduction to the Bible in Context* (Louisville, KY: Westminster John Knox Press, 2001), p. 112.

3. For exploration of David's repentance within the narratives in the book of Samuel, see Hayyim Angel, "The Yoke of Repentance: David's Post-Sin Conduct in the Book of Samuel and Psalm 51," at http://www.yutorah.org/lectures/lecture.cfm/818982/Rabbi_Hayyim_Angel/The_Yoke_of_Repentance:_David%E2%80%99s_Post-Sin_Conduct_in_Sefer_Shemuel_and_Tehillim_51; Ari Mermelstein, "Retribution, Repentance, Restoration: The Motives and Message Underlying Absalom's Rebellion," *Nahalah* 1 (1999), pp. 51-64.

4. Rabbi Lookstein shared this insight during my class on Psalm 51 at Congregation Kehilath Jeshurun in Manhattan on August 29, 2015. Rabbi Lookstein confirmed this formulation for the article by email on February 21, 2016.

5. Amos Hakham likens this superscription to that of Psalm 34: "Of David, when he feigned madness in the presence of Abimelech,

who turned him out, and he left." It is more likely that David composed this Psalm after his initial encounter with Abimelech (who is called Achish in the book of Samuel) (Da'at Mikra: Psalms vol. 1 [Hebrew] [Jerusalem: Mosad Harav Kook, 1979], p. 296).

6. *Da'at Mikra*, p. 304.

7. The imagery of washing away sin is also found in Isa. 1:16; 4:4 (with the root *r-h-tz*), and Jer. 2:22; 4:14 (with the same root as here, *k-b-s*).

8. See also Ibn Ezra and Malbim.

9. See also Rabbi Isaiah of Trani.

10. See also Amos Hakham, *Da'at Mikra*, p. 298.

11. See, for example, *Nedarim* 64b, *Exod. Rabbah* 1:34; *Tanhuma Tzav* 13.

12. This practice traces back to the third-century Amora Rabbi Yohanan in *Berakhot* 4b; 9b.

13. See, for example, 1 Sam. 15:22; Isa. 1:10-17; 43:22-24; 61:8; Jer. 7:22; Hos. 6:6; Amos 5:21-25 Mic. 6:4-8. See also Ps. 40:7.

14. One of the great Siddur translators of the 20th century, Dr. David de Sola Pool, expressed his ambivalence over how to interpret these last two verses in relation to the rest of the Psalm. In his translation of the Rosh Hashanah Siddur, he set off the last

two verses with a line and parentheses. Here is his translation of verses 18-21 as laid out in his Siddur:

> For Thou takest no delight in a sacrifice,
>> Else would I give it;
>> A burnt-offering Thou dost not desire.
> The sacrifices of God are a contrite spirit,
>> A broken and a contrite heart, O God, Thou wilt
>>> not despise.

> (Do good unto Zion in Thy loving will,
>> Build up the walls of Jerusalem.
> Then Thou wilt be pleased with sacrifices of righteousness,
>> Burnt-offering and whole offering;
>> Then bulls shall be offered on Thine altar.)

(*New Year Book of Prayers,*
Union of Sephardic Congregations, page 8)

In his Yom Kippur Siddur, however, Dr. Pool used the same translation but did not insert a line or parentheses to set off the final two verses (*Day of Atonement Book of Prayers,* Union of Sephardic Congregations, page 100).

15. The issue of dating of the book of Psalms goes far beyond the parameters of this essay. Suffice it to say here that several traditional sources maintain that parts of the book of Psalms were composed after the time of David. For further discussion, see Hayyim Angel, "Authorship and Structure of Psalms," in Angel, *Vision from the*

Prophet and Counsel from the Elders: A Survey of Nevi'im and Ketuvim (New York: OU Press, 2013), pp. 210-219. For extensive discussion of Ibn Ezra's view of the authorship of Psalms, as well as the positions of two of his illustrious predecessors, Rabbi Saadiah Gaon and Rabbi Moshe ibn Gikatilah, see Uriel Simon, *Four Approaches to the Book of Psalms: From Saadiah Gaon to Abraham ibn Ezra* (New York: SUNY Press, 1991).

THE ETERNAL DAVIDIC COVENANT IN 2 SAMUEL CHAPTER 7 AND ITS LATER MANIFESTATIONS IN THE BIBLE[1]

The Book of Samuel vs. the Book of Kings

After informing King David that he would not build the Temple, Nathan prophesied God's eternal covenant with the Davidic kingdom:

> When your days are done and you lie with your fathers, I will raise up your offspring after you, one of your own issue, and I will establish his kingship. He shall build a house for My name, and I will establish his royal throne forever. I will be a father to him, and he shall be a son to Me. When he does wrong, I will chastise him with the rod of men and the affliction of mortals; but I will never withdraw My favor from him as I withdrew it from Saul, whom I removed to make room for you. Your house and your kingship shall ever be secure before you; your throne shall be established forever (2 Sam. 7:12-16).

---

1. This article appeared originally in *Jewish Bible Quarterly* 44:2 (2016), pp. 83-90.

If future kings sin, God will punish them but eternally preserve the Davidic throne. Although the Davidic kings impressively reigned for over four centuries, the second-longest dynasty in ancient Near Eastern history,[1] it came to an end in 586 BCE with the destruction of Jerusalem and the Temple and the exile of Zedekiah.

In addition to the conflict with historical events, Nathan's prophecy also conflicts with a series of passages in the book of Kings. On his deathbed, David exhorted Solomon to be faithful to the Torah, and quoted God as saying that faithfulness is a necessary prerequisite for the existence of the Davidic monarchy:

> Then the Lord will fulfill the promise that He made concerning me: "If your descendants are scrupulous in their conduct, and walk before Me faithfully, with all their heart and soul, your line on the throne of Israel shall never end!" (1 Kings 2:4).

This prophecy appears to contradict Nathan's original prophecy, which states later kings would suffer punishment if they sin but the Davidic kingship would endure eternally.

At the Temple dedication ceremony, Solomon refers to the prophecy that David had told him (1 Kings 8:25). God then responds to Solomon's prayer and corroborates David's formulation:

> As for you, if you walk before Me as your father David walked before Me, wholeheartedly and with uprightness,

doing all that I have commanded you [and] keeping My laws and My rules, then I will establish your throne of kingship over Israel forever, as I promised your father David, saying, "Your line on the throne of Israel shall never end." (1 Kings 9:4-5).[2]

Of course, this formulation of the prophecy was fulfilled, since the monarchy ended after Zedekiah.

To summarize, there are two questions confronting Nathan's original formulation of God's covenant with the Davidic kingdom:

1. It conflicts with several passages in Kings.
2. It conflicts with history.

Before addressing these questions, it must be noted that even within Kings, God's eternal covenant with the Davidic monarchy is repeatedly stressed. When the prophet Ahijah told Jeroboam that he would inaugurate a new kingdom, he emphasized that God would preserve the Davidic dynasty over the Southern Kingdom as a result of the covenant (1 Kings 11:32). We find similar formulations with Abijam (1 Kings 15:4) and Joram (2 Kings 8:19). Thus, it appears even in Kings that some aspect of the covenant is permanent.

Addressing the apparent conflict between Nathan's prophecy of eternal reign and the conditional formulations in Kings, Professor Michael Avioz maintains that Nathan's original covenant was conditional as well.[3] Nathan also calls for faithfulness to God, and therefore there is less daylight between the prophecies as is commonly held. Avioz is correct, that faithfulness to the Torah is central to both prophecies. However, it is specifically regarding the consequences of unfaithfulness where there is a discrepancy between the books of Samuel and Kings. In the book of Samuel, Nathan predicts punishment but an eternal dynasty. In Kings, David, Solomon, and God proclaim the monarchy itself to be conditional on righteous behavior. Therefore, Avioz's argument is unconvincing.

Proposing a more persuasive alternative, Antti Laato suggests that the prophecies in Kings teach that Davidic reign over *all* Israel is conditional on the kings' righteous behavior, but Davidic reign over Judah is unconditional.[4] He also suggests that the release of Jehoiachin from prison at the end of Kings (2 Kings 25:27-30) expresses hope for the continuation of the Davidic dynasty following the destruction of the Temple. Laato's interpretation is consistent with Nathan's prophecy, and also with the passages in Kings that reflect God's permanent covenant with David and his dynasty.

Laato's resolution appears to be the most faithful to the prophecies in Samuel and Kings, but we are left with the problem of history: With the exile of Zedekiah, Davidic kingship ended over the Southern Kingdom as well. Psalm 89 and Jeremiah 33 take up this problem directly, offering strikingly different responses.

Psalm 89 and Jeremiah 33:
Responses to the Cessation of the Davidic Monarchy

Psalm 89 is one of the most jarring of the psalms. For 38 verses, the psalmist speaks elatedly of God's eternal covenant with the

Davidic monarchy. God swore that it would endure forever, like the sun, moon, and heavens. The psalmist reflects formulations in Nathan's prophecy regarding God's promise of an eternal monarchy to David, and also regarding the consequences of sin—that God would punish sinful kings but still preserve the monarchy eternally (89:30-34).[5]

The psalm then turns abruptly, and in verses 39–52 the psalmist explodes at the abrogation of the covenant when the monarchy ended:

> Yet You have rejected, spurned, and become enraged at Your anointed. You have repudiated the covenant with Your servant; You have dragged his dignity in the dust. You have breached all his defenses, shattered his strongholds (Ps. 89:39–41).

It appears that the psalmist is directly accusing God of violating His oath.

Ibn Ezra (on 89:2) mentions a Spanish sage who considered this psalm blasphemous and therefore censored it: "In Spain, there was a great and pious sage, and this psalm was difficult for him. He would not read it, nor was he able to listen to it since the psalmist speaks sharply against God...." Ibn Ezra agrees that those verses are blasphemous, but he is unwilling to entertain the possibility that an inspired biblical psalmist would speak inappropriately. Therefore, he asserts that the psalmist is quoting the words of the enemies of God who blaspheme.

Radak (on 89:39), in turn, censures the anonymous sage and Ibn Ezra:

Many have expressed astonishment over how this psalmist could speak these words against God.... I am astonished by their astonishment, for the psalms were written through divine inspiration, and it is unthinkable that something in them is untrue!

Rabbi Isaiah of Trani and Amos Hakham likewise consider these words to be of the psalmist. Hakham quotes talmudic passages stating that the righteous do not flatter God. Rather, they stand honestly before their Creator, pouring out all their emotions.[6]

Thus, Psalm 89 is consistent with Nathan's prophecy, but it does not take into account the conditional passages in Kings. No doubt many Judeans had similar thoughts at the time of the destruction, and were shocked that God had broken His eternal covenant with the Davidic dynasty. The sense of betrayal in this psalm is palpable.

At the brink of the destruction, the prophet Jeremiah recognized the despair of the people who thought that God's covenant with the Davidic monarchy was coming to an end. In one of his prophecies of restoration, Jeremiah states:

Thus said the Lord: If you could break My covenant with the day and My covenant with the night, so that day and night should not come at their proper time, only then could My covenant with My servant David be broken— so that he would not have a descendant reigning upon his throne—or with My ministrants, the levitical priests. Like the host of heaven which cannot be counted, and the sand of the sea which cannot be measured, so will I multiply the offspring of My servant David, and of the Levites who minister to Me (Jer. 33:20-22).

Jeremiah appears to offer a new interpretation to Nathan's prophecy. Psalm 89, and many people in Jeremiah's generation, understood Nathan's prophecy that the Davidic kingdom would last *ad olam*, "forever," to mean "always." However, Jeremiah prophetically explains that no other dynasty ever will supplant the Davidic kingship, even if there is no king on the throne. Additionally, the Davidic dynasty will be restored. Therefore, God's covenant with the Davidic dynasty is forever, as explained in Nathan's prophecy. The actual continuation of the monarchy, however, is conditional on faithfulness to the covenant, as explained in the prophecies in Kings. This prophecy thus addresses the conflicting prophecies in Samuel and Kings, and also responds to the concerns of Psalm 89.

In the same prophecy, Jeremiah predicts the future coming of a *tzemah*, "branch," from David (Jer. 33:15). The Second Temple prophet Zechariah adopted this imagery, holding out hopes that Zerubbabel could be that branch (Zech. 3:8; 6:12).[7] It also is significant that the book of Chronicles, written in the Second Temple period, continues to stress God's eternal covenant with the Davidic dynasty despite the lapse that had occurred at the time of the first destruction. Nathan's prophecy is repeated (1 Chron. 17:11-14), and the Davidic kingdom is associated with God's kingdom (1 Chron. 28:5; 29:11; 2 Chron 13:8). God's relationship to the Davidic dynasty is a permanent "covenant of salt" (2 Chron. 13:5; cf. 2 Chron. 21:7).[8] Jeremiah's prophetic interpretation emerged victorious. God's covenant with the Davidic dynasty was eternal, even though there presently was no king on the throne.[9]

Jacob's Promise of Kingship to Judah

We find the roots of the divergent views of understanding Nathan's prophecy by Psalm 89 and Jeremiah 33 in the Torah. On his deathbed, Jacob prophetically gave the kingship to the Tribe of Judah:

> *Lo yasur shevet mi-Yehudah u-mehokek mi-ben raglav ad ki yavo Shiloh ve-lo yikkehat ammim.*

> The scepter shall not depart from Judah, nor the ruler's staff from between his feet; so that tribute shall come to him and the homage of peoples be his (Gen. 49:10).

In a syntactical discussion of the possible meanings of this verse, Professor Richard Steiner explores whether the main break should be after *raglav*, as per the *te'amim*; or whether it should go after *ad*.[10] In the first reading, *ad* means "until," yielding the meaning, "The scepter shall not depart from Judah…, until…."

Alternatively, if the break comes after *ad*, then *ad* would mean *la-ad*, "to eternity, forever." This latter reading yields two distinct possibilities:

1. The scepter shall not depart from Judah… ever…, i.e., the scepter shall never depart from Judah;
2. The scepter shall not depart from Judah…forever…., i.e., if the scepter departs from Judah, it shall not do so permanently.

We may apply Steiner's analysis to Psalm 89 and Jeremiah 33. Psalm 89 understands Nathan's prophecy like the first reading with the break after *ad*: The scepter shall never depart from Judah. Since the scepter *did* depart after Zedekiah, the psalmist viewed the abrogation of the Davidic monarchy as a violation of God's covenant. In contrast, Jeremiah adopts the second reading with the break after *ad*: The scepter shall not depart from Judah permanently. This reading accepts the possibility of a temporary cessation of the Davidic monarchy, while stressing that in the future the monarchy will return because of God's eternal covenant with David.

Human and Divine Perspectives
on the Loss of the Monarchy

Another way of understanding the contrast between the perspectives of Psalm 89 and Jeremiah 33 is that Psalm 89 expresses an immediate, human reaction to the shocking cessation of the monarchy. In contrast, Jeremiah adopts a prophetic perspective that transcends the moment of the destruction to build a long-term vision. In this vein, Rabbi Samson Raphael Hirsch contextualizes the tone of protest against God in Psalm 89 to the time close to the destruction, when all seemed lost:

> But in the early days of the dark centuries of exile, the experience of the collapse of everything that had been created for man's elevation, and the sight of the descent of all national life to ever more abject nothingness, might well have given rise to questions concerning the

fulfillment of God's promises and to a search for the resolution of such doubts. The verses that follow express this questioning and seeking (on Ps. 89:39).[11]

To cite a parallel example from the time of the destruction: Many exiled Judeans harbored feelings of revenge against their vicious Babylonian captors:

Fair Babylon, you predator, a blessing on him who repays you in kind what you have inflicted on us; a blessing on him who seizes your babies and dashes them against the rocks! (Ps. 137:8-9).

Contrast that immediate, violent reaction with Jeremiah's prophetic perspective:

And seek the welfare of the city to which I have exiled you and pray to the Lord in its behalf; for in its prosperity you shall prosper (Jer. 29:7).

Looking beyond the present moment, Jeremiah understood that, despite the hostility Judeans harbored toward Babylonia, the stability of Babylonia would ultimately make conditions better for the Judean exiles to build a future for their nation while in captivity.[12]

Conclusion

There appears to be a tension between Nathan's prophecy of eternal reign to the Davidic dynasty, and the conditional formulations in Kings. Within the context of Samuel and Kings, the various passages appear best explained by positing that God promised eternal monarchy to the Davidic dynasty over at least David's own tribe of Judah, but Davidic reign over all Israel was conditional on faithfulness to the Torah.

However, the cessation of the monarchy at the time of the destruction of the First Temple undermined that assumption and led to two responses. Psalm 89 focuses on Nathan's prophecy of eternality and therefore accuses God of breaking His oath. In contrast, Jeremiah prophetically interprets Nathan's prophecy to mean that God's covenant with the Davidic dynasty is eternal, even if there is a temporary cessation in the monarchy. In addition to providing a viable understanding of the prophecies in Samuel and Kings, Jeremiah's prophecy also paved the way for Zechariah and Chronicles, who likewise understood that God's covenant with the Davidic dynasty endures even though there was no Davidic king.

Additionally, the Bible creates a distinction between the human response of Psalm 89 and the prophetic, long-term response of Jeremiah. Both perspectives are necessary to reflect the multifaceted relationship between God and the Davidic dynasty.

NOTES

1. Cyrus Gordon and Gary Rendsburg, *The Bible and the Ancient Near East* (New York: W.W. Norton, 1997), p. 223.

2. Psalm 132 also reflects this conditional aspect of the monarchy: "The Lord swore to David a firm oath that He will not renounce,

'One of your own issue I will set upon your throne. If your sons keep My covenant and My decrees that I teach them, then their sons also, to the end of time, shall sit upon your throne'" (vv. 11-12).

3. Michael Avioz, "The Davidic Covenant in 2 Samuel 7: Conditional or Unconditional?" in *The Ancient Near East in the 12th-10th Centuries BCE: Culture and History*, ed. Gershon Galil et al. (Ugarit-Verlag: Munster, 2012), pp. 43-51.

4. Antti Laato, "Psalm 132 and the Development of the Jerusalemite/Israelite Royal Ideology," *Catholic Biblical Quarterly* 54 (1992), pp. 49-66.

5. See, for example, Nahum Sarna, "Psalm 89: A Study in Inner Biblical Exegesis," in Sarna, *Studies in Biblical Interpretation* (Philadelphia: Jewish Publication Society, 2000), pp. 377-394; Michael Fishbane, *Biblical Interpretation in Ancient Israel* (Oxford: Clarendon Press, 1985), pp. 465-467; Jon D. Levenson, *Sinai and Zion: An Entry into the Jewish Bible* (San Francisco: Harper, 1985), pp. 209-216.

6. Amos Hakham, *Daʾat Mikra: Psalms* vol. 2 (Hebrew), (Jerusalem: Mosad HaRav Kook, 1979) pp. 156–157. See, for example, JT *Berakhot* 7:4 (11c); BT *Yoma* 69b. See further discussion in Hayyim Angel, "God Insists on Truth: Rabbinic Evaluations of Two Audacious Biblical Prayers," *Jewish Bible Quarterly* 38 (2010), pp. 3-9; reprinted in Angel, *Creating Space between Peshat and Derash: A Collection of Studies on Tanakh* (Jersey City, NJ: Ktav-Sephardic Publication Foundation, 2011), pp. 154-162.

7. When that failed to occur, Jewish tradition incorporated this prophetic formulation in expressing messianic hopes for the restoration of the Davidic monarchy into the Amidah: *Et tzemah David avdekha meherah tatzmi'ah*, "May the offshoot of Your servant David soon flower."

8. See further references and discussion in Gary N. Knoppers, "David's Relation to Moses," in *King and Messiah in Israel and the Ancient Near East: Proceedings of the Oxford Old Testament Seminar*, ed. John Day (Sheffield: Sheffield Academic Press, 1998), pp. 91-118; Gary N. Knoppers, "Ancient Near Eastern Royal Grants and the Davidic Covenant: A Parallel?" *Journal of the Americal Oriental Society* 116 (1996), pp. 670-696.

9. For a similar analysis and conclusion, see Rabbi Amnon Bazak, *Shemuel Bet: Malkhut David* (Hebrew) (Jerusalem: Maggid, 2014), pp. 99-104.

10. Richard C. Steiner, "Four Inner-Biblical Interpretations of Genesis 49:10: On the Lexical and Syntactic Ambiguities of עד as Reflected in the Prophecies of Nathan, Ahijah, Ezekiel, and Zechariah," *Journal of Biblical Literature* 132 (2013), pp. 33-60.

11. Translation from *The Hirsch Tehillim*, trans. Gertrude Hirschler, revised edition (Nanuet, NY: Feldheim, 2014), pp. 754-755.

12. It is noteworthy that when Jeremiah speaks personally against his enemies, rather than through prophetic revelation, he exhibits similar human feelings for revenge and justice as Psalm 137. See, for example, Jer. 11:20; 12:3; 15:15; 17:18; 18:21-23; 20:11-12.

JEREMIAH'S TRIAL AS A
FALSE PROPHET (CHAPTER 26)

A WINDOW INTO THE COMPLEX
RELIGIOUS STATE OF THE PEOPLE[1]

Introduction

When reading the book of Jeremiah, it is easy to assume that all of Jeremiah's adversaries must have been wicked for opposing God's prophet. However, there potentially was a wide range of motivations underlying the actions of Jeremiah's opponents. Some may have been wicked, but others were sincerely religious, even if they were misguided.

Jeremiah chapter 26 provides a window into the complex religious state of the society that Jeremiah confronted at the beginning of Jehoiakim's reign. In this essay, we will explore three approaches of commentators—Abarbanel, Malbim, and Menahem Boleh[1]—who suggest comprehensive explanations of the narrative. Each interpreter presents different understandings of the religious state of the people.

1. This article appeared originally in *Jewish Bible Quarterly* 45:1 (2017), pp. 13-20.

How Were Jeremiah's Opponents
Certain that Jeremiah was a False Prophet?

Jeremiah entered the Temple precincts at the beginning of Jehoiakim's reign (c. 609 BCE)[2] to prophesy the destruction of the Temple if the people failed to repent. Just as God allowed the holy city of Shiloh to be destroyed because of Israel's sins,[3] so too Jerusalem was vulnerable. The priests, prophets, and people were outraged by Jeremiah's message and wanted him executed immediately as a false prophet:

> And when Jeremiah finished speaking all that the Lord had commanded him to speak to all the people, the priests and the prophets and all the people seized him, shouting, "You shall die! How dare you prophesy in the name of the Lord that this House shall become like Shiloh and this city be made desolate, without inhabitants?" (Jer. 26:8-9).

Since all these people opposed a prophet of God, one might conclude that they all were wicked people who hated Jeremiah for criticizing them and for threatening their religious authority. Although this explanation may account for some of their motivation, nobler factors also may have been involved.

In chapter 7—likely a parallel prophecy to the narrative in Jeremiah 26[4]—Jeremiah censured the people for believing that the Temple would never be destroyed:

> Don't put your trust in illusions and say, "The Temple of the Lord, the Temple of the Lord, the Temple of the

Lord are these [buildings]." No, if you really mend your ways and your actions; if you execute justice between one man and another… (Jer. 7:4-5).

The people also served God as pagans would serve their deities by offering sacrifices while persisting in their immoral and even idolatrous behavior (Jer. 7:9-11).

Although such individuals were both misguided in their service of God and immoral, even fully righteous individuals might have suspected that Jeremiah was a false prophet. Jeremiah prophesied the destruction of the Temple soon after the righteous King Josiah's abrupt death (609 BCE). Jeremiah's critique of Judean society, then, came in the wake of Josiah's reformation (622 BCE). Were the people already so wicked to warrant the destruction of the Temple? Addressing this concern early in his career, Jeremiah censured the insincerity of the ostensibly penitent Judeans:

The Lord said to me in the days of King Josiah: Have you seen what rebellious Israel did, going to every high mountain and under every leafy tree, and whoring there? … And after all that, her sister, treacherous Judah, did not return to Me wholeheartedly, but insincerely— declares the Lord (Jer. 3:6, 10).

However, it is likely that many believed that the people were generally righteous at that time.[5]

Furthermore, Jeremiah stated this prophecy of destruction less than a century after the miraculous salvation of Jerusalem in Isaiah's time (701 BCE):

"I will protect and save this city for My sake and for the
sake of My servant David." [That night] an angel of the
Lord went out and struck down one hundred and eighty-
five thousand in the Assyrian camp, and the following
morning they were all dead corpses (Isa. 37:35-36).

In principle, the religious establishment could have cited this
prophecy of divine protection of Jerusalem as a further precedent
against Jeremiah's prophecy.[6] Jeremiah would respond that
Isaiah's prophecy was intended for Isaiah's generation, but times
had changed and Jeremiah's new prophetic revelation called for
the destruction of Jerusalem. However, such a claim from an
unproven prophet would be difficult to accept, even for the most
righteous members of that society. Thus, Jeremiah's adversaries
could have been anything from purely evil, to misguided and
immoral God-worshippers, to sincerely religious individuals
who believed that Jeremiah must be a false prophet since he
contradicted their worldview and their perception of the
religious state of the post-Josiah society.

The Trial
In response to the accusations, Jeremiah insisted that God sent
him. Jeremiah was powerless against his accusers; nevertheless,
he calmly and heroically retained his prophetic integrity in the
face of intense hostility and danger:

As for me, I am in your hands: do to me what seems
good and right to you. But know that if you put me to
death, you and this city and its inhabitants will be guilty

of shedding the blood of an innocent man. For in truth the Lord has sent me to you, to speak all these words to you (Jer. 26:14-15).

The officials ruled in Jeremiah's favor, and the people supported the prophet as well:

Then the officials and all the people said to the priests and prophets, "This man does not deserve the death penalty, for he spoke to us in the name of the Lord our God" (26:16).

From this verdict, it appears that the story should be over. Jeremiah prophesied the impending destruction of Jerusalem if the people would not repent, the people insisted that Jeremiah should be executed as a false prophet, Jeremiah maintained that God sent him, and the officials ruled in his favor. However, the narrative surprisingly continues with an ensuing discussion that provides precedents in support of and against Jeremiah:

And some of the elders of the land arose and said to the entire assemblage of the people, "Micah the Morashtite, who prophesied in the days of King Hezekiah of Judah, said to all the people of Judah: 'Thus said the Lord of Hosts: Zion shall be plowed as a field, Jerusalem shall become heaps of ruins and the Temple Mount a shrine in the woods.' Did King Hezekiah of Judah, and all Judah, put him to death? Did he not rather fear the Lord and implore the Lord, so that the Lord renounced the punishment He had decreed against them? We are about to do great injury to ourselves!" (vv. 17-19).

There was also a man prophesying in the name of the Lord, Uriah son of Shemaiah from Kiriath-jearim, who prophesied against this city and this land the same things as Jeremiah. King Jehoiakim and all his warriors and all the officials heard about his address, and the king wanted to put him to death. Uriah heard of this and fled in fear, and came to Egypt. But King Jehoiakim sent men to Egypt, Elnathan son of Achbor and men with him to Egypt. They took Uriah out of Egypt and brought him to King Jehoiakim, who had him put to the sword and his body thrown into the burial place of the common people (vv. 20-23).

However, Ahikam son of Shaphan protected Jeremiah, so that he was not handed over to the people for execution (v. 24).

Commentators prior to Abarbanel[7] focus primarily on one question: Who is the speaker in verses 20-23? The elders in verses 17-19 presented a positive precedent in Jeremiah's favor, whereas Jehoiakim's killing of Uriah is a precedent against Jeremiah. The Tosefta (*Sotah* 9:5), followed by medieval commentators including Rashi and Radak, suggests that after the righteous elders spoke, the wicked priests and prophets countered with the Jehoiakim-Uriah precedent as an argument against Jeremiah. It was a genuine trial, with defense and prosecution supplying arguments against one another.[8]

However, the text does not indicate a change in speaker. Consequently, Rabbi Joseph Kara suggests that the narrator relates the Jehoiakim-Uriah incident to inform the reader that Jeremiah was indeed in great peril at the beginning of Jehoiakim's reign, which explains why Ahikam urgently needed to intervene.[9]

Also concerned with the omission of a change in speaker in the text, Rabbi Joseph ibn Caspi alternatively suggests that the elders quoted both precedents in verses 17-23 to argue that Hezekiah's righteous response of repentance after Micah's prophecy was preferable to Jehoiakim's wicked response of killing Uriah for his prophecy.

The aforementioned commentators do not address additional questions: (1) What did the elders contribute by citing the positive precedent of Hezekiah-Micah? After all, the officials already had reached a favorable verdict in verse 16! (2) What role did Ahikam play in saving Jeremiah, if the prophet already had been deemed innocent by the court? Abarbanel, Malbim, and Menahem Boleh offer different ways of understanding how the details fit together.

In his review of the predominant position of his predecessors, including Rashi and Radak, Abarbanel surmises that after the officials' ruling in favor of Jeremiah, the elders jumped onto the bandwagon by citing the Hezekiah-Micah precedent. The elders meant well by supporting Jeremiah, but unwittingly reopened the discussion after the verdict. The wicked priests and prophets seized the opportunity by invoking the precedent of Jehoiakim-Uriah (following the reading of the Tosefta, that they were the speakers in vv. 20-23). The masses, who initially had accepted the judges' verdict (v. 16), now began to turn against Jeremiah. Therefore, Ahikam intervened to turn the tide back in Jeremiah's favor.

In this reading, the elders were righteous but somewhat cowardly by waiting until the officials' verdict before speaking on Jeremiah's behalf. The priests and prophets were wicked and determined to silence Jeremiah. In contrast, the masses were genuinely unsure who was right—Jeremiah or his adversaries. This view of the masses is supported from the fact that Jeremiah addressed both the officials and the people (v. 12), evidently trying to win them over; and from the decision of the officials and the people that Jeremiah was not a false prophet (v. 16).

After presenting his reconstruction of the view of his predecessors, Abarbanel rejects their approach since he is troubled by the omission of a change in speaker in verse 20. Therefore, he adopts a view similar to that of Ibn Caspi, that the elders cited both precedents and preferred Hezekiah's righteous response to Jehoiakim's wicked response. Unfortunately, the people were not swayed by the elders' argument, so Ahikam needed to intervene.

Adopting a different reading, Malbim claims that the priests and prophets sincerely believed that Jeremiah was a false prophet, while the masses believed that Jeremiah was a true prophet. However, the masses were wicked and did not want his rebuke. Thus, the priests, prophets, and people all wanted Jeremiah to be killed (vv. 8-9), but they had very different motivations.

Once the officials ruled in favor of Jeremiah, the priests and prophets accepted the verdict. However, the masses then attempted to lynch Jeremiah, believing that he was a true prophet but wanting to stifle him. The elders therefore intervened by invoking Hezekiah's repentance as the proper response. The narrator then explains that the climate at the beginning of Jehoiakim's reign was antagonistic to Jeremiah (following the reading of Kara, that the narrator is speaking in vv. 20-23). Emboldened by this royal precedent, the mob ignored the elders and surged toward Jeremiah. Ahikam therefore forcefully rescued Jeremiah from the mob. Verse 24 states that Ahikam saved Jeremiah from *ha-am*, "the people," which supports Malbim's reading that the masses, rather than the priests and prophets, posed the final threat to the prophet.

In Malbim's reading, the elders were righteous and heroic. The priests and prophets were more righteous and law-abiding but misguided, and they accepted the officials' verdict. The masses agreed with the officials that Jeremiah was a true prophet and therefore did not deserve legal execution. However, they were wicked people who wanted to silence the true prophet, and attempted to lynch him.

Although there are significant differences between the perspectives of Abarbanel and Malbim, both read the narrative in sequential order. In contrast, Menahem Boleh suggests that the narrative moves from general to specific. The officials' verdict in verse 16 in fact came *after* hearing the arguments recorded in verses 17-24. The elders defended Jeremiah with the Hezekiah-Micah precedent, and then the wicked priests and prophets accused Jeremiah with the Jehoiakim-Uriah precedent (following the reading of the Tosefta, that they were the speakers in vv. 20-23). Because the precedent of the prosecution was so recent, the officials were inclined to accept their argument.

Therefore, Ahikam intervened to the court and convinced them to rule in Jeremiah's favor.[10] The masses accepted the ruling of the court after that, whereas the priests and prophets evidently did not (v. 16).[11]

According to Boleh, all of Jeremiah's opponents were wicked. The priests wanted Jeremiah executed since he prophesied the destruction of the Temple—the source of their livelihood. The false prophets opposed Jeremiah since he contradicted their prophecies of peace. The masses were wicked, and opposed Jeremiah because he criticized them.[12] Within Boleh's reading of the narrative moving from general to specific, one also could argue that some of Jeremiah's adversaries were religiously motivated, yet mistaken.

Conclusion

Abarbanel, Malbim, and Boleh offer three significantly different interpretations of the narrative in Jeremiah chapter 26. In their attempts to make sense of the account in verses 16-24, they explain not only the respective roles of the characters, but also the religious state of the priests, prophets, and masses at that time. In Abarbanel's reconstruction of the view of his predecessors, the priests and prophets were wicked, whereas the masses were unsure who was right and therefore gave everyone a fair hearing. In Malbim's reading, the priests and prophets were religiously mistaken but sincere and law-abiding, and could not believe that Jeremiah was a true prophet. In contrast, the masses believed that Jeremiah was a true prophet but they were wicked so they attempted to kill the prophet in order to silence him. Boleh personally maintains that all parties were wicked and wanted to silence Jeremiah. However, within his reading that the debate in verses 17-24 influenced the officials in verse 16, one may argue that some of Jeremiah's adversaries were religiously motivated, albeit misguided.

According to Malbim and Boleh, the elders played a heroic role in standing up for Jeremiah. In contrast, Abarbanel suggests that while righteous, the elders were cowardly in not defending Jeremiah until after he received a favorable verdict. They also unwittingly caused more harm than good.

Through this debate, Abarbanel, Malbim, and Boleh open possibilities for understanding not only this chapter, but also the religious state of Jeremiah's audience—both the leadership and the masses. In so doing, they bring the dramatic scene in chapter 26 to life.

NOTES

1. Menahem Boleh, *Da'at Mikra: Jeremiah* (Hebrew) (Jerusalem: Mosad HaRav Kook, 1983).

2. Boleh, p. 331, Yair Hoffman, *Mikra le-Yisrael: Jeremiah* vol. 2 (Hebrew) (Tel Aviv: Am Oved, 2001), p. 520, and Jack R. Lundbom, *Jeremiah 21-36* Anchor Bible 21B (New York: Doubleday, 2004), pp. 285-286, maintain that the "beginning" of Jehoiakim's reign might indeed refer to his first year (609), but it need not and may refer to one of the early years of his reign.

3. Cf. Ps. 78:58-60. The book of Samuel does not mention the actual destruction of Shiloh (chapter 4). However, the Ark was not brought there after the Philistines returned it to Israel (chapter 7).

4. For a list of literary parallels between the two chapters, see Yair Hoffman, p. 518.

5. The Talmud suggests that Josiah himself overestimated the positive religious state of the people: "Josiah, however, did not know that his generation found but little favor [in the eyes of God]" (*Ta'anit* 22b; cf. *Lam. Rabbah* 1:53).

6. Cf. Jack R. Lundbom, p. 288.

7. I have used the critical editions of Rashi, Rabbi Joseph Kara, Radak, Rabbi Isaiah of Trani, Rabbi Joseph ibn Caspi, and Rabbi Menahem b. Shimon from the *Mikraot Gedolot ha-Keter* edition, ed. Menahem Cohen (Ramat-Gan, Bar-Ilan, 2012).

8. Cf. Michael Fishbane, *Biblical Interpretation in Ancient Israel* (Oxford: Clarendon Press, 1985), p. 246.

9. Cf. S.D. Luzzatto, Yair Hoffman, pp. 516-517; Jack R. Lundbom, p. 285. Lundbom adds that the narrator wishes to contrast Uriah's fate with Jeremiah's salvation, serving as a reminder of God's promise to Jeremiah that he would protect him from his enemies (Jer. 1:8, 18-19; 15:20-21).

10. Boleh, p. 340.

11. Boleh, p. 336.

12. Boleh, p. 333.

'REBUKE YOUR MOTHER': BUT WHO IS SHE?

THE IDENTITY OF THE
"MOTHER" AND "CHILDREN" IN HOSEA 2:4-7[1]

Introduction

The book of Hosea begins with God's commanding the prophet to marry a "wife of whoredom," symbolizing God's relationship with unfaithful Israel prior to the exile of the Northern Kingdom in the eighth century BCE. The prophet obeys by marrying Gomer, and has three children—bearing the symbolic names Jezreel, Lo-ruhamah, and Lo-ammi—that form prophecies of doom in chapter 1 and then prophecies of restoration in chapter 2.

Throughout his book, Hosea likens Israel to God's wife and also to God's children. Generally, these imageries express different aspects of the God-Israel relationship. For example, marriage is the ideal love bond, but a bad marriage can dissolve. In contrast, the bond between parents and children is permanent, no matter how strained the relationship becomes.[1]

---

1. This article appeared originally in *Jewish Bible Quarterly* 44:1 (2016), pp. 13-20.

However, Hosea 2:4-7 stands out in that the prophet appears to give distinct identities to the mother and children. Hosea calls upon the children to rebuke their mother, lest everyone suffer exile. To whom does each group refer?

In this essay, we will analyze the views of Rashi, Ibn Ezra, and Abarbanel. We then will consider how the interrelationship between 1:2, 2:4-7, and 4:4-9 suggests a different possibility, namely, that the mother in 2:4-7 represents the corrupt religious leadership and the children represent the masses. A midrashic tradition cited by Rashi offers this interpretation, and what had initially appeared to be a *derash* wordplay may have impact on the primary meaning of the text.

A Wife of Whoredom and Children of Whoredom

> When the Lord first spoke to Hosea, the Lord said to Hosea, "Go, get yourself a wife of whoredom and children of whoredom; for the land will stray from following the Lord" (Hos. 1:2).

Both expressions, *eshet zenunim*, "wife of whoredom," and *yaldei zenunim*, "children of whoredom," are unique to the book of Hosea. Most classical commentators interpret *eshet zenunim* as synonymous with *zonah*, "prostitute."[2] However, this is the only biblical occurrence of the term *eshet zenunim*. It is similar to expressions such as *eshet ne'urim*, "wife of youth" (Prov. 5:18; Mal. 2:14-15) and *eshet medanim*, "wife of contentions" (Prov. 21:9; 25:24). These instances indicate characteristic behavior, and therefore *eshet zenunim* suggests an unfaithful wife, rather than a prostitute from beforehand.[3] Even had Gomer been a prostitute before she married Hosea, that detail is irrelevant to the ensuing prophecy. Gomer evidently cheated on Hosea after they were married, parallel to Israel's cheating on their "marriage" to God.

More significant for our purposes is the meaning of *yaldei zenunim*, "children of whoredom." Are the children innocent victims of their mother's adulterous behavior like *mamzerim* (Rashi, Rabbi Isaiah of Trani, and Yehudah Kiel,[4] following *Pesahim* 87b),[5] or were the children promiscuous like their mother (Kara, Radak)? Since both wife and children are identically described with the same term *zenunim*, the view of Kara and Radak appears more likely. We will revisit this discussion below.

The Mother and Children in 2:4-7

Chapter 2 presents God's tormented feelings over Israel's infidelity. God oscillates between wanting to banish Israel, to punish her, to block her from her lovers, and to win Israel back to a permanent, loving relationship.

Amidst the vivid descriptions of God's emotions, Hosea calls upon the children to rebuke their mother, lest both be punished:

Rebuke your mother, rebuke her—for she is not My wife and I am not her husband—and let her put away her harlotry from her face and her adultery from between her breasts. Else will I strip her naked and leave her as on the day she was born: and I will make her like a wilderness, render her like desert land, and let her die of thirst. I will also disown her children; for they are now a harlot's brood [*benei zenunim*], in that their mother has played the harlot, she that conceived them has acted shamelessly [*hovishah horatam*]... (Hos. 2:4-7).

Who are the mother and children in this prophecy? Since Hosea generally uses both wife and children imagery to describe all of Israel, Rashi suggests that the mother refers to the collective nation of Israel, whereas the children are individual people.[6] The prophet thus calls upon Israelites to rebuke one another and repent, lest they all suffer national exile. In Rashi's reading of 2:4-7, the mother and children represent the same sinful people. Therefore, he interprets *benei zenunim* as "promiscuous children."

Rashi's interpretation gains support from the fact that throughout the book of Hosea, mother and children both refer to all Israel, rather than to different subsets of the population. Additionally, both mother and children are contemporaries of Hosea, and therefore are the prophet's audience. Abarbanel objects to this reading, however, since Hosea specifically distinguishes between mother and children in 2:4-7, whereas Rashi views both as referring to the same group of people.

Offering a different interpretation, Ibn Ezra proposes that the mother refers to Hosea's generation who were sinning and later exiled by the Assyrians. The children are the descendants of Hosea's generation who were born in exile.[7] Although later generations inherited exile through no fault of their own, they still are sinful like their mother and therefore must repent. Like

Rashi, Ibn Ezra interprets *benei zenunim* in 2:6 to mean that the children are sinful themselves.

Ibn Ezra's interpretation gains over that of Rashi because mother and children appear to be different groups of people in 2:4-7. However, Abarbanel objects to Ibn Ezra's reading, since Hosea addresses both mother and children in the present tense, and both were threatened with exile were they not to repent. According to Ibn Ezra, however, the children were not contemporaneous with Hosea. Additionally, the mother had not yet been exiled and Hosea's point is that repentance still could potentially ward off the exile.

The views of Rashi and Ibn Ezra each have significant relative strengths and weaknesses in comparison with the other. Unable to navigate between the two views, Radak simply cites both Rashi and Ibn Ezra without favoring either position.[8]

Attempting to break out of this impasse, Abarbanel proposes that the mother refers to wicked Israelites, whereas the children refer to righteous Israelites. In his reading, Hosea calls upon the righteous members of his generation to encourage repentance among the sinners. If they fail to do so, everyone will be exiled, and the righteous will suffer along with the wicked.[9]

Unlike Rashi and Ibn Ezra, Abarbanel maintains that the *benei zenunim* are innocent victims of their mother's promiscuity, rather than active sinners. They are faithful to God, but tragically live in an age when most people are wicked and therefore the impending destruction of the Northern Kingdom will cause them to suffer as well if they fail to improve their society.

Thus, Abarbanel proposes independent identities for the mother and children, and also identifies both groups as contemporaries of Hosea. He thereby overcomes the respective weaknesses of the interpretations of Rashi and Ibn Ezra. Because of the clear advantages of Abarbanel's position, later commentators, including *Metzudat David*, Malbim, and Yehudah Kiel[10] accept it as most likely.

However, Yehudah Kiel expresses concern with Abarbanel's understanding of *benei zenunim* to mean innocent victims of the mother's sins. Their punishment in 2:6 suggests that the children are sinful, as in the reading of Rashi and Ibn Ezra.[11] Although this question is not nearly as decisive as the difficulties that beset the views of Rashi and Ibn Ezra, there may be another approach to the issue that addresses all the variables more comprehensively.

A Different Meaning of Mother in Chapter 4

Yehudah Kiel suggests that the first three chapters in the book of Hosea shed light on interpreting chapters 4-14, and the reverse also is true.[12] In this spirit, chapter 4 may illuminate our discussion of 2:4-7:

"Let no man rebuke, let no man protest!" For this your people has a grievance against [you], o priest! So you shall stumble by day, and by night a prophet shall stumble as well, and I will destroy your kindred [*immekha*]. My people is destroyed because of [your] disobedience! Because you have rejected obedience, I reject you as My priest; because you have spurned the teaching of your God, I, in turn, will spurn your children [*banekha*]. The more they increased, the more they sinned against Me: I will change their dignity to dishonor. They feed on My people's sin offerings, and so they desire its iniquity. Therefore, the people shall fare like the priests: I will punish it for its conduct, I will requite it for its deeds (Hos. 4:4-9).

In this prophecy, Hosea condemns the wicked priests. Although the NJPS translation above renders *immekha* (4:5) as "your *kindred*," the expression literally means "your mother." Similarly, God will "spurn your children" in 4:6. The meaning of the terms "mother" and "children" in these verses is uncertain, but they may symbolically refer to Israel or to subsets of Israel.[13] Perhaps the corrupt priests and prophets are the mother, and the masses whom they lead are the children. This reading gains support from 4:9, where "the people shall fare like the priests." Evidently, the people are held accountable for their own sins despite the fact that their religious leaders are wicked (Radak, Abarbanel, Kiel[14]). A.A. Macintosh eloquently summarizes the passage:

> The notion of primary responsibility does not excuse the sins of those who are guilty because they have allowed themselves to be misled. It is precisely the lack of conscientious objection to wickedness throughout society that is the main focus of God's complaint and its origin is traced to the baleful relationship between priests and people.[15]

We may apply the likening of the corrupt religious leadership to the mother and the sinful masses to children in chapter 4 to our discussion of 2:4-7. In this reading, Hosea calls upon the masses to criticize their wicked leaders for their corruption. If they do not, they will be held accountable for their own sins and all will suffer exile.

If the wicked religious leaders are the mother and the masses are the children in 2:4-7, then Hosea addresses two different groups who are his contemporaries. Additionally, the mother and children both are sinful. This reading overcomes all of the weaknesses in the views of Rashi, Ibn Ezra, and Abarbanel.

A Midrashic Insight on 2:7

There is a further dimension of this interpretation in 2:7: *ki zanetah immam, hovishah horatam*. At the level of *peshat*, these two stiches are poetic parallels, and therefore most commentators interpret *horatam* to mean "she that conceived them" (e.g., Kara, Rabbi Isaiah of Trani, Kiel[16]). The NJPS translation follows suit, rendering "in that their mother has played the harlot, she that conceived them has acted shamelessly."

A Midrash, however, links Hosea's condemnation of the religious leadership in chapter 4 with 2:7, and plays on the word "*horatam*" to mean "teachers," from *le-horot*:

> "The more they increased [*ke-rubam*], the more they sinned against Me: I will change their dignity to dishonor" (Hos. 4:7). What is *ke-rubam*? Rabbi Samuel b. Nahmani said, whatever the leaders did, so did the generation....Rabbi Simlai said, it is written, "in that their mother has played the harlot, she that conceived them has acted shamelessly [*hovishah horatam*]" (Hos.

2:7). They [i.e., the religious leadership] disgraced their own words before the masses. How? The sage would publicly teach, "do not lend with interest," but he would lend with interest. He would say, "do not steal," but he would steal…. (*Deut. Rabbah* 2:19).

Quoting Targum, Rashi on 2:7 adopts this midrashic reading as well. Thus, *Deuteronomy Rabbah*, Targum, and Rashi suggest a multivalent wordplay with *horatam*. At its primary level, the term means "the one who conceived them." However, *horatam* also suggests the metaphorical meaning of their teachers. This interpretation fits our identification of the mother as the corrupt religious leadership, and the children as the sinful masses. Hosea ascribes religious and moral responsibility to the masses to make the right choices despite their leaders' wicked teachings.

Yehudah Kiel observes that Hosea distinguishes himself from his contemporaries by holding his entire generation accountable for their sins: the parents/teachers as the corrupt leaders and the children/pupils as the wicked laity. In contrast, Amos and Micah generally depict groups of wicked oppressors and the innocent oppressed, providing a sympathetic portrayal of at least some members of their society.[17]

Conclusion

Through most of the Book of Hosea, the prophet likens all of Israel to God's wife and children. In 2:4-7, however, Hosea appears to distinguish between mother and children, leading to a debate as to the meaning of each term. We analyzed the views of Rashi, Ibn Ezra, and Abarbanel in light of the local text evidence.

Although Abarbanel's reading is preferable to the alternatives of Rashi and Ibn Ezra, it appears that chapter 4 opens a new interpretive possibility, namely, that the mother refers to the corrupt religious leadership, whereas children refers to the sinful masses. Applying this interpretation to 2:4-7, the respective weaknesses of the views of Rashi, Ibn Ezra, and Abarbanel are overcome.

The midrashic reading of *horatam* referring to teachers quoted by Rashi on 2:7 initially appears to stray from the primary meaning of that term. However, by understanding this interpretation as a secondary layer of meaning based on wordplay is consistent with the distinction between mother and children in 2:4-7 in conjunction with the prophecy in chapter 4.

If this interpretation is correct, Hosea's prophecy dignifies all Israelites by insisting that they are not innocent sheep blindly misled by corrupt priests and prophets. Rather, Hosea calls upon each individual to live righteously, even when their leaders teach and act otherwise.

NOTES

1. Cf. *Kiddushin* 36a: "'You are children of the Lord your God' (Deut. 14:1): when you behave as sons you are designated sons; if you do not behave as sons, you are not designated sons: this is Rabbi Judah's view. Rabbi Meir said: In both cases you are called sons, for it is said… 'and instead of being told, "You are Not-My-People," they shall be called Children-of-the-Living-God' (Hos. 2:1)."

2. See Rashi, Kara, Ibn Ezra, Radak, Abarbanel, Malbim, Yehudah Kiel (*Da'at Mikra: Twelve Prophets vol. 1, Hosea* [Hebrew] [Jerusalem: Mosad HaRav Kook, 1990], p. 3).

3. See Francis I. Andersen and David N. Freedman, *Hosea* Anchor Bible 24 (New York: Doubleday, 1980), p. 159; A.A. Macintosh, *International Critical Commentary: Hosea* (Edinburgh: T&T Clark, 1997), p. 8. Kiel also acknowledges the possibility that the term might mean wife of whoredom.

4. Kiel, pp. 3-4.

5. Cf. Gen. 38:24 regarding Tamar: *ki harah li-zenunim*, "she is with child by harlotry."

6. Cf. Andersen and Freedman, p. 219.

7. Isaiah 50:1 similarly uses mother imagery to refer to the generation who experienced the destruction of the Temple: "Thus said the Lord: Where is the bill of divorce of your mother whom I dismissed? And which of My creditors was it to whom I sold you off? You were only sold off for your sins, and your mother dismissed for your crimes." The children therefore would refer to subsequent generations.

8. Macintosh also cites these two views as the most likely (pp. 40, 46).

9. Shortly before the destruction of the First Temple, Ezekiel prophesies: "Say to the land of Israel: Thus said the Lord: I am going

to deal with you! I will draw My sword from its sheath, and I will wipe out from you both the righteous and the wicked" (Ezek. 21:8).

The Talmud offers two fundamental approaches to this verse. *Bava Kamma* 60a states that destruction is indiscriminate: "Once permission has been granted to the Destroyer, he does not distinguish between righteous and wicked. Moreover, he even begins with the righteous at the very outset, as it says: 'And I will wipe out from you both the righteous and the wicked.'" Alternatively, *Avodah Zarah* 4a maintains that the righteous are held accountable if they do not rebuke the wicked: "'And I will wipe out from you both the righteous and the wicked,' that refers to one who is not thoroughly righteous….It was in their power to protest against [the wickedness of the others] and they did not protest, they are not regarded as thoroughly righteous." Both approaches work well within Abarbanel's reading. Hosea could mean that if the righteous do not rebuke the wicked, all will be exiled indiscriminately; he also can mean that the righteous will be held accountable for their failure to attempt to improve the religious state of their generation.

10. Kiel, p. 9.

11. Kiel, p. 10.

12. Kiel, introduction, p. 10.

13. See Kiel, pp. 28-29; Zeev Weissman *et al.*, *Olam ha-Tanakh: Twelve Prophets vol. 1* (Hebrew) (Tel Aviv: Dodson-Iti, 1997), p. 41.

14 Kiel, p. 29.

15. Macintosh, p. 146.

16. Kiel, p. 10.

17. Kiel, introduction, p. 13.

PERSPECTIVES ON PSALM 19[1]

Psalm 19 is straightforward on its surface. Verses 2-7 proclaim that God's glory is revealed through nature. Verses 8-15 then praise God's Torah and its effects on people. The relationship between the sections of the psalm has elicited various responses by commentators throughout the ages. How one connects them reflects and affects one's religious outlook in significant ways. In this essay we explore several facets of interpretation.

Connecting the Two Halves of the Psalm

Rabbi Elhanan Samet[1] divides the first half of the psalm into two subsections: the heavens' declaration of God's glory (2-5a), and the daily activity of the sun (5b-7):

> [1]For the leader. A psalm of David. [2]The heavens declare the glory of God, the sky proclaims His handiwork. [3]Day to day makes utterance, night to night speaks out. [4]There is no utterance, there are no words, whose sound goes unheard. [5a]Their voice carries throughout the earth, their words to the end of the world.

1. This article appeared originally in *MiTokh Ha-Ohel, From Within the Tent: The Shabbat Prayers*, ed. Daniel Z. Feldman and Stuart W. Halpern (Jerusalem: Maggid, 2015), pp. 135-141.

Heavens speak, but without words. Consequently, we must pay special attention to hear the praises that the heavens utter. Rabbi Samet quotes from the Talmud: "Were it not for the sound of the tumult of Rome, the sound of the revolution of the sun would be heard" (*Yoma* 20b). It is possible to drown out the sounds of God's glory with too much emphasis on day-to-day existence. The opening verses of this psalm describe the glory of God manifest throughout the cosmos, and how people need to direct their attentiveness in order to hear the beauty of nature and how it glorifies God.

The psalmist then praises the sun for its joyful obedience of God's command. It perfectly fulfills its role to illuminate:

> 5bHe placed in them a tent for the sun, 6who is like a groom coming forth from the chamber, like a hero, eager to run his course. 7His rising-place is at one end of heaven, and his circuit reaches the other; nothing escapes his heat.

The section concludes *ve-en nistar me-hamato*, translated by several commentators as "nothing escapes its heat." Rabbi Samet notes that everything else describing the sun is positive. He therefore adopts the reading of Rabbi Samson Raphael Hirsch, who explains that *hamato* means God's sun and not the sun's heat. No place on earth is hidden from the sun's light. Alternatively, Amos Hakham explains that nobody hides from the sun's warmth and rays, also conveying a positive tone.[2]

Moving to the second half of the psalm, verses 8-11 praise the Torah, its commandments, and its influence on people.

Verses 12-14 then are a prayer to God to save the psalmist from sin, and verse 15 concludes with a prayer that the psalmist's words should be acceptable to God:

> [8]The teaching of the Lord is perfect, renewing life; the decrees of the Lord are enduring, making the simple wise; [9]The precepts of the Lord are just, rejoicing the heart; the instruction of the Lord is lucid, making the eyes light up. [10]The fear of the Lord is pure, abiding forever; the judgments of the Lord are true, righteous altogether, [11]more desirable than gold, than much fine gold; sweeter than honey, than drippings of the comb. [12]Your servant pays them heed; in obeying them there is much reward. [13]Who can be aware of errors? Clear me of unperceived guilt, [14]and from willful sins keep Your servant; let them not dominate me; then shall I be blameless and clear of grave offense. [15]May the words of my mouth and the prayer of my heart be acceptable to You, O Lord, my rock and my redeemer.

Commentators adopt different strategies for linking the two halves of our psalm. Some see a similarity between the two halves. Within those who see the two halves as parallel, there is discussion whether the religious values of nature and Torah are different but equal ways of approaching God, or whether the psalm presents the Torah as a superior means of developing a relationship with God. Rashi (first view) and Amos Hakham[3] parallel the two halves: just as the sun illuminates, so does the Torah. Similarly, Radak (second view) argues that just as the sun is necessary for physical existence, the Torah is vital for our souls. Ibn Ezra, Radak (first view), and Meiri view the Torah as superior to nature: we find testimony to God's greatness in nature, and the Torah is even greater testimony.

Rabbi Samson Raphael Hirsch suggests that the study of nature teaches any thoughtful person that there is a God. However, heavens and earth cannot provide people with answers to the question of why we should praise God, or why we should recognize God as Master. Nature cannot answer the question of what people should do with their free will. The contemplation of nature never will teach us our purpose in this world. It is only Torah that can shape people in accordance with God's will.

Other commentators view the two halves of the psalm as contrasting. Rashi (second view) interprets the final expression in the first half, *ve-en nistar me-hamato*, "nothing escapes his heat" (v. 7), as negative. The sun can burn, whereas the Torah heals and restores the soul. A more dramatic contrasting approach is found in Rabbenu Bahya ben Asher's *Kad ha-Kemah* in his entry on Torah. Rabbenu Bahya quotes Psalm 19:8-10, and gives a detailed analysis of how each aspect of Torah is superior to some aspect of the sun. For example, one looking directly at the sun can be blinded, but the Torah brightens our eyes. The sun shines only during the day, whereas the Torah perpetually illuminates. As noted above, Rabbi Samet disagrees with the negative reading of *ve-en nistar me-hamato*. The first half of the psalm appears entirely positive in its praise of all nature, including the sun.

Rabbi Samet explains that the heavens attest to God's greatness. The sun is the ideal model of the heavenly realm, serving God with perfection and enthusiasm. This paradigm is not identical in the human realm. The psalmist longs for the sun's perfection and enthusiasm in serving God, but knows that as a person he cannot be perfect. People are liable to error, and sometimes those errors are hidden (*nistarot*) even from themselves. In contrast, nothing is hidden (*nistar*) from the sun's light.[4] The sun therefore rejoices like a bridegroom, whereas the religious person worries. The parallel between the two halves of the psalm is that God created perfection in nature, and in the Torah. The religious individual considers the sun as a role model in serving God, and prays that he or she will avoid error in the effort to likewise attain perfection in serving God through the Torah.

Whereas the aforementioned medieval commentators do not interpret this psalm in this manner, *Sifrei Deuteronomy* 306 explicitly expresses this idea:

"Give ear, O heavens, and I will speak" (Deut. 32:1)— The Holy One, blessed be He, said to Moses: Say to Israel: Look into the heavens that I created to serve you. Have they perhaps changed their ways? Did perhaps the sphere of the sun say: I shall not rise in the east and illuminate the entire world? Rather as it is stated, "The sun also rises, and the sun goes down" (Ecc. 1:5). And what is more, it is happy to do My will, as it is stated: "And it is like a bridegroom coming out of his chamber" (Ps. 19:6). Surely there is an *a fortiori* argument: If they who do not act for reward nor for loss—if they merit they do not receive reward, and if they sin they do receive punishment—and do not have compassion for their sons and daughters—if they do not change their ways, then you, who if you merit you receive reward, and if you sin you receive punishment, and you have compassion for your sons and for your daughters, all the more so you must not change your ways.

In this Midrash, God views the sun as a model for humanity. As the sun always perfectly fulfills God's will, people should strive to do so all the more. When people use their free will properly in the service of God, then humanity is in harmony with the cosmos. Rabbi Samson Raphael Hirsch similarly concludes that all of nature acts in accordance with God's will. In contrast, people need God's word to achieve their purpose.

Amos Hakham observes that the blessings before the *Shema* follow this pattern, as well. The first blessing praises God as the Creator of the cosmos, whereas the second focuses on Israel's intimate personal relationship with God. Armed with both aspects, we can accept the yoke of Heaven by reciting the *Shema*.[5]

Breaking the Psalm into Three Parts

J. Ross Wagner and Philip Nel offer additional insight into Psalm 19 by dividing it into three sections rather than two.[6] Wagner observes that verses 2-7 speak about nature as objectively awesome, and do not refer to people. These verses refer to God as *El*, in God's capacity as the Creator of the cosmos. Verses 8-11 bring God closer to people, exulting in how God's Torah benefits people. In these verses, the psalmist does not address God directly, but talks about Him using God's personal name Y-H-V-H, implying a more personal, intimate, covenantal relationship. Verses 12-15 bring God still closer, as the psalmist directly addresses God for the first time. The psalm's seventh and final reference to God's personal name (v. 15) is the only time that the psalmist addresses God directly by name. The concluding address to God as *Tzuri ve-Go'ali,* "my Rock and my Redeemer," appeals to God's intimate relationship with the psalmist and his nation. Thus, the psalmist is awed by the cosmos, then by the Torah, and then he internalizes these means to shape and transform his own religious life. The psalmist wants to take his place in this infinite and eternal order in perfect service to God.

Adopting a different approach that also divides the psalm into three sections, Philip Nel argues that the cosmos (2-7) and Torah (8-11) both are perfect, whereas people are not (12-14). Instead of remaining mute, however, people can and should speak God's praises and meditate on God's greatness (15). We are inconstant but when we pray we join nature and the Torah in glorifying God.

Combining Torah and Madda

Rabbi Norman Lamm discusses an apparent conflict within Rambam's writings.[7] Rambam writes that one attains love of God through contemplating nature (*Hilkhot Yesodei ha-Torah* 2:2; see also *Guide of the Perplexed* 3:28 and 3:52). However, in his *Sefer ha-Mitzvot,* Rambam includes both mitzvah observance and contemplation of nature as means to attaining love of God (positive commandment 3). Why is Rambam inconsistent?

Rabbi Lamm adopts an approach common in Rambam scholarship, and distinguishes between the masses and the intellectual elite. The masses love God through observance of the *mitzvot*, whereas the philosophical elite love God through nature. The *Guide* is elitist, whereas *Sefer ha-Mitzvot* was written as a popular work. What about the *Mishneh Torah*, a work similarly intended for everyone? Rabbi Lamm answers that its opening chapters are philosophical, and therefore can be understood properly only by an exclusive elite.

One may question this solution. Even the simplest soul can be overwhelmed by the cosmos. Several psalms—Psalm 19 included—express that sentiment. Perhaps the discrepancy in Rambam's writings has more to do with the context of each book. *Sefer ha-Mitzvot* teaches how Jews develop a love of God—through the Torah's commandments and through the contemplation of nature. In contrast, the opening chapters in *Mishneh Torah* and the *Guide* focus on how any religious person attains the love and fear of God. Therefore, they highlight the universal aspects of God's glory in nature.

In his book *Torah UMadda*,[8] Rabbi Lamm quotes the Mishnah in *Avot* 3:7: "Rabbi Yaakov used to say: One who is studying Torah as he walks by the way, and who interrupts his studies to say, 'How beautiful is this tree,' or 'how beautiful is this furrow,' it is as though he is guilty with his life." Rabbi Lamm adopts Rashi's interpretation: nature certainly helps us appreciate God, but the Torah is God's revealed word and therefore it has religious primacy. This interpretation of the Mishnah is in line with Ibn Ezra, Radak (first view), and Meiri we considered earlier, who view the Torah as superior to nature in Psalm 19.

Rabbi Marc D. Angel pointed out to me an alternate interpretation of the Mishnah in *Avot*. One who views nature as an *interruption* from Torah errs. One who perceives nature as part of a Torah worldview has a proper understanding. As Psalm 19 teaches, Torah and nature are different manifestations of God's voice. Because they are different, the psalm separates them into two categories. However, they are two means of hearing God's voice that work together in harmony. This interpretation is in line with that of Rashi (first view), Radak (second view), and Amos Hakham, who see the Torah and nature as parallel means of reaching God in Psalm 19.

Psalm 19 teaches that the Torah and nature are different manifestations of God's voice. Concurrently, they are two means of hearing God's voice that work together in harmony. The job of humanity is to perceive God's glory in nature and the Torah, and speak out God's praises. In this manner, all creation harmoniously unites in the service of God.

NOTES

1. Rabbi Elhanan Samet, *Iyyunim be-Mizmorei Tehillim* (Hebrew) (Tel Aviv: Yediot Aharonot, 2012), pp. 41-69.

2. Amos Hakham, *Da'at Mikra: Psalms* vol. 1 (Hebrew) (Jerusalem: Mosad HaRav Kook, 1979), p. 99.

3. *Ibid.*, p. 102.

4. In a similar vein, C.S. Lewis suggests that the psalmist feels that one cannot hide from the searching light of the sun, nor can one hide one's soul from the all-encompassing light of the Torah (*Reflections on the Psalms: The Celebrated Musings on One of the Most Intriguing Books of the Bible* [Boston: Mariner Books, 2012 edition of the 1958 publication]), p. 64.

5. *Ibid.*, pp. 102-103.

6. J. Ross Wagner, "From the Heavens to the Heart: The Dynamics of Psalm 19 as Prayer," *Catholic Biblical Quarterly* 61 (1999), pp. 245-261; Philip Nel, "Psalm 19: The Unbearable Lightness of Perfection," *Journal of Northwest Semitic Languages* 30 (2004), pp. 103-117.

7. Rabbi Norman Lamm, "Maimonides on the Love of God," *Maimonidean Studies* 3 (1992-1993), pp. 131-142.

8. Rabbi Norman Lamm, *Torah UMadda: The Encounter of Religious Learning and Worldly Knowledge in the Jewish Tradition* (Lanham, MD: Rowman and Littlefield, 2004), pp. 146-147.

PERSPECTIVES ON PSALM 145[1]

We recite our beloved Psalm 145 (which makes up the majority of the *Ashrei* prayer) three times daily, which led Shelomo Goitein to dub it the "*Shema* of the Psalms."[1] It is the only psalm that begins *tehillah*, "praise,"[2] and Amos Hakham suggests that perhaps the Sages named the book "*Tehillim*" after this psalm.[3] In this essay we consider different perspectives on this psalm as a chapter in Tanakh and then as part of our liturgy.

Alternation between Calls to Praise and Praise

Rabbi Avia Hacohen offers several ways of structuring the psalm.[4] The most convincing of these readings frames Psalm 145 as alternating between calls to praise and actual praise. The psalm would be set up as follows:

---

1. This article appeared originally in *MiTokh Ha-Ohel: The Weekday Prayers*, ed. Daniel Z. Feldman and Stuart W. Halpern (New Milford, CT: Maggid, 2014), pp. 127-137.

Call to praise:

[1]I will extol You, my God and king, and bless Your name
forever and ever.

[2]Every day will I bless You and praise Your name forever
and ever.

Praise:

[3]Great is the Lord and much acclaimed; His greatness
cannot be fathomed.

Call to praise:

[4]One generation shall laud Your works to another and
declare Your mighty acts.

[5]The glorious majesty of Your splendor and Your
wondrous acts will I recite.

[6]Men shall talk of the might of Your awesome deeds,
and I will recount Your greatness.

[7]They shall celebrate Your abundant goodness, and sing
joyously of Your beneficence.

Praise:

[8]The Lord is gracious and compassionate, slow to anger
and abounding in kindness.

[9]The Lord is good to all, and His mercy is upon all His
works.

Call to praise:

[10]All Your works shall praise You, O Lord, and Your
faithful ones shall bless You.

[11]They shall talk of the majesty of Your kingship, and speak of Your might,

[12]to make His mighty acts known among men and the majestic glory of His kingship.

Praise:

[13]Your kingship is an eternal kingship; Your dominion is for all generations.

[14]The Lord supports all who stumble, and makes all who are bent stand straight.

[15]The eyes of all look to You expectantly, and You give them their food when it is due.

[16]You give it openhandedly, feeding every creature to its heart's content.

[17]The Lord is beneficent in all His ways and faithful in all His works.

[18]The Lord is near to all who call Him, to all who call Him with sincerity.

[19]He fulfills the wishes of those who fear Him; He hears their cry and delivers them.

[20]The Lord watches over all who love Him, but all the wicked He will destroy.

Summary call:

[21]My mouth shall utter the praise of the Lord, and all creatures shall bless His holy name forever and ever.

In this structure, there is a growing trend of praise. The first round of praise is one verse, the second is two verses, and the third is eight verses. In the first call to praise, the psalmist refers to himself: "I will extol You… and [I] will bless… I bless You and [I] praise Your name forever and ever." The second call combines the psalmist as an individual with a group: "One generation shall laud… will I recite… men shall talk… I will recount… they shall celebrate." The third call is to the collective, rather than the individual: "All Your works shall praise You… Your faithful ones shall bless You… They shall talk… and speak." The psalm thus moves outward from the psalmist himself, to his joining the community in prayer, to focusing entirely on the community.

A similar progression occurs with the root *b-r-k*, "bless." In verses 1-2, the psalmist will bless God. In verse 10, the righteous bless God. Verse 21 expands to a longing that all people should bless God.[5] The psalm's final verse teaches that although individuals form a community through prayer, each individual retains his or her voice: "*My* mouth shall utter."[6]

The psalm's final verse also anticipates the day when "all creatures shall bless His holy name forever and ever." The individual at the beginning of the psalm will "bless Your name forever and ever," omitting "holy." God's name is referred to as "holy" with communal prayers, anticipating the concept of holy matters, *devarim she-bi-kedushah*, which require a quorum to praise God publicly (*Megillah* 23b). By coming together as a community, people have the power to sanctify God's name.

Pote'ah et Yadekha: You Give it Openhandedly

> Rabbi Yosi [also] said: May my portion be of those who
> recite the entire *Hallel* every day. But that is not so, for a
> Master said: He who reads *Hallel* every day blasphemes
> and reproaches [the Divine Name]? We refer to the
> Verses of Song (*Pesukei de-Zimra*) (*Shabbat* 118b).[7]

Why would someone who recites the *Hallel* (Psalms 113-118)
each day be considered a blasphemer? Rabbi Joseph Soloveitchik
explains that Psalms 113–118 include praise for God's great
miracles, including the exodus from Egypt and the crossing
of the Jordan River in Joshua's time. We refer to this liturgy
as *Hallel Mitzri*, the "Egyptian Hallel" (*Berakhot* 56a). We risk
lessening the impact of God's acts if we equate all miracles—
the daily and the supernatural. The daily recital of *Hallel*, then,
would be a form of blasphemy. By treating it as a daily prayer,
we would indicate that we no longer appreciate God's unusual
acts as special. In contrast, Psalms 145–150 praise God for daily
miracles, such as sustaining His creation and other natural
phenomena.[8]

Similarly, the Talmud suggests that the optimal praises of
God bless Him for the mundane:

> Rabbi Eleazar b. Avina says: Whoever recites [the psalm]
> "Praise of David" (Psalm 145) three times daily, is sure
> to inherit the world to come. What is the reason? Shall
> I say it is because it has an alphabetical arrangement?
> Then let him recite, "Happy are they that are upright in

the way" (Ps. 119), which has an eightfold alphabetical arrangement. Again, is it because it contains [the verse], "You open Your hand [*pote'ah et yadekha*]"? Then let him recite the great *Hallel* (Ps. 136), where it is written: "Who gives food to all flesh!" (136:25). Rather, [the reason is] because it contains both (*Berakhot* 4b).

Replete with praise for God for the Creation and exodus, Psalm 136 receives honorable mention for its penultimate verse that praises God for day-to-day sustenance. Human nature revels in the supernatural and finds little to get excited about in the mundane. In contrast, Jewish thought gives primacy to the miracles of every day, rather than the extraordinary. The *Tur* explains that the verse "*pote'ah et yadekha*" is the primary reason that the Sages mandated reading Psalm 145 each day (*Orah Hayyim* 51). The *Shulhan Arukh* rules that if one does not have proper intention when reading this verse, he should return to recite it again (*Orah Hayyim* 51:7).

Rabbi Elhanan Samet[9] further observes similarities between Psalms 145 and 104. Both psalms stress the dependence of all creatures on God's sustenance. However, Psalm 104 notes that while God takes care of all creation, not every individual creature receives what it needs. Psalm 145, in contrast, is purely positive. The psalmist celebrates how God sustains all creatures without further qualification.

145	104
15: The eyes of all look to You expectantly, and You give them their food when it is due (*enei kol elekha yesabberu, ve-attah noten lahem et okhlam be-itto*).	27: All of them look to You to give them their food when it is due (*kullam elekha yesabberun, la-tet okhlam be-itto*).
16: You give it openhandedly, feeding every creature to its heart's content (*pote'ah et yadekha u-masbia le-khol hai ratzon*).	28-29: Give it to them, they gather it up; open Your hand, they are well satisfied (*tiftah yadekha yisbe'un tov*); hide Your face, they are terrified; take away their breath, they perish and turn again into dust.

The Acrostic and the Missing *Nun*

Psalm 145 is an acrostic, illustrating a complete praise of God from the letters *aleph* to *tav*. Adele Berlin writes:

> The poet praises God with everything from A to Z; his praise is all-inclusive. More than that, the entire alphabet, the source of all words, is marshalled in praise of God. One cannot actually use all of the words in a language, but by using the alphabet one uses all potential words.[10]

The psalm also is a literary *inclusio* that begins and ends with similar formulations. It begins with *tehillah*, a song of "praise," and ends *tehillat Hashem yedabber pi*, "my mouth shall utter the praise of the Lord." It begins *va-avarekha shimka le-olam va-ed*, 'I will bless Your name forever and ever," and ends *vi-varekh kol basar shem kodsho le-olam va-ed*, "and all creatures shall bless His holy name forever and ever." Psalms that begin and end with the same wording are a sign of completeness, and the Talmud considers them to be special (*Berakhot* 9b-10a, cf. *Tosafot* s.v. *kol*). Another element of completeness in this psalm is its frequent use of the term *kol*, "all." The word *kol* appears seventeen times, including sixteen from verses 9-21. Adele Berlin suggests that this theme teaches that God does good to all, and therefore all always should praise Him.[11]

Psalm 145 contains verses beginning with each letter of the *aleph-bet* with the exception of *nun*. The Talmud offers a midrashic explanation which connects it to a verse in the book of Amos:

> Rabbi Johanan says: Why is there no *nun* in *Ashrei*? Because the fall of Israel's enemies [i.e., Israel] begins with it. For it is written: Fallen is the virgin of Israel, she shall no more rise (Amos 5:2).... Rabbi Nahman b. Isaac says: Even so, David refers to it by inspiration and promises them an uplifting. For it is written: The Lord upholds all that fall (Ps. 145:14) (*Berakhot* 4b).

In this passage, the Sages homiletically link Psalm 145 to Amos 5:2 to explain that although Amos prophesied that Israel shall rise no more, God raises *all* who fall—which would include Israel.

However, this is not likely a *peshat* explanation for the absence of the *nun*. Radak and Meiri (on Ps. 145:1) state that we do not know the reason for the omission of the *nun*[12] and the talmudic passage is a comment according to the ways of *derash*. Some acrostics in the book of Psalms use the entire *aleph-bet*, whereas others—such as 25 and 34—omit letters (*Ecc. Rabbah* 1:13).[13] We do not know why some are complete while others are not.[14]

However, there is extra-biblical evidence that reflects the presence of a verse beginning with a *nun*. The discovery of the Dead Sea Scrolls (DSS) provided a Hebrew version of the verse: *Ne'eman Elokim bi-devarav ve-hasid be-khol ma'asav*, "God is faithful in His words/deeds and gracious in all His works." Similarly, in the Septuagint (LXX), the Greek translation of Tanakh, there is a verse that reflects the reading "*ne'eman*."[15] It is possible that the original psalm omitted a verse beginning with *nun*. A later writer was troubled by that omission, and added this verse to complete the *aleph-bet*. From this vantage point, our Masoretic Text (MT) contains the original version. Alternatively, it is possible that the original psalm contained the verse beginning with *nun*, but a scribe accidentally omitted it. From this vantage point, the MT does not contain the original version and the LXX and DSS preserve the more authentic text.

Contemporary scholars debate which of these alternatives is more likely.[16] The best arguments in favor of the authenticity of the *nun* verse are: (1) It contains a new idea from the rest of the psalm. (2) The first blessing we recite after *haftarot* is "*ha-El ha-ne'eman be-khol devarav*," which is strikingly similar to the wording of this *nun* verse. Perhaps the formula of the blessing originates from this verse.[17]

The best arguments against the authenticity of the *nun* verse are: (1) other acrostics in the book of Psalms (e.g., 25, 34, 37) also are incomplete, so the missing *nun* in 145 is not unusual. While true, however, this is not an argument against the *nun* as much as one demonstrating the plausibility of a missing letter in an acrostic. (2) The *nun* verse sounds suspiciously similar to *tzaddik Hashem be-khol derakhav ve-hasid be-khol ma'asav* (verse 17). Perhaps this similarity suggests that a later author copied a nearby verse in a feeble effort to supply a verse beginning with *nun*. However, there are other repetitions in the book of Psalms that serve as a chorus (e.g., 24:7, 9; 67:4, 6), so the near-repetition of a verse is plausible here as well. (3) It is more likely for a later writer or translator to smooth out a difficulty than for a scribe to accidentally omit a verse. (4) The Talmud already attests to the absence of a *nun* (*Berakhot* 4b), so this omission is ancient. Given that we recite the psalm regularly in our liturgy, an accidental omission of the *nun* becomes less likely. Overall, it appears more likely that the MT contains the original text, whereas the LXX and DSS reflect a later addition.

In his introduction to the book of Leviticus, Rabbi David Zvi Hoffmann addresses the general issue of variant texts. Although he grants the possibility of scribal errors in Tanakh, as a matter of religious policy we should not emend biblical texts or it will open a Pandora's box that cannot be closed. It would be very difficult to learn Tanakh religiously if we never could be certain about the authenticity of the text. Therefore, in practice we treat the MT as the original, even when we know of plausible variants.[18]

Universalism and Particularism in Psalms 145-150

The themes of universalism and particularism run throughout all Tanakh. Psalms 145-150, which comprise the heart of the morning *Pesukei de-Zimra*, reflect those two themes as well.[19] Psalm 145 is purely universalistic, as God sustains all creation. There is no special mention of Israel in this psalm.

In contrast, Psalms 146-149 contain elements of God's special relationship with Israel. Psalm 146 refers to God as the God of Jacob (146:5), and the concluding verse likewise mentions Israel: "The Lord shall reign forever, your God, O Zion, for all generations. Hallelujah" (146:10). Although the rest of the psalm applies to Jews and non-Jews alike, these verses add a distinctly Israelite element. While much of Psalm 147 praises God in nature, it also highlights Israel:

The Lord rebuilds Jerusalem; He gathers in the exiles of Israel (147:2).

He issued His commands to Jacob, His statutes and rules to Israel. He did not do so for any other nation; of such rules they know nothing. Hallelujah (147:19-20).

Psalm 148 resembles universalistic psalms such as 8 and 104, which praise God as the Creator of the cosmos. Its closing verse, however, stresses the special God-Israel relationship: "He has exalted the horn of His people for the glory of all His faithful ones, Israel, the people close to Him. Hallelujah" (148:14). Psalm 149 contrasts Israel and her foes: "Let Israel rejoice in its maker; let the children of Zion exult in their king" (149:2). The psalm then focuses on God's future retribution against Israel's enemies.

Finally, Psalm 150 returns to universalism: "Let all that breathes praise the Lord. Hallelujah" (150:6). Thus, the bookends of these six psalms are universalistic, whereas the middle four psalms contain more particularistic elements, as well.[20]

Psalm 145 as Liturgy

The Talmud (*Berakhot* 4b) teaches that "whoever recites [the psalm] Praise of David three times daily is sure to inherit the world to come." Amos Hakham[21] notes that our printed text is not the original talmudic text. The original passage read, "whoever recites [the psalm] Praise of David daily." Rabbi Amram Gaon had the original version in his Siddur (c. 875 CE). In the Geonic period, the practice developed to recite this psalm three times daily to increase the likelihood of saying it at least once (*Shibbolei ha-Leket* 7). Evidently, this new practice crept into the text of the Talmud. The daily practice reflects the psalm's second verse, *be-khol yom avarakheka*, "every day will I bless You."

In addition to the completion that the psalm exhibits with its acrostic and inclusio, our tradition to append verses at the beginning and end of the psalm adds a new dimension of completion. Prior to the psalm, we open with the verses in Psalm 84:5 and 144:15, which both begin with the word "*ashrei*." At the conclusion of the psalm, we add 115:18, which ends in "Hallelujah." In the liturgical form that we recite it, Psalm 145 now begins with the first word of the book of Psalms, and ends with the final word in the book of Psalms. By reading Psalm 145, then, we symbolically read the entire book.

Tosafot suggest that *ashrei yoshevei betekha*, "Happy are those who dwell in Your house" (Ps. 84:5), was added to refer to the idea that the saintly people of old used to prepare themselves for one hour before prayer (*Berakhot* 32b, s.v. *kodem*). By reciting that verse, we symbolically use Psalm 145 as our preparation for prayer.

Additionally, by adding the verses at the beginning and end of the psalm, we shift the universalistic psalm to a more Israel-centered focus. "Happy the people who have it so; happy the people whose God is the Lord" (144:15) prefaces Psalm 145 with Israel's joy in serving God. The psalm concludes by expressing a longing for all humanity to serve God: "all creatures shall bless His holy name forever and ever" (145:21). We follow that with an expression that we currently do so: "But we will bless the Lord now and forever. Hallelujah" (115:18).[22] Finally, Rabbi Amram Gaon explained that adding 115:18 to the end of Psalm 145 has it conclude with "Hallelujah" in order to connect it to the following five psalms of *Pesukei de-Zimra,* which begin and end with "Hallelujah" (quoted in *Tur, Orah Hayyim* 51).[23]

The array of perspectives on this beloved psalm is not surprising. Its love of God and its ability to move the individual into a growing community of worshippers who accept God's kingship have indeed made it into the "*Shema* of the psalms."

NOTES

1. Shelomo D. Goitein, *Biblical Studies* (Hebrew) (Tel Aviv: Yavneh, 1957), p. 228.

2. In contrast, fifty-seven psalms contain the word *mizmor* in their opening verses.

3. Amos Hakham, *Da'at Mikra: Psalms* vol. 2 (Hebrew) (Jerusalem: Mosad HaRav Kook, 1979), p. 570, n. 2.

4. Rabbi Avia Hacohen, *Tefillah le-El Hai: The Journey of the Soul and the Spirit of the Song in the Book of Psalms* (Hebrew) (En Tzurim: Yeshivat HaKibbutz HaDati, 2007), pp. 93-111.

5. Nahum M. Sarna et al. (*Olam HaTanakh: Psalms* vol. 2 [Hebrew] [Tel Aviv: Dodson-Iti, 1999], p. 267) notes that Psalms 146-150 present the community praising God rather than the individual, and suggests that one may view Psalms 145-150 as a unit where the individual calls on others to praise God in chapter 145, and the following five psalms respond to that call.

6. Cf. Binyamin Gezundheit and Reuven Kimelman, "A Praise of David: Structure and Meaning" (Hebrew), *Megadim* 49 (2008), pp. 61-62. A similar progression from the individual to the community occurs in Psalm 103, and that psalm also concludes with the voice of the individual still present.

7. Rashi understands the *Pesukei de-Zimra* as referring specifically to Psalms 148 and 150, which feature the word *hallelu*. Most others

understand this passage as referring to all of Psalms 145-150, which are recited in the daily liturgy (Rif; Rambam *Hilkhot Tefillah* 7:12; *Soferim* 18:1). *Halakhah* codifies the recitation of Psalms 145-150 as the "daily Hallel" but if someone comes late to services and does not have time to recite them all, we follow Rashi in giving priority to chapters 148 and 150 (*Shulhan Arukh, Orah Hayyim* 52:1).

8. Arnold Lustiger, *Derashot HaRav: Selected Lectures of Rabbi Joseph B. Soloveitchik*, 2003, pp. 153–156.

9. Rabbi Elhanan Samet, at http://vbm-torah.org/archive/tehillim70/51tehillim.htm.

10. Adele Berlin, "The Rhetoric of Psalm 145," in *Biblical and Related Studies Presented to Samuel Iwry*, ed. Ann Kort and Scott Morschauser (Winona Lake, IN: Eisenbrauns, 1985), p. 18.

11. Ibid., p. 19.

12. Uriel Simon (*Four Approaches to the Book of Psalms: from Saadiah Gaon to Abraham Ibn Ezra*, trans. Lenn. J. Schramm [New York: SUNY Press, 1991], p. 104, n. 45) quotes the tenth century Karaite Yefet ben Ali, who speculated that the omission of the *nun* verse suggests that it is impossible to fully praise God. Although it is a nice idea homiletically, there are acrostics in the book of Psalms (111, 112, and 119) that do complete the *aleph-bet* so Yefet's explanation is inadequate at the level of *peshat*.

13. Gezundheit and Kimelman ("A Praise of David," p. 64, n. 19) quote Yaakov Bazak who observes that the acrostics ascribed to

David (25, 34, 37, 145) omit letters whereas those not ascribed to David (111, 112, 119) have complete *aleph-bet* acrostics.

14. For further discussion, see Ronald Benun, "Evil and the Disruption of Order: A Structural Analysis of the Acrostics in the First Book of Psalms," *Journal of Hebrew Scriptures* 6:5 (2006). Alternatively, Rabbi Shalom Carmy suggests that the psalmist may have intentionally deviated from the expected acrostic pattern to subtly allude to the brokenness from which God saves him ("The Manufacture of Sulphurous Acid: On Wisdom as a Catalyst in Torah Study," in *Wisdom from All My Teachers: Challenges and Initiatives in Contemporary Torah Education*, ed. Jeffrey Saks and Susan Handelman [Jerusalem: Urim Publications, 2003, ATID], pp. 79-80).

15. The Greek reflects the reading, "*Ne'eman Hashem be-khol devarav ve-hasid be-khol ma'asav.*"

16. See Sarna et al., *Olam ha-Tanakh: Psalms* vol. 2, pp. 268-269, for a summary of both sides of the argument.

17. Reuven Kimelman ("Psalm 145: Theme, Structure, and Impact," *Journal of Biblical Literature* 113 [1994], p. 50) argues that a later writer drew from the blessing of the *haftarah* and added it to the text of the psalm, rather than the reverse.

18. For a broader discussion of traditional sources pertaining to text variants in Tanakh, see Rabbi Amnon Bazak, *Ad ha-Yom ha-Zeh: Until This Day: Fundamental Questions in Bible Teaching* (Hebrew), ed. Yoshi Farajun (Tel-Aviv: Yediot Aharonot, 2013), pp. 183-243.

19. See also Sarna et al., *Olam ha-Tanakh: Psalms* vol. 2, p. 267.

20. For further analysis of the interrelationship between Psalms 145-150, see Binyamin Gezundheit, *"Pesukei de-Zimra:* A Literary and Conceptual Unit Based on Contextual Interpretation" (Hebrew), *Megadim* 54 (2013), pp. 85-109.

21. Hakham, *Da'at Mikra: Psalms* vol. 2, p. 579. Cf. Rabbi Akiva Eiger (*Gilyon ha-Shas* on *Berakhot* 4b), who notes that Rosh, *Tur*, and *Roke'ah* likewise did not have "three times" in their versions.

22. Cf. Hakham, *Da'at Mikra*, p. 580; Gezundheit and Kimelman, "A Praise of David," p. 68.

23. For a conceptual approach to the additional verses, see Rabbi Joseph B. Soloveitchik, *Al ha-Tefillah* (Hebrew), ed. Reuven Grodner (New York: OU Press, 2012), pp. 27-39.

AFTERLIFE IN JEWISH THOUGHT

THE EVOLUTION OF AN IDEA AND IMPLICATIONS
FOR CONTEMPORARY RELIGIOUS LIFE[1]

Afterlife in Tanakh

There is a paucity of explicit references to afterlife—whether a bodily resurrection or a soul world—in Tanakh. The Torah promises this-worldly rewards and punishments for faithfulness or lack thereof to God and the Torah. It does not promise heaven for righteousness, nor does it threaten hell or the absence of heaven for sinfulness. The prophetic ideal is the messianic era in this world. Given the ancient world's belief in, and even obsession with, immortality and afterlife, the Torah's silence is all the more remarkable.

Aside from the lack of explicit references to afterlife in the Torah, one might have expected an appeal to afterlife in the book of Job. For all the arguments raised by Job's so-called friends to vindicate Job's unfair suffering, they never say that

1. This article appeared originally in *Conversations* 23 (Autumn 2015), pp. 216-226; reprinted in Angel, *Increasing Peace Through Balanced Torah Study. Conversations* 27 (New York: Institute for Jewish Ideas and Ideals, 2017), pp. 72-82.

Job will be rewarded in the afterlife. Rather, Job and his friends agree with the biblical premise that ultimate justice is supposed to occur during one's lifetime. Job insisted that his suffering was unjust, whereas his friends assumed that he must have deserved his punishment.[1]

Assessing the Near Absence of
Explicit References to Afterlife in Tanakh

Daniel, a late biblical book, explicitly mentions a bodily resurrection: "Many of those that sleep in the dust of the earth will awake, some to eternal life, others to reproaches, to everlasting abhorrence. And the knowledgeable will be radiant like the bright expanse of sky, and those who lead the many to righteousness will be like the stars forever and ever" (Dan. 12:2–3). In his *Treatise on the Resurrection*, Rambam considers this passage to be the only explicit reference to resurrection in Tanakh.[2]

For some time, academic scholars generally concluded that since Tanakh does not explicitly mention resurrection until the book of Daniel, it must have been a later belief that crept into Jewish thought toward the end of the biblical period, most likely from Zoroastrianism.[3] Until that point, Israel's prophets believed that when people die, they cease to exist. This academic position ran against rabbinic tradition, which insists that belief in resurrection traces back to the Torah, even if it is only alluded to and not mentioned explicitly: "The following have no portion [in the World to Come]: He who maintains that resurrection is not a biblical doctrine,[4] the Torah was not divinely revealed, and an *epikoros*…" (*Sanhedrin* 90a).

In 2006, however, Professor Jon D. Levenson published a book, *Resurrection and the Restoration of Israel: The Ultimate Victory of the God of Life*. He demonstrates that Israel's belief in resurrection has an extensive range of biblical antecedents, and did not simply appear late in the biblical period. Resurrection is an essential component of Israel's redemption, which itself vindicates history.

Levenson explains that contemporary academic scholarship, rooted in the modern world with its emphasis on individualism, has a difficult time understanding the biblical concept of identity. If one asks, "Will I have life after death?" one already misses the heart of the matter. The biblical conception of afterlife is grounded in a corporate identity inextricably linked to the nation of Israel; ancestors and descendants are completely connected. Jewish belief in resurrection is rooted in God's promises to Israel, His power over life and death, and His preference for life. Although Daniel was the first to mention resurrection explicitly, the ideas underlying this resurrection trace back to the earliest texts in Tanakh. Thus, the classical rabbinic position is fundamentally correct.

Tanakh Assumes Afterlife

In addition to Levenson's thesis, Professor James Kugel cites a number of biblical verses that presume an existence beyond life in this world.[5] For example, "And Abraham breathed his last, dying at a good ripe age, old and contented; and he was gathered to his kin" (Gen. 25:8). Abraham was "gathered to his kin," regardless of where his ancestors were buried or how righteous they were. Abraham rose to religious heights vastly above his pagan father Terah, and they were buried hundreds of miles apart.

Numerous other biblical references similarly suggest that death is not absolutely final. There are two mysterious deaths in Tanakh: God took Enoch (Gen. 5:24), and Elijah was taken to heaven in a fiery chariot (2 Kings 2:11). Malachi prophesies that Elijah will return in the future as the harbinger of the messianic era (Mal. 3:23–24). A witch evidently conjured up Samuel's spirit (1 Sam. 28:11–14), and Elijah and Elisha revived dead children (1 Kings 17:19-23; 2 Kings 4:32–36).

From these and other references, Kugel concludes that "some decades ago, the cliché about the Hebrew Bible was that it really has no notion of an afterlife or the return of the soul to God or a last judgment or a world to come. But such a claim will not withstand careful scrutiny."[6]

Why Does Tanakh Give Afterlife So Little Attention?

We have seen that Tanakh regularly alludes to a belief in an afterlife despite its not discussing it explicitly until the late book of Daniel. Additionally, the notion of resurrection is fundamentally connected to beliefs that span back to the beginning of the biblical period. We now must ask, however, why does Tanakh give afterlife such little overt attention, and why is the covenant of the Torah predicated entirely on this-worldly existence?[7]

Professor Moshe David (Umberto) Cassuto sheds light on this issue in his analysis of the Garden of Eden narrative. There were two trees at the center of Eden. The Tree of Life seems supernatural. Were Adam and Eve to eat from it, they would have become immortal (Gen. 3:23). An expert in the literature of the ancient Near East, Cassuto observed that nearly every ancient mythology had a tree, a plant, or something else of life. This element reflects the obsessive quest for immortality prevalent in the ancient world.

In stark contrast with Israel's surrounding cultures, the Torah decisively downplays the Tree of Life. That tree becomes significant to the narrative only after Adam and Eve sinned by eating from the Tree of Knowledge and were expelled from the Garden of Eden. God then sends Cherubim to prevent Adam and Eve from eating of the Tree of Life (Gen. 3:22–24).

To understand why the Torah would diminish the role of the Tree of Life, we must consider the tree that is central to the narrative, namely, the Tree of Knowledge. Whereas the Tree of Life appears supernatural, the Tree of Knowledge seems to have been a regular fruit tree. The Sages suggested that the Tree of Knowledge was either a fig tree, a grapevine, wheat, or an *etrog* (citron) tree (*Gen. Rabbah* 15:7). The effects of the fruit derived from God's prohibition, rather than from any inherent supernatural property.

Whereas the Tree of Life was prevalent in other ancient literatures, the Tree of Knowledge is otherwise unattested. The Torah is a revolution in human history, shifting focus away from nonexistent mythical fruits that give immortality, and replacing them with an emphasis on developing a genuine relationship with God. It teaches that we must live religious-moral lives and take personal responsibility for our actions. The ultimate vision of the prophets is a messianic world, which will achieve a perfected, religious-moral society, returning humanity to the harmonious state in the Garden of Eden.

In this spirit, the book of Proverbs transforms the Tree of Life into Torah and wisdom: "She is a tree of life to those who grasp her, and whoever holds on to her is happy" (Prov. 3:18).[8] The Jewish Tree of Life is Torah and wisdom, representing a lifelong religious quest, rather than a supernatural fruit. It also is significant that the Ark, which contains the tablets of the Ten Commandments, is guarded by Cherubim. The Tabernacle represents the only other appearance of Cherubim in the Torah aside from the Garden of Eden, where they guard the Tree of Life (Gen. 3:24).

Despite the purposeful emphasis on this-worldly conduct and reward and punishment throughout Tanakh, rabbinic Judaism incorporated afterlife as an essential part of its system of understanding divine justice in this world. When did this change occur?

Malachi and Daniel:
Using Afterlife to Vindicate Unfairness

The problem of the righteous suffering and the wicked prospering runs throughout Tanakh. The classical biblical wisdom approach to justify unfairness, particularly emphasized in Psalms and Proverbs, is that the suffering of the righteous or the success of the wicked was only a temporary state. Any injustices would be rectified during the lifetimes of the individuals. Job and Ecclesiastes challenge this approach, leaving unfairness as a matter that lies beyond human comprehension.[9]

Toward the end of the biblical period, the books of Malachi and Daniel addressed a new situation. For the first time, Israel's faithful suffered precisely because they were righteous, whereas the sinners prospered as a consequence of their wickedness. Divine justice was under siege, and many righteous Jews were sinking into despair and losing faith. No longer could one appeal to the classical prophetic responses rooted in the Torah, that national suffering occurs when Israel sins.

Rather than offering short-term solutions, Malachi appeals to the messianic redemption to vindicate history:

> You have wearied the Lord with your talk. But you ask, "By what have we wearied [Him]?" By saying, "All who do evil are good in the sight of the Lord, and in them He delights," or else, "Where is the God of justice?" Behold, I am sending My messenger to clear the way before Me, and the Lord whom you seek shall come to His Temple suddenly. As for the angel of the covenant that you desire, he is already coming.... He shall act like a smelter and purger of silver; and he shall purify the descendants of Levi and refine them like gold and silver, so that they shall present offerings in righteousness. Then the offerings of Judah and Jerusalem shall be pleasing to the Lord as in the days of yore and in the years of old.... And you shall come to see the difference between the righteous and the wicked, between him who has served the Lord and him who has not served Him (Mal. 2:17; 3:1–4, 18).

Daniel invokes the resurrection that would occur during this period of redemption to vindicate injustices (Dan. 12:2–3). The innovation of Malachi and Daniel was not belief in the Messiah or resurrection. Rather, their primary innovation was in linking the classical problem of unfairness with the future messianic era.

Their appeal to an ideal future to vindicate today's unfairness was a formal concession that ultimate justice does not necessarily occur during one's lifetime.

The Sages follow in this spirit, concluding that afterlife vindicates injustices in this world:

> It was taught: Rabbi Jacob says, there is no precept in the Torah, where reward is stated by its side, from which you cannot infer the doctrine of the resurrection of the dead. Thus, in connection with honoring parents it is written: "That your days may be prolonged, and that it may go well with you" (Deut. 5:16). Again in connection with the law of letting [the dam] go from the nest it is written: "That it may be well with you, and that you may prolong your days" (Deut. 22:7). Now, in the case where a man's father said to him, "Go up to the top of the building and bring me down some young birds," and he went up to the top of the building, let the dam go and took the young ones, and on his return he fell and was killed—where is this man's length of days, and where is this man's happiness? But "that your days may be prolonged" refers to the world that is wholly long, and "that it may go well with you" refers to the world that is wholly good (*Hullin* 142a).

Heaven and Resurrection: A Medieval Debate

A second major development in the Jewish discussion of afterlife arose with Rambam's efforts to bridge Torah and Greek philosophy.[10] Rambam was enamored by the Platonic notion of a soul-world afterlife, and he discusses heaven with great passion. Simultaneously, Rambam espouses the classical Jewish belief in Messiah and the resurrection, which create an ideal this-worldly existence. To reconcile these positions, he concludes that in the messianic era there will be a resurrection, but then everyone will die again and return to the ideal existence in heaven.

In order to conflate the prophetic ideal of Messiah with the Platonic ideal of a heavenly afterlife, Rambam insists that the prophets and sages longed for the messianic age so that they could live without distraction and thereby work on earning a share in the World to Come:

> The prophets and sages longed for the messianic era, not so that they could rule the world, not that they could dominate pagans, not to receive honor from the nations, nor to eat and drink and be merry. Rather, [they longed for it] so that they would be free to learn Torah and wisdom, and there would be no oppressor or distraction. In this way they would earn a share in the World to Come, as we explained in *the Laws of Repentance* [chapter 8] (*Hilkhot Melakhim* 12:4).

Rambam's preference of a soul-world over the biblical ideas of a this-world messianic era and resurrection did not go unnoticed or unchallenged. Some of Rambam's critics accused him of denying the resurrection altogether, leading Rambam to compose a scathing retort in his *Treatise on Resurrection*. Granting his resolute belief in the resurrection, however, there is little question that Rambam radically shifted emphasis away from the biblical conception of a this-world ideal society to a soul-world ideal for each individual.[11] Additionally, Rambam's view highlights personal religious development and prefers it to societal perfection.

This debate runs throughout Tanakh. For example, the most prevalent metaphorical interpretation in Jewish tradition casts the Song of Songs as symbolizing the historical covenantal relationship between God and Israel as a community (e.g., Targum, Rabbi Saadiah Gaon, Rashi, Rashbam, Ibn Ezra). In contrast, Rambam interprets the Song of Songs as a symbol of the love between the religious individual and God.[12]

Rambam also insists that a prophet had to reach the highest intellectual and religious levels as a prerequisite to receiving prophetic revelation (*Guide of the Perplexed* 2:32–45). In contrast, Rabbi Judah Halevi maintains that prophecy is a divine gift. Were God to deem it necessary to send a prophet on a mission, anyone could receive a prophetic message (*Kuzari*, e.g., 1:4; 1:87). Abarbanel (on Amos 1:1; 7:14) endorses Rabbi Halevi's view, insisting that a prophet's mission to his people, and not his personal perfection, is the defining characteristic of biblical prophecy. Abarbanel concludes that Rambam derived his conception of prophecy, which favors individual spirituality over one's communal mission, from Greek philosophy, and this understanding is inconsistent with traditional Jewish thought.

To summarize, the Torah and prophets emphasize communal perfection. The ideal of Tanakh is the messianic age, a perfected society and world harmony. The plain sense of the biblical texts certainly favors the position of Rambam's opponents over that of Rambam, who shifted attention to individual perfection and the soul-world.

Contemporary Applications

This debate is not simply an unverifiable, abstract philosophical disagreement. One's belief in afterlife profoundly affects how one lives life in this world. If one's foremost goal is the attainment of a personal heaven, one could live in a cave completely removed from society, study Torah, pray, observe the Torah's commandments, and reflect philosophically on God.[13] In contrast, the prophets always lived among the people despite all the heartache that entailed, as their abiding goal was to improve their society and bring it closer to the ideas of the Torah. They longed for Israel to become a model nation that would inspire all humanity to serve God.

More broadly, the discussion of afterlife has direct implications on how contemporary society functions. Much of secular society denies or downplays afterlife. This position leads to the conclusion that this life is all there is. Some idealists use this conclusion to do everything they can to make a positive impact during their lifetimes. Many others conclude that life has little ultimate purpose, and therefore overemphasize this-worldliness and self-indulgence.

At the other side of the spectrum, some religious communities teach that this world is only a way station where we strive to earn eternal heavenly reward. This system of belief dangerously gives too much power to the religious clerics, who can tell their followers what it takes to earn a place in heaven. When clerics have upright ethical values, they can achieve phenomenal results. However, when clerics preach murder or other immorality in the name of their religion, it is truly evil.

In a completely different arena that should not in any way be likened to the above discussion, the Orthodox Jewish yeshiva system confronts a different challenge pertaining to belief in the afterlife. In many *yeshivot*, Tanakh receives woefully inadequate attention.[14] Yet, many learn the eighteenth-century work by Rabbi Moshe Hayyim Luzzatto, the *Mesillat Yesharim* (*Path of the Just*).

This remarkable book focuses on piety and self-perfection, and is worthy of careful study. However, learning *Mesillat Yesharim* without Tanakh creates an imbalance in the yeshiva curriculum. Rabbi Luzzatto introduces his work by stating that the purpose of our existence is to gain afterlife:

> Our Sages of blessed memory have taught us that man was created for the sole purpose of rejoicing in God and deriving pleasure from the splendor of His Presence; for this is true joy and the greatest pleasure that can be found. The place where this joy may truly be derived is the World to Come, which was expressly created to provide for it; but the path to the object of our desires is this world (*Mesillat Yesharim* chapter 1).[15]

Students of the prophets never would stop there, since the prophets were concerned with the perfection of their society. Learning *Mesillat Yesharim* without learning the soaring visions of the prophets sends the message that personal religious growth lies at the heart of religious Jewish experience. While of course we aspire to individual personal growth (and should learn *Mesillat Yesharim*!), this aspiration must be accompanied by the prophetic imperative to channel our religious energies to improve the broader community.[16] It is the longing for the messianic era, and not a personal afterlife, that should shape the heart of our religious experience and actions. Lacking this prophetic vision, students may become connected to God and the Torah, but isolate themselves from the broader community.

If there is hope for understanding and resolution, it is through serious engagement with Tanakh, which forms the basis of the Jewish vision. Individual religious strengths must be developed and channeled toward the betterment of society. The messianic visions of the prophets are for all humanity, and not just Israel. These beliefs foster a love for humanity, rather than just those who share our particular beliefs.

Tragically, we live in a world where too many people overemphasize afterlife, and too many others underemphasize it. Most Jews no longer stand by or even understand the alternative of the Torah and the prophets. But the vision of Tanakh has the power to change the world if we will listen to its message and promote it.

NOTES

1. There are several passages where Job seems to accept the finality of death. For example, "As a cloud fades away, so whoever goes down to Sheol does not come up; he returns no more to his home; his place does not know him" (Job 7:9). Based on this verse, Rava insisted that "this shows that Job denied the resurrection of the dead" (*Bava Batra* 16a). Cf. Job 10:20–22; 14:1–10.

2. Several other biblical verses employ resurrection terminology. Three prominent examples are, (1) "He will destroy death forever.

My Lord God will wipe the tears away from all faces and will put an end to the reproach of His people over all the earth—for it is the Lord who has spoken" (Isa. 25:8). (2) "Oh, let Your dead revive! Let corpses arise! Awake and shout for joy, you who dwell in the dust!—for Your dew is like the dew on fresh growth; You make the land of the shades come to life" (Isa. 26:19). (3) Ezekiel's celebrated vision of the Dry Bones (Ezek. 37:1–14). However, these prophecies likely refer to God's miraculous restoration of Israel in the messianic era, rather than the bodily resurrection of individual people. In contrast, Daniel refers specifically to the bodily resurrection of individuals so that God can mete out ultimate justice onto them.

3. See, e.g., Neil Gillman, *The Death of Death: Resurrection and Immortality in Jewish Thought* (Woodstock, VT: Jewish Lights, 1997), p. 96. See also Jon D. Levenson, *Resurrection and the Restoration of Israel: The Ultimate Victory of the God of Life* (New Haven, CT: Yale, 2006), p. x, where he cites the widespread scholarly view that Zoroastrianism is the likely candidate for having influenced Jewish thought regarding resurrection. Levenson proceeds to reject much of that scholarly consensus.

4. Not all versions of the Mishnah contain the text that one must believe that resurrection is *min ha-Torah*, "from the Torah." Rambam states that one must believe in the resurrection, but does not insist that one must believe that it is from the Torah. See Marc Shapiro, *The Limits of Orthodox Theology: Maimonides' Thirteen Principles Reappraised* (Oxford: Littman Library of Jewish Civilization, 2004), p. 152, n. 62.

5. James L. Kugel, *The Great Poems of the Bible: A Reader's Companion with new Translations* (New York: Free Press, 1999), pp. 192–210.

6. *Ibid.*, pp. 209–210.

7. For a survey of classical responses to this question, see Nehama Leibowitz, *New Studies in Vayikra–Leviticus*, trans. Rafael Fisch and Avner Tomaschoff (Jerusalem: Eliner Library), pp. 572–579. See also Noah H. Rosenbloom, "Rationales for the Omission of Eschatology in the Bible," *Judaism* 43:2 (1994), pp. 149–158.

8. See also Prov. 11:30; 13:12; 15:4.

9. For discussion and sources pertaining to this issue in Psalms, Proverbs, Job, and Ecclesiastes, see Hayyim Angel, *Vision from the Prophet and Counsel from the Elders: A Survey of Nevi'im and Ketuvim* (New York: OU Press, 2013), pp. 227–234, 241–248, 249–257, 288–300.

10. See sources and discussion in Neil Gillman, *The Death of Death*, pp. 143–172.

11. Louis Jacobs maintains that Rambam was the only medieval Jewish philosopher who committed to the idea that the future existence is in an incorporeal state in a soul world rather than in this world (*Principles of the Jewish Faith* [New York: Basic Books, 1964], p. 407).

12. See *Hilkhot Teshuvah* 10:3; *Guide of the Perplexed* 3:51. See Yosef Murciano, "Rambam and the Interpretation of the Song of Songs" (Hebrew), in *Teshurah le-Amos: A Collection of Studies*

in Biblical Interpretation Presented in Honor of Amos Hakham, ed. Moshe Bar-Asher et al. (Alon Shevut: Tevunot, 2007), pp. 85–108. For an exploration of the value of adopting the views of Rashi and Rambam in one's religious experience, see Rabbi Shalom Carmy, "Perfect Harmony," *First Things* (December 2010); "On Cleaving as Identification: Rabbi Soloveitchik's Account of *Devekut* in *U-Vikkashtem Mi-Sham*," *Tradition* 41:2 (Summer 2008), pp. 100–112.

13. It should be emphasized that Rambam did not advocate that lifestyle, and was deeply involved in communal affairs himself. Nevertheless, his philosophical position is vulnerable to this conclusion.

14. For analysis of why this has been so, see, for example, Rabbi Mordechai Breuer, "Bible in the Curriculum of the Yeshiva" (Hebrew), in *Mehkarim ba-Mikra u-va-Hinnukh: Presented to Prof. Moshe Ahrend*, ed. Dov Rappel (Jerusalem: Touro College, 1996), pp. 223–235; Frederick E. Greenspahn, "Jewish Ambivalence towards the Bible," *Hebrew Studies* 48 (2007), pp. 7–21; Rabbi Moshe Sokolow, "*U-Va Le-Tzion Go'el, Kedushah De-Sidra*, and the Yeshiva Curriculum," in *MiTokh Ha-Ohel: The Weekday Prayers*, ed. Daniel Z. Feldman and Stuart W. Halpern (New Milford, CT: Maggid, 2014), pp. 293–301.

15. Translation in Shraga Silverstein, *The Path of the Just* (Jerusalem: Feldheim, 1980), p. 17.

16. As per our caveat regarding Rambam (see above note 13), this discussion also is not a critique of Rabbi Luzzatto or his work. Rather, it is a yeshiva curriculum that teaches *Mesillat Yesharim* while excluding serious study of Tanakh that creates this problem.

'THE DISCIPLES OF THE WISE INCREASE PEACE IN THE WORLD'

THE USE OF TRADITIONAL SCHOLARSHIP TO BUILD BRIDGES AND MEND RIFTS[1]

Introduction

At the end of five different tractates of the Talmud, we find the following teaching:

Rabbi Eleazar said in the name of Rabbi Hanina: The disciples of the wise increase peace in the world, as it says, And all your children shall be taught of the Lord, and great shall be the peace of your children [*banayikh*] (Isa. 54:13). Read not *banayikh* ["your children"] but *bonayikh* ["your builders"] (*Berakhot* 64a, cf. *Yevamot* 122b, *Nazir* 66b, *Keritot* 28b, *Tamid* 32b).

---

1. This article appeared originally in *Conversations* 26 (Autumn 2016), pp. 20-32.

Genuine Torah scholars are supposed to be builders of society, and increase peace in the world. When rabbis and scholars are seeking heaven and communal unity, their Torah scholarship is the ideal tool to unite diverse people.

The Talmud celebrates the diversity of the Jewish people by coining a blessing:

> Rabbi Hamnuna further said: If one sees a crowd of Israelites, he should say: Blessed is He who discerns secrets (*Berakhot* 58a).

Rather than considering conformity a blessing, the Talmud idealizes diversity as something for which God deserves praise. We seek Jewish unity, but not conformity.[1]

Command of a multiplicity of opinions, the hallmark of a Torah scholar, can be used to teach the many legitimate avenues into Torah. The sixteenth-century commentator Rabbi Samuel Eidels (Maharsha) explains that God revealed the Torah in the presence of 600,000 Israelites because the Torah can be interpreted in 600,000 different ways![2] Although the cliché "two Jews, three opinions" may be true, a more telling adage would be, "one learned Jew, dozens of opinions." When Torah scholars learn sources in their depth, they realize that every single point is debated by the greatest rabbinic minds. The dazzling range of possibilities teaches uncertainty, and also that people can hold significantly different opinions and still be unified under the roof of the Torah.

We live in an age of terrible fragmentation. Whereas debates are hardwired into Jewish tradition, rifts are detrimental to the

Jewish community. Often, rifts arise when each side adopts a partial truth from within tradition to the near-exclusion of another partial truth held by the other side. Good Torah scholarship, in its attempt to navigate the two halves, offers an opportunity to build bridges and mend these rifts.

In this essay, we will briefly survey a few areas pertaining to (1) relations between Orthodox Jews; (2) relations between Orthodox and non-Orthodox Jews; and (3) relations between Jews and non-Jews. The guiding principle is that a faithful commitment to Torah and unity coupled with the range of opinions from within tradition offers models to build bridges and mend rifts without demanding conformity.

WITHIN ORTHODOXY

Religious Authority of Midrash

Jewish tradition venerates earlier rabbinic scholarship, and places a premium on the Talmud and other midrashic collections. Simultaneously, the *peshat* school from the post-talmudic Geonim down to the present has established that the biblical text remains at the center of inquiry, and non-legal rabbinic teachings are not binding. The scholarly pursuit of truth in Torah is imperative.[3]

Many within the Orthodox world adopt only half of that truth at the expense of the other. One side dogmatically adopts talmudic and midrashic teachings as literal, and insists that this position is required as part of having faith in the teachings of the Sages. Another group dismisses the talmudic traditions as being far removed from biblical text and reality. The first group accuses the second of denigration of the Sages, whereas the second group accuses the first of being fundamentalists who ignore science and scholarship.

The truth is, this rift has been around for a long time. Rambam lamented this very imbalance in the twelfth century in his introduction to *Perek Helek* in tractate *Sanhedrin*. He divided Jews into three categories:

> The first group is the largest one…They understand the teachings of the sages only in their literal sense, in spite of the fact that some of their teachings when taken literally, seem so fantastic and irrational that if one were to repeat them literally, even to the uneducated, let alone sophisticated scholars, their amazement would prompt them to ask how anyone in the world could believe such things true, much less edifying. The members of this group are poor in knowledge. One can only regret their folly. Their very effort to honor and to exalt the sages in accordance with their own meager understanding actually humiliates them. As God lives, this group destroys the glory of the Torah of God and says the opposite of what it intended. For He said in His perfect Torah, "The nation is a wise and understanding people" (Deut. 4:6)…

Such individuals are pious, but foolish. They misunderstand the intent of the Sages, and draw false conclusions in the name of religion.

Misguided as this first group is, at least it is preferable to the second group, which also takes the words of the Sages literally but rejects their teachings as a result:

> The second group is also a numerous one. It, too, consists of persons who, having read or heard the words of the sages, understand them according to their simple literal sense and believe that the sages intended nothing else than what may be learned from their literal interpretation. Inevitably, they ultimately declare the sages to be fools, hold them up to contempt, and slander what does not deserve to be slandered.... The members of this group are so pretentiously stupid that they can never attain genuine wisdom.... This is an accursed group, because they attempt to refute men of established greatness whose wisdom has been demonstrated to competent men of science....

The first group is reverent to the Sages, whereas the second group is open to science and scholarship and therefore rejects the Sages and their teachings. Both groups fail because of their fundamental misunderstanding of the Sages.

Rambam then celebrates that rare ideal scholar, who combines those two half-truths into the whole truth:

> There is a third group. Its members are so few in number that it is hardly appropriate to call them a group.... This group consists of men to whom the greatness of our sages is clear.... They know that the sages did not speak

nonsense, and it is clear to them that the words of the sages contain both an obvious and a hidden meaning. Thus, whenever the sages spoke of things that seem impossible, they were employing the style of riddle and parable which is the method of truly great thinkers....[4]

In addition to Rambam's insistence on the fact that the Sages did not always mean their words literally, we must add that the greatest *peshat* commentators, from Rabbi Saadiah Gaon to Rashi to Ibn Ezra to Ramban to Abarbanel and so many others, venerated the Sages without being bound by all of their non-legal comments. These rabbinic thinkers combine reverence for the Sages with a commitment to scholarship and integrity to the text of the Torah.[5]

OPENNESS TO NON-ORTHODOX
AND NON-JEWISH SCHOLARSHIP[6]

Jewish tradition's commitment to truth should lead us to accept the truth from whoever says it. Rambam lived by this axiom,[7] and many great rabbinic figures before and after him similarly espoused this principle.[8] On the other hand, it is difficult to distinguish between knowledge and theory. Scholarship invariably is accompanied by conscious and unconscious biases of scholars, some of which may stray from traditional Jewish thought and belief.

This tension is expressed poignantly in an anecdote cited by Rabbi Joseph ibn Aknin (c. 1150-c. 1220). After noting the works of several rabbinic predecessors who utilized Christian and Muslim writings in their commentaries, he quotes a story related by Shemuel Ha-Nagid:

> Rabbi Mazliah b. Albazek the rabbinic judge of Saklia told [Shemuel Ha-Nagid] when he came from Baghdad… that one day in [Rabbi Hai Gaon's] yeshiva they studied the verse, "let my head not refuse such choice oil" (Ps. 141:5), and those present debated its meaning. Rabbi Hai of blessed memory told Rabbi Mazliah to go to the Catholic Patriarch and ask him what he knew about this verse, and this upset [Rabbi Mazliah]. When [Rabbi Hai] saw that Rabbi Mazliah was upset, he rebuked him, "Our saintly predecessors who are our guides solicited information on language and interpretation from many religious communities— and even of shepherds, as is well known!"[9]

All scholarship is valuable, but all scholars are necessarily biased. There is no easy solution to this dilemma, and rabbinic scholars continue to espouse different approaches for the proper balance in this issue.[10]

Sins of Biblical Heroes

In recent years, particularly in Israel, there has been a raging debate regarding the sins of biblical heroes. One side insists that even ostensibly egregious sins, such as David and Bathsheba-Uriah (2 Samuel 11), Solomon and idolatry (1 Kings 11), and others should not be taken at face value. On the contrary, numerous rabbinic sources insist that these biblical figures did not violate cardinal sins as the plain sense of the text suggests.

Others maintain that the biblical texts speak for themselves. The Bible exposes the flaws of its greatest heroes, teaching that nobody is above the law, and nobody is perfect. There also are many rabbinic sources in support of this position.

In this instance, each side of the debate represents a half-truth. One group properly teaches a deep sense of awe and reverence for our heroes, whereas the other group correctly insists that nobody is above the Torah, and even the greatest figures are vulnerable to sin. Both of these messages emerge from the biblical texts and rabbinic tradition. However, people who adopt only one or the other half-truth cannot even engage with one another. The first group accuses the other of irreverence, whereas the second group protests that the first ignores the biblical text and its commentaries, and also justifies the immorality of religious leaders in the name of tradition.

Responsible rabbis and educators carefully weigh those two half-truths into a balanced picture more in tune with the biblical texts and rabbinic tradition, teaching that nobody is above the Torah, while maintaining proper awe and reverence for our heroes.[11]

ORTHODOX AND NON-ORTHODOX JEWS

Judaism includes the basic tenets of belief in one God, divine revelation of the Torah, and a concept of divine providence and reward-punishment. Although there have been debates over the precise definitions and contours of Jewish belief, these core beliefs are universally accepted as part of our tradition.[12]

The question for believing Jews today is: How should we relate to the overwhelming majority of Jews, who likely do not fully believe in classical Jewish beliefs? Two medieval models shed light on this question.

Rambam insists that proper belief is essential. Whether one intentionally rejects Jewish beliefs, or whether one simply is mistaken or uninformed, non-belief leads to exclusion from the community of believers:

> When a person affirms all these Principles, and clarifies his faith in them, he becomes part of the Jewish People. It is a mitzvah to love him, have mercy on him, and show him all the love and brotherhood that God has instructed us to show our fellow Jews. Even if he has transgressed out of desire and the overpowering influence of his base nature, he will be punished accordingly but he will have a share in the World to Come. But one who denies any of these Principles has excluded himself from the Jewish People and denied the essence [of Judaism]. He is called a heretic, an *epikoros*, and "one who has cut off the seedlings." It is a mitzvah to hate and destroy such a person, as it says (Ps. 139:21), "Those who hate You, God, I shall hate" (*Introduction to Perek Helek*).

For Rambam, belief in the principles of Jewish belief are necessary, and sufficient, to gain afterlife. Scholars of Rambam generally explain that Rambam did not think afterlife was a reward. Rather, it is a natural consequence of one's religious-intellectual development. Although Rambam did not invent Jewish beliefs, he did innovate this dogmatic position of Judaism being a community of believers in a set of propositions.[13]

Professor Menachem Kellner explains that Rambam's position was not the only rabbinic response to Jews who do not espouse Jewish beliefs. Ra'avad, Rabbi Simon b. Tzemah Duran, and Rabbi Joseph Albo maintain that if one makes a well-intentioned error based on a misunderstanding of sources, that person is wrong but not a heretic. One is a heretic only when one willfully denies a principle of faith or willfully affirms a principle denied by the Torah.[14] Kellner argues that the majority of medieval rabbinic thinkers support this latter view, rather than the exclusionary dogmatic position of Rambam.[15]

Halakhah, of course, defines Jewishness by birth and nationhood, and not by belief. Every Jew is part of the family even if he or she is mistaken in belief. We ideally want all Jews to learn, observe, and believe in the Torah and tradition. However, we should not exclude as heretics those who fall short unless they intentionally wish to exclude themselves from the community.[16]

The approach espoused by Ra'avad, Duran, and Albo reflects a productive means of addressing today's fragmented society from within tradition. We stand for an eternal set of beliefs and practices, and we embrace and teach all Jews as we build community together.[17]

JEWS AND NON-JEWS

The Torah embraces universalistic values that apply to all humanity. All people are descended from one couple, so there is no room for bigotry (*Sanhedrin* 37a). All people are created in God's image (Gen. 1:26).[18] There is a universal morality demanded by the Torah, codified in the Talmud as the Seven Noahide Laws. The messianic visions of the prophets foresee that all humanity will one day live in harmony by accepting God and the requisite moral life demanded by the Torah.[19]

Simultaneously, God made a singular covenant with the people of Israel through the Torah. Israel plays a unique role as a "kingdom of priests and holy nation" (Exod. 19:6), has a separate set of laws revealed by God, and occupies a central role in the covenantal history between God and humanity.

Many within the Jewish community focus almost exclusively on the particularistic elements of tradition, and consequently look down upon all non-Jews and non-observant Jews. Many other Jews focus almost exclusively on the universalistic vision of Judaism, ignoring Jewish belief, law, and values in favor of modern Western values. Needless to say, the respective espousing of half-truths again leads to rifts within the community.

Tradition teaches a sensitive balance of universalism and particularism.[20] The Torah has a special vision for Jews and simultaneously embraces all of humanity in an effort to perfect society.[21]

Conclusion

We have seen several areas where traditional scholarship can build bridges between half-truths that divide people. Within the Orthodox world, reverence toward heroes and the Sages must be balanced with fidelity to the biblical text, commitment to prophetic integrity, and commitment to truth in scholarship.

In relating to non-observant or non-believing Jews, we must espouse and teach traditional belief and observance, but not exclude those who are not yet fully connected. The Torah teaches both particularistic and universalistic values, and it is critical to adopt both in a faithful religious worldview. This position enables believing Jews to sincerely love all humanity and to long for universal morality and harmony.

It is easier to espouse a half-truth than to struggle for the whole truth. The perils of this approach are not theoretical, but an unfortunate and avoidable part of our current reality. It is up to the disciples of the wise to build the ideological basis for increasing peace in the world by upholding and promoting the eternal values of the Torah.

NOTES

1. See further in Rabbi Marc D. Angel, "Orthodoxy and Diversity," *Conversations* 1 (Spring 2008), pp. 70-81.

2. Maharsha, *Hiddushei Aggadot* on *Berakhot* 58a.

3. See, for example, Rabbi Marc D. Angel, "Authority and Dissent: A Discussion of Boundaries," *Tradition* 25:2 (Winter 1990), pp. 18-27; Rabbi Hayyim David Halevi, *Aseh Lekha Rav*, vol. 5, resp. 49 (pp. 304-307); Rabbi Michael Rosensweig, "*Elu va-Elu Divre Elokim Hayyim*: Halakhic Pluralism and Theories of Controversy," *Tradition* 26:3 (Spring 1992), pp. 4-23; Marc Saperstein, *Decoding the Rabbis: A Thirteenth-Century Commentary on the Aggadah* (Cambridge MA: Harvard University Press, 1980), pp. 1-20; Rabbi Moshe

Shamah, "On Interpreting Midrash," in *Where the Yeshiva Meets the University: Traditional and Academic Approaches to Tanakh Study*, ed. Hayyim Angel, *Conversations* 15 (Winter 2013), pp. 27-39.

4. Translation from the Maimonides Heritage Center, https://www.mhcny.org/qt/1005.pdf. Accessed March 15, 2016.

5. See further in Rabbi Marc D. Angel, "Reflections on Torah Education and Mis-Education," *Conversations* 24 (Winter 2016), pp. 18-32; Rabbi Nahum E. Rabinovitch, "Faith in the Sages: What Is It?" (Hebrew), in *Mesilot Bilvavam* (Ma'alei Adumim: Ma'aliyot, 2014), pp. 103-114.

6. See Hayyim Angel, "The Use of Non-Orthodox Scholarship in Orthodox Bible Learning," *Conversations* 1 (Spring 2008), pp. 17-19; Rabbi Nathaniel Helfgot, "Reflections on the Use of Non-Orthodox Wisdom in the Orthodox Study of Tanakh," in *Where the Yeshiva Meets the University: Traditional and Academic Approaches to Tanakh Study*, ed. Hayyim Angel, *Conversations* 15 (Winter 2013), pp. 53-61.

7. In his introduction to *Pirkei Avot* (*Shemonah Perakim*), Rambam writes, "Know that the things about which we shall speak in these chapters and in what will come in the commentary are not matters invented on my own.... They are matters gathered from the discourse of the Sages in the Midrash, the Talmud, and other compositions of theirs, as well as from the discourse of both the ancient and modern philosophers and from the compositions of many men. Hear the truth from whoever says it." Translation in *Ethical Writings of Maimonides*, Raymond Weiss and Charles Butterworth (New York: Dover, 1983), p. 60.

8. See, for example, Ephraim E. Urbach, "The Pursuit of Truth as a Religious Obligation" (Hebrew), in *Ha-Mikra va-Anahnu*, ed. Uriel Simon (Ramat-Gan: Institute for Judaism and Thought in Our Time, 1979), pp. 13-27; Uriel Simon, "The Pursuit of Truth that Is Required for Fear of God and Love of Torah" (Hebrew), *ibid.*, pp. 28-41; Marvin Fox, "Judaism, Secularism, and Textual Interpretation," in *Modern Jewish Ethics: Theory and Practice*, ed. Marvin Fox (Columbus: Ohio State University Press, 1975), pp. 3-26. See also Hayyim Angel, "The Yeshivah and the Academy: How We Can Learn from One Another in Biblical Scholarship," in Angel, *Revealed Texts, Hidden Meanings: Finding the Religious Significance in Tanakh* (Jersey City, NJ: Ktav-Sephardic Publication Foundation, 2009), pp. 19-29; reprinted in *Peshat Isn't So Simple: Essays on Developing a Religious Methodology to Bible Study* (New York: Kodesh Press, 2014), pp. 28-35.

9. *Hitgalut ha-Sodot ve-Hofa'at ha-Me'orot*, ed. Abraham S. Halkin (Jerusalem: Mekitzei Nirdamim, 1964), pp. 493-495. In *Hagigah* 15b, God Himself initially refused to quote Rabbi Meir in the heavenly court since Rabbi Meir continued to learn from his teacher Elisha b. Avuyah, though the latter had become a heretic. However, Rabbah instantly rejected God's policy, stressing that Rabbi Meir carefully sifted out the valuable teachings from the "peel." Consequently, God reversed His policy and began quoting "His son" Rabbi Meir in the heavenly court.

10. See further discussion in Hayyim Angel, "From Black Fire to White Fire: Conversations about Religious Tanakh Learning Methodology," in Angel, *Revealed Texts, Hidden Meanings: Finding the Religious Significance in Tanakh* (Jersey City, NJ: Ktav-

Sephardic Publication Foundation, 2009), pp. 1-18; *Peshat Isn't So Simple: Essays on Developing a Religious Methodology to Bible Study* (New York: Kodesh Press, 2014), pp. 11-27; Hayyim Angel, "The Literary-Theological Study of Tanakh," afterword to Moshe Sokolow, *Tanakh: An Owner's Manual: Authorship, Canonization, Masoretic Text, Exegesis, Modern Scholarship and Pedagogy* (Brooklyn, NY: Ktav, 2015), pp. 192-207; also in Angel, *Peshat Isn't So Simple: Essays on Developing a Religious Methodology to Bible Study* (New York: Kodesh Press, 2014), pp. 118-136; Hayyim Angel, "Faith and Scholarship Can Walk Together: Rabbi Amnon Bazak on the Challenges of Academic Bible Study in Traditional Learning," *Tradition* 47:3 (Fall 2014), pp 78-88; reprinted in this volume; Rabbi Shalom Carmy, "Always Connect," in *Where the Yeshiva Meets the University: Traditional and Academic Approaches to Tanakh Study*, ed. Hayyim Angel. *Conversations* 15 (Winter 2013), pp. 1-12; Rabbi Shalom Carmy, "A Room with a View, but a Room of Our Own," in *Modern Scholarship in the Study of Torah: Contributions and Limitations*, ed. Shalom Carmy (Northvale, NJ: Jason Aronson Inc., 1996), pp. 1-38.

11. See, for example, Rabbi Amnon Bazak, *Ad ha-Yom ha-Zeh: Until This Day: Fundamental Questions in Bible Teaching* (Hebrew), ed. Yoshi Farajun (Tel Aviv: Yediot Aharonot, 2013), pp. 432-470; Rabbi Shalom Carmy, "To Get the Better of Words: An Apology for *Yir'at Shamayim* in Academic Jewish Studies," *Torah U-Madda Journal* 2 (1990), pp. 7-24; Rabbi Aharon Lichtenstein, "A Living Torah" (Hebrew), in *Hi Sihati: Al Derekh Limmud ha-Tanakh*, ed. Yehoshua Reiss (Jerusalem: Maggid, 2013), pp. 17-30; Rabbi Yaakov Medan, *David u-Vat Sheva: Ha-Het, ha-Onesh, ve-ha-Tikkun* (Hebrew) (Alon Shevut: Tevunot, 2002), pp. 7-24; Rabbi Joel B. Wolowelsky,

"*Kibbud Av* and *Kibbud Avot*: Moral Education and Patriarchal Critiques," *Tradition* 33:4 (Summer 1999), pp. 35-44.

12. See Marc B. Shapiro, *The Limits of Orthodox Theology: Maimonides' Thirteen Principles Reappraised* (Oxford: Littman Library of Jewish Civilization, 2004). Review Essay, Rabbi Yitzchak Blau, "Flexibility with a Firm Foundation: On Maintaining Jewish Dogma," *Torah U-Madda Journal* 12 (2004), pp. 179-191.

13. See Menachem Kellner, *Dogma in Medieval Jewish Thought: From Maimonides to Abravanel* (Oxford: Littman Library of Jewish Civilization, 1986); Menachem Kellner, *Must a Jew Believe Anything?* (London: Littman Library of Jewish Civilization, 1999). Book Review by David Berger, *Tradition* 33:4 (Summer 1999), pp. 81-89.

14. Menachem Kellner, *Dogma in Medieval Jewish Thought*, pp. 99-107.

15. Menachem Kellner, *Must a Jew Believe Anything?*, p. 68.

16. Menachem Kellner, *Must a Jew Believe Anything?*, pp. 111-126. See also Marc B. Shapiro, "Is There a '*Pesak*' for Jewish Thought?" in *Jewish Thought and Jewish Belief* (*Mahshevet Yisrael ve-Emunat Yisrael*), ed. Daniel J. Lasker (Be'er Sheva: Ben-Gurion University of the Negev Press, 2012), pp. 119*-140*.

17. See also Rabbi Dov Linzer, "The Discourse of Halakhic Inclusiveness," *Conversations* 1 (Spring 2008), pp. 1-5; Menachem Kellner, "Must We Have Heretics?" *Conversations* 1 (Spring 2008), pp. 6-10.

18. See Rabbi Yuval Cherlow, *In His Image: The Image of God in Man* (New Milford, CT: Maggid, 2015).

19. See especially Rabbi Jonathan Sacks, *The Dignity of Difference: How to Avoid the Clash of Civilizations* (London: Continuum, 2002). See also Alan Brill, *Judaism and Other Religions: Models of Understanding* (New York: Palgrave MacMillan, 2010); Alan Brill, *Judaism and World Religions: Encountering Christianity, Islam, and Eastern Traditions* (New York: Palgrave MacMillan, 2012); Alan Brill, "Many Nations Under God: Judaism and Other Religions," *Conversations* 2 (Autumn 2008), pp. 39-49.

20. See Rabbi Marc D. Angel, "The Universalistic Vision of Judaism," *Conversations* 12 (Winter 2012), pp. 95-100; Rabbi Marc D. Angel, *Voices in Exile: A Study in Sephardic Intellectual History* (Hoboken, NJ: Ktav, 1991), pp. 197-207; Rabbi Marc D. Angel with Hayyim Angel, *Rabbi Haim David Halevi: Gentle Scholar, Courageous Thinker* (Jerusalem: Urim, 2006), pp. 189-198.

21. See Hayyim Angel, "'The Chosen People': An Ethical Challenge," *Conversations* 8 (Fall 2010), pp. 52-60; reprinted in Angel, *Creating Space between Peshat and Derash: A Collection of Studies on Tanakh* (Jersey City, NJ: Ktav-Sephardic Publication Foundation, 2011), pp. 25-34.

Made in the USA
Columbia, SC
26 February 2018